# RACING
## MY FATHER

FOR Ansley

# RACING
## MY FATHER

### Growing Up With a Riding Legend

BY PATRICK SMITHWICK

Lexington, Kentucky

ECLIPSE
PRESS

Library of Congress Cataloging-in-Publication Data

Smithwick, Patrick, 1951–
  Racing my father : growing up with a riding legend / by Patrick Smithwick.
      p. cm.
  Includes bibliographical references.
  ISBN-13: 978-1-58150-140-7 (hardcover)
  ISBN-10: 1-58150-140-4 (hardcover)
  1. Smithwick, Patrick, 1951– 2. Jockeys—United States—Biography. 3. Horse racing—United States.  I. Title.
  SF336.S623S65  2006
  798.40092—dc22

                                                              2005033996


Printed in the United States of America
First Edition: 2006


Distributed to the trade by
National Book Network
4501 Forbes Blvd., Suite 200, Lanham, MD 20706
1.800.462.6420

A Division of
Blood-Horse Publications
Publishers Since 1916

# CONTENTS

*What you want, above all things on a raft, is for everyone to be satisfied, and feel right and kind towards the other.*

— Huck Finn
*Adventures of Huckleberry Finn*, by Mark Twain

*... I remember the way he'd pull on a rubber shirt over a couple of jerseys and a big sweat shirt over that, and get me to run with him in the forenoon in the hot sun. He'd have, maybe, taken a trail trip with one of Razzo's skins early in the morning after just getting in from Torino at four o'clock in the morning and beating it out to the stables in a cab and then with the dew all over everything and the sun just starting to get going, I'd help him pull off his boots and he'd get into a pair of sneakers and all these sweaters and we'd start out.*

*"Come on, kid," he'd say, stepping up and down on his toes in front of the jock's dressing room, "let's get moving."*

— Joe Butler
"My Old Man," by Ernest Hemingway

*... the problems of the human heart in conflict with itself ... alone can make good writing because only that is worth writing about, worth the agony and the sweat.*

— William Faulkner
Noble Prize Speech, Stockholm, Sweden, December 10, 1950

# Preface

During my childhood days, whether seated at the bar in Esposito's or waiting for my father outside the jocks' room at Saratoga, I listened to tales of my father that were as influential and character forming as those heard by a Greek boy about the exploits of Odysseus. The stories I heard were about a living legend, and they had several major themes: To be a man one must ride, one must drink, one must take daily life-threatening risks, one must push himself to the utmost, one must attract women, one must have no fear, one must have nerve. Nerve was everything. To be a man you had to be like one of the early astronauts or, better yet, be like the great test pilot Chuck Yeager. You had to be able to stay up all night carousing, arise early, lose five pounds driving in a hot car, and then go out and ride that horse better than anyone in the world. You did it calmly, all in a day's work, knowing that the week before a fellow rider-pilot had been killed on this horse. You had to have The Right Stuff. And you had to be able to do this whether you had pneumonia, bronchitis, a broken shoulder, a cracked collarbone, no peripheral vision, or were so stiff from being run over by a whole field of racehorses the day before that you could barely walk.

There was also another side to the stories. My father gave. He helped people without expecting anything back. He gave people second and third chances. He gave them money. He gave them jobs. He gave them meals. He gave them drinks. He gave them the benefit of the doubt. He gave them loyalty and love. My father gave his life to that which he loved — the sport of racing and the Thoroughbred horse.

# Preface

# PART I

# DOING LIGHT WITH POP

# 1

## Awakening

Our alarm went off at 5:15, as it did every morning. I lay there, pretending to be asleep. Pop propped himself up on an elbow, reached across my shoulders, and pushed in the alarm button. He lay down again on his back. I listened to the old air-conditioning window unit rumbling, struggling to blow in cool air. I could hear Pop's great friend, Scotty Schulhofer, rustling in the other bed a few feet away. Then I heard his friend Marvin Green, who had the little room across the hall, thump his big feet onto the floor, let out a groan, walk to the bathroom, shut the door, and take a leak. Pop sat up on the edge of our bed in the dark and coughed. He felt around the bedside table for his Pall Malls, smacked the pack to get a cigarette out, and clicked open his lighter. I rolled over, opened my eyes, and saw him lean forward, his expression serious, and light the cigarette. He inhaled and the tip of the cigarette lit up. He exhaled, coughed, and cleared his throat. Marvin padded out of the bathroom. Scotty, who used to ride races with Pop and was now training, got up and went in.

Pop leaned toward me and gently rubbed my shoulder. "You awake, Bud?" he asked.

"Yeah."

## Chapter 1

"Okay, it's time to get going."

He turned on the lamp and took another pull on the cigarette. I closed my eyes and turned away from the light. The relaxed autumn scent of the burning tobacco wafted toward me. Pop coughed.

"Pop," I said, "you've got to stop smoking so much."

"I will, Cowboy. I will."

The four of us had been out to dinner the night before, and it seemed that I had just fallen asleep, that it was still the middle of the night. Scotty came out of the bathroom. "Good morning, Little Paddy. Good morning, Paddy," he said in his soothing South Carolinian accent. He sat on the edge of his bed and started dressing.

"Good morning," I mumbled, head still on pillow.

"Morning, Scotty," said Pop.

The huge, fully dressed frame of Marvin Green appeared in the doorway. He had his hands on his hips and was frowning, looking at Pop sitting on the edge of the bed with his cigarette. "Little Paddy," he said. "You awake?"

"Not quite," I said.

"Your dad's getting too old for this race riding. You'd better get ready to take over."

"It won't be long," Pop said. As he stood up, I felt the mattress rise and along with it a slight hollowing of my chest and quickening of my heart. He always told me he'd ride his last race on the day I rode my first.

"How's your eye, Paddy?" Marvin asked. I'd forgotten all about the eye; Pop had scratched it the day before and had worn a patch over it at dinner and to bed.

"It's okay, Marvin."

"Yeah, okay. Well, just okay doesn't make it in your business, Smithwick. You need to be a hundred percent. You know those stewards won't let you ride today if they know you can't see straight."

"It's a long way from my heart, Marvin."

"Damn, you're stubborn. I ought to call those stewards myself. Give me that phone, Paddy." Marvin reached for the phone beside our bed.

"Oh, go on, Marvin," Pop laughed, pushing Marvin's big hand away. "You're not calling any damn stewards."

"See you at the track, boys — that is if you get there before it closes," Marvin joked. The main track and the training track opened at 5:30 a.m. for training and closed at 10:30 a.m.

"Ah, go on now," Scotty told Marvin. We knew he was headed for the track kitchen, where he'd have a full breakfast of pancakes, eggs, and coffee with a few fellow trainers, all garrulous big-morning eaters like himself.

I sat up on my side of our bed. Pop came out of the bathroom, his black hair wetted down and cleanly parted on the side. I went in, took a leak, brushed my teeth, and rubbed cold water on my face. I saw the eye patch we had rigged the night before; Pop had thrown it in the trashcan. When I came out, Scotty was gone. Pop was sitting on the edge of the bed, dressed in khakis and a light-blue Oxford shirt rolled up at the sleeves. He stretched one leg out and pulled an elastic legging up over one foot and onto his calf. I sat on my side of the bed and got dressed. I pulled on my leggings and slid my feet into my dark brown, thin-leathered over-the-ankle riding boots. They were my first new pair. My favorite ones as a kid had been hand-me-downs: My grandmother had worn them as a teenager; she'd saved them for twenty years and passed them on to Mom, who wore them as a teenager. Granny then stored them in her shoe closet for another twenty years, keeping them well oiled and polished. She gave them to me when I was twelve.

Pop had gotten me the new pair just a couple of weeks earlier. We ordered them off the Thyben's Saddlery truck, which circulated around the track area. They were well made and fit perfectly. The foot tapered at my high arch, and once I laced them, the thin tops felt molded to the hand-width of leg above my ankle.

As I focused on lacing the top holes of the boots, I looked forward to

# Chapter 1

the day. I was fifteen and spending my first full summer with Pop at the track. It was my first year of galloping racehorses. I was going from working with my mother — riding show ponies and show horses and then selling them — to spending more time around racehorses with my father. I was very happy.

Pop, Marvin, and Scotty had rented this apartment for years. It was actually just the top floor, almost an attic, of a small house in a development. The gabled roof slanted down over our heads. You could only stand up straight in the exact middle of our room. There were two windows and one was clogged with an old air-conditioning unit; it could get hot. It was a half-mile from the back gates of Belmont Park racetrack in Elmont, New York, and a ten-minute walk from Esposito's Bar. Off and on that summer, another boarder, Joe Canty, squeezed into these tight quarters. He was galloping horses and working at becoming an assistant trainer for a flat-racing outfit. Occasionally, one of Pop's fellow jumping riders, Tommy Walsh, spent a few nights. Tommy kept things lively when he stayed. We were packed in there, and we were a happy family.

It was still dark out when we got in the car. Pop turned the key, starting the engine. He pushed in the car lighter, stuck a cigarette in his mouth, and started backing out the entrance. The lighter popped back out a fraction of an inch as we coasted onto the street. He put on the brakes, brought the round band of heated coils to the tip of the cigarette, and the tip reddened. Without giving the car time to stop fully, he shifted into drive, and as we picked up speed on the empty street, he stuck the lighter back in the hole. We headed for the coffee shop five minutes away.

Over past summers, when I wasn't helping my mother, I had put in my time working with Pop and his brother, Mikey, at the track as the number one hot-walker and "gopher" around the barn. I'd also occasionally ride Rex, the stable pony, out onto the track beside Pop, who'd be on a racehorse. This summer I was bigger and stronger, weighing

138. Pop was training the Belmont Park string of steeplechase and flat horses for Smithwick Stables, comprising the triumvirate of my father's mother, Emma Smithwick; my Uncle Mikey; and Pop. At the same time, my father was also riding steeplechase races for Smithwick Stables at Monmouth Park, New Jersey. My Uncle Mikey was on the racing farm at Hydes, Maryland, training a barn full of horses, and he and Pop also had a stable of horses at Delaware Park, and another at Mrs. Ogden Phipps' farm farther out on Long Island, in Westbury. Smithwick Stables was a big outfit of fifty to sixty horses running in races up and down the East Coast during the spring, summer, and fall. In July they were running at Belmont Park, Monmouth Park, and Delaware Park, preparing for Saratoga Springs in August.

Pop swung the car into a parking place. The keys jingled as he dropped them on the floor to await our return. As soon as we entered the coffee shop, Nick, the whiskery Greek owner, poured us two cups of scalding coffee. "Good morning, Smithwicks," he said, from behind the counter, setting the cups in their saucers before us. There were six or seven other men, mainly racetrackers, sitting quietly at the counter. They looked up at us and the conversation among them rose. I could hear, "That's Paddy Smithwick — the jumping rider." And, "… in here every morning." Nick gave the group a scowl and the talk died down. I was very proud; everyone knew my father. Nick took an ashtray off the counter, dumped the cigarette butts in the trash can, cleaned the ash tray with a rag, and set it to the right of Pop's coffee. He bent over, took the *Morning Telegraph* — a companion paper to *Daily Racing Form* — out from under the counter, and set it down to the left of Pop's coffee. He leaned forward, close to Pop, and asked in a low voice, "Think you got a shot today, Paddy?"

Nick was looking for a bet. "No, not on much today, Nick," Pop said.

All that summer of 1966, if Pop were on a good horse, he'd say, "Got my good luck with me today, Nick," and he'd nod in my direction. That was code for go ahead and place your bet. I'd grin, happy to get credit for my hard work, happy to participate in and be a part of his winning, and I'd know that many of the Greeks in Elmont would be calling their bookmakers later in the morning.

This "good luck" business had gotten serious the summer before. After we'd shipped out of Saratoga Springs at the end of August, I'd stayed a couple of weeks into September at Belmont. There was one jumping race per day. Pop won a race the first day I was there and then continued to win a race day after day. He set a record. He was winning on horses that weren't even that good. He wouldn't let me go home and go back to school. I was his good luck. I was his sidekick. I went everywhere with him. Quite a few late mornings after work, he brought me by the jocks' room. It was a magical place. The jocks would be walking around naked, relaxed, going to the masseur, coming out of the hot box, or sitting with towels around their waists at the counter ordering a poached egg on a slice of toast. Older jocks would be quietly shooting a game of pool or reading that day's *Morning Telegraph*. Younger jocks might be dancing around, playing ping-pong with no clothes on. The valets would be cleaning boots and tack, and Pop's valet, Dick Dwyer, would inquire how Pop was doing — what weight he was so he could decide which saddle Pop would use that afternoon. Dick would wink at me and ask Pop to put his foot up on the bench alongside the open lockers. Pop would unzip his riding boots, slide a foot out and put it up on the bench. Dick would pull up the leg of Pop's pants, look at the calf with the legging still on it, and run his hand down it. Then, Merlin-like, he would pronounce Pop's weight. "One forty-two and a half," he'd say. "You've got to lose three pounds, brother."

Pop would pull off his clothes, and I'd follow him through the gauntlet of naked and half-dressed jockeys to the scales. Braulio Baeza, Manuel Ycaza, Johnny Rotz, Bill Boland, Eddie Maple were all there — and sometimes Willie Shoemaker. The greatest of them, Eddie Arcaro, had hung up his tack. Pop knew him well. I'd met Arcaro a couple of times. The Turf writers called him "the Master," and they called Pop "the Eddie Arcaro of the Steeplechase Set."

Pop knew best of all those who had to fight the weight; they suffered together through hours in the "hot-box" — the sauna — and sometimes they hit the road together in a "hot car." Besides the broken bones, the weight was the worst part. At five-foot-eleven-and-a-half, Pop was tall for a jumping rider, and he was not naturally thin. He was muscular, built more like a middleweight boxer. When he was not reducing, he had a square, ruddy Irish face, strong neck, and well-defined shoulders. When casually reducing, he was built like a lithe boy: cheeks taut, neck thin, shoulders gawky, the thinness of his legs making him look tall. When doing light, he appeared gaunt, the bones of his skull looking as if they'd puncture the tight skin, his eyes retreating back and leaving a void, his shoulders consisting of just bones and blades. His clothes would look loose, the shoulders of his jackets sagging. All he ate was a steak and a salad at night.

Pop would stand on the scales; the long needle would swing up to 145 or so, down to 138, back up, back down, and settle on 142 and a half. We'd walk back to Pop's locker. Dick was so sure of himself he would have Pop's lightest and favorite saddle out, and be lacing the stirrup leathers through the stirrups. Pop would sit down on the bench. "Got to lose three pounds, Cowboy. Got to get in the box," he'd tell me.

I didn't mind not going back to school that fall. But finally someone was driving back to Maryland and I had to go home. Pop's winning streak ended. I did catch a ride in a car instead of having to go in the back of a horse van.

* * *

Pop took a last morning cough and put out his cigarette in the ashtray. He set a five-dollar bill on the counter, just like in a bar. Nick rang up our bill, took the money, put it in the cash register, and set a couple of dollar bills and some change back on the counter. Pop left it there.

Pop sipped his coffee, and I sipped mine. He scanned the front page of the *Telegraph*, reading up on the racing news across the country. He

## Chapter 1

looked over at me, "You sure you don't want some eggs, Cowboy, or at least a doughnut?"

I set the cup down in the saucer. "No thanks, I'm fine," I said. I didn't want any because I knew he couldn't. Later in the morning while he was out on a horse, I'd get a soda and some doughnuts from Red, who drove the coffee truck, a wild Dr. Seuss-like kitchen on wheels.

Pop opened up the paper and folded it against the counter. Drinking his coffee slowly, he relaxed, first studying the results of the previous day's races, particularly the one he'd ridden in, and then looking at the chart for that day's races to see what kind of competition he was up against. He'd also double-check what weight he had to make.

I sat there sipping my coffee, listening to the men talking around me and watching Pop take a pull of his cigarette. Nick set a plate of three fried eggs, sunny side up, hash browns, bacon, and buttered toast in front of the man on my right. My mouth watered as I breathed in the fried-egg-and-bacon scent. I took another drink of the rich, hot coffee. I wanted to ask Pop some questions about Mom. She'd had a bad fall a few days earlier in a horse show and had broken her leg. Pop had explained to me that Dr. Jerry Johnson — the best — had set her leg and she was now in traction at Union Memorial Hospital in Baltimore, but I hadn't really understood what all this meant. I wondered about Mom, what she was doing at this moment. I breathed in the smoke from Pop's cigarette and the scent from the eggs and bacon, and I didn't interrupt Pop's reading of the paper.

This particular morning Pop wasn't too happy: He had to be at Monmouth Park — a couple of hours down the New Jersey Turnpike and the Garden State Parkway — in the afternoon to ride Totem II. The horse was rank — ornery and uncooperative — and a bad jumper, but Pop was the leading steeplechase jockey in the country and the best rider, especially on rank, bad-jumping horses, and the owner wanted him to ride Totem II. Also, his eye still hurt.

The day before he had taken me shopping for some shirts, and I'd seen what struck me as an odd logo for a button-down Oxford shirt. On the wrapping of the shirt was a photograph of a man with a black patch over one eye, his other eye caught in a piercing stare. It had bothered me. Later that day Pop scratched his eye while taking a shower. After dinner that night we were in Esposito's Bar, and everyone in the Esposito family kept coming out from the kitchen and behind the bar to look at Pop's eye. Mom and Pop Esposito and their three adult sons urged him to call off his ride for the next day and go see a doctor. Pop had a couple of drinks, and Junior, the youngest of the Esposito sons, rigged up an eye patch out of one of those Zorro-mask things people pull over their eyes to keep the light out so they can sleep. There Pop was, in a damn eye patch, looking like that man on the package.

Slowing as we drove through the big gates of Belmont Park, Pop saluted the Pinkerton security guards, keeping his hand on the steering wheel. One waved to us and called out, "Good morning, Smithwicks." The other held his hand up for us to stop. He leaned toward us and said, "Careful up ahead, Paddy." Here we go again, I thought. Some men on the backstretch had joined a union, and now we had to cross the picket line. A line of men came into our view; they started to march toward the car. A few of them carried signs nailed to two-by-fours. I leaned back, braced my feet against the floor, and gripped the edge of the seat with both hands — not wanting Pop to notice. I had heard some unsavory stories about these union men — including threats of lighting barns on fire. A day earlier an exercise rider had had a bad "spill" after being hit by a rock thrown by a union member. Pop looked at the Pinkerton, whom we saw every morning. The Pinkerton held his hands up — gesturing there was nothing he could do. Pop reached across the seat, set his hand firmly on my leg, just above my knee, and said, "Hold on, Cowboy." He revved the engine and drove, picking up speed, straight at the union line, and it dissolved before us, as did most problems when we took them head on.

We pulled up outside the barn at six o'clock sharp. It was an enclosed barn, about seventy-five yards long. I walked through the big open doorway, onto the shed row — a dirt walkway that encircled the entire barn — and took a right, heading for the tack room. On my left, a line of stalls, in the center of the barn, stretched out before me, with the horses all looking out their doors. On my right was a sturdy wooden wall — I knew it was sturdy because I'd smacked into it more than once on a misbehaving horse — lined with open windows at shoulder-height. Above, a gabled roof extended over the shed row to the wall. In the winters the windows in the wall could be shut, and when the track was closed due to bad weather, we'd ride the horses at a fast trot around and around the shed row.

I said good morning to Emmett Grayson, our foreman, who had been at the barn since 4:30, when he'd fed the horses and started mucking out stalls. Tanza, our groom, was busy cleaning and refilling water buckets, acting as if he'd been there a while. His cup of coffee, set on the top edge of the stall door, was steaming. Emmett and Tanza lived in the cinder block bunkhouse next to the barn. Emmett had been patrolling our section of the shed row, day and night, looking for any funny business from the union men.

Emmett was also dealing with Lenny, a new trainer next to us who had half a dozen horses. You got to know the trainers and the men who worked near your stalls. Lenny was an ex-flat rider, ex-pony boy, and about to be an ex-trainer, but the main thing was that he was loud, noisy, raucous, and always seemed to be fighting with his men. He had one very sour and very big man in his twenties who rubbed for him, and Lenny would berate him all morning long. During the haranguing, Emmett would mutter, "His time is going to come. His time is going to come," and let it be known to me that he thought Lenny picked on the man more because of his color — black, as were Emmett and Tanza — than because of his performance.

I stepped into the fresh straw of our first stall, gave the horse a pat on the neck, and prepared to take off the bandages that Emmett and Tanza had wrapped around the horse's front legs the day before. I kneeled, undid the safety pin that held the bandage on, and uncoiled about eight feet of wrap, going around and around the horse's leg. Beneath was an inch-thick, fluffy, white cotton bandage, which I removed in just three turns around the leg. And beneath that was a cool, clean, straight tendon onto which Emmett or Tanza had gently massaged rubbing alcohol. I ducked under the horse's neck (sometimes, I crawled right under their bellies, something my Uncle Mikey often did. This way you didn't have to stand up and squat down again, but it was a little risky), unwrapped the other bandage, and ran my hand down the tendon as I'd seen Pop do. Then I moved on to the next horse. Pop followed behind me, feeling each horse's front legs, checking on tender or sore spots, and making sure there was no heat in the knees, tendons, or ankles. Emmett had already taken the temperatures of the horses, a job I didn't like much since you couldn't exactly take them orally and sometimes the horses did not cooperate when you were attempting to get the thermometer where it belonged.

Emmett and I "knocked off" — brushed off — and tacked up two horses, he working on one side of the horse and I on the other. Emmett's hands swept in strong massaging strokes over the horse, first with a currycomb, then a stiff brush and a soft brush, and finally a rub rag that snapped and cracked. Then his long sinewy fingers delicately and precisely set the saddlecloth, saddle pad, and pommel pad on the horse's back before slapping the exercise saddle on top. We talked about whether the great Jack Dempsey would be by later in the morning. He owned a few horses that Lenny trained, but we hadn't seen him for a week. I'd met Dempsey on my first day of work that summer. I'd been in the tack room picking out a bridle for the next horse I would ride, and Pop had said to me, "Hey Bud, come here a minute." I'd stepped out, and there, alongside five-foot-tall Lenny, was this huge man in a black pinstriped suit. He had a craggy face and gray hair, and his long legs moved purposefully down the shed row as he looked in at the horses in their stalls.

"Do you know who that is?" Pop had asked.

"No," I'd said.

"That's Jack Dempsey. Lenny has a few horses for him."

Lenny and Dempsey had continued walking down the shed row, looking in the stalls, until they were just a few stalls down from our tack room. I'd nervously stepped out of the tack room, with a saddle and bridle draped over my arm. Pop was unsnapping the webbing across the opening to a stall, and we were preparing to go in and tack up the horse. Dempsey had looked our way, stepped away from Lenny and toward Pop, and put his hand out. "Paddy Smithwick," Dempsey had said, as they shook. "It's good to meet you. I admire how you've stayed at the top of your game all these years."

"Thank you, Mr. Dempsey," Pop had said, half-bowing as he always did when he first met someone or was being complimented.

"Jack — just call me Jack."

"Jack, this is my son, Paddy, who has always been a great admirer of your career," Pop had glanced toward me, then back at Dempsey, and added, "and your heart."

It'd been like a dream. I'd reached up, and this big hand had clamped around mine; he'd grinned and looked me in the eye and we shook. I'd had one thousand questions to ask him, but I didn't say a word. I was starting to prepare some sort of a remark when a deep voice from outside the barn had called, "Hey, Jack, where the hell are you?" And then a short, roly-poly man in a dark pinstriped, double-breasted suit had stepped into the shed row. He was not as old or weathered as Dempsey but had a thickened and slightly crooked nose that must've been broken once or twice. Dempsey had introduced his friend to us — he was part owner of a couple of the horses — and they'd walked back down the shed row to Lenny's stalls.

Tanza was quiet this time of the morning, his expression sad and sleepy. He was setting up for when we returned with the hot horses:

filling wash buckets with steaming water from the faucet over by the bunk house, pouring in the antiseptic, dropping in sponges and scrapers, taking breathers between tasks. He slowly lugged the heavy buckets as the foamy water splashed out of them. I knew he'd come to life after we got the first set of horses out.

About this time, a gentle-looking, neatly dressed, light-skinned black man came walking down our shed row. He ambled past Tanza, into the side door of Tanza and Emmett's bunkhouse, and to the bathroom we all shared. Emmett started muttering to himself, and Tanza chuckled and looked over at Emmett. "There he goes," said Emmett, raking up outside a stall. "He's on the hop, smack. Damn dope head oughtn't to be allowed on the track." He stopped raking and looked at me, "Little Paddy, don't you go into that bathroom alone."

Soon the man was back, leading a horse around the shed row. As he passed our stall, he nodded to me, and said, "Good morning." I said, "Good morning," to him, and that was it. He walked on by, looking neat and clean in his khakis and long-sleeve shirt. For the next four hours, he'd continue walking "hots" — horses that have just exercised — around and around the shed row until they cooled out. He always wore long sleeves, no matter how hot it was.

"No need to be making friends with him, Little Paddy," Emmett said, glaring at the man as he walked away from us. "I've seen him in the bathroom stall sticking in the needle. His arm looks like Swiss cheese. Veins are so shot, he's got to stick the needle in his leg now." Emmett could be as judgmental about this sort of thing as one of the Puritans we read about at school last year in *The Scarlet Letter*; Tanza just shrugged it off.

Pop and I got the first set out early. Our barn was far from the track, and as we walked down the horse path side-by-side — Pop on a big bay gelding, me on a fine-boned black filly — the owners, trainers, jockeys, exercise boys, grooms, and hot-walkers talked to Pop and kidded with us.

Pop had a lot of old riding buddies who had quit. A few who quit early had become successful trainers. But riding had become a way of life for the ones who had been doing it more than ten years. Pop had explained to me they could neither adapt to a new lifestyle nor work off their drinking as they had when riding. Some of them had never become real horsemen — they'd just lived in the present moment of riding — unlike Pop, who had been a knowledgeable horseman since he was a teenager and who had been training along with his brother, Mikey, for years. Pop had been race-riding for twenty years and knew all the riders well.

We walked down the wide pathway in a surging stream of horses headed for the track. Hot horses that had just galloped were coming toward us, headed back to the barns, their riders relaxed in the saddle. We passed barn after barn. Horses were being tacked up. Horses were being washed off. Chestnut horses. Bay horses. Black horses. Gray horses. Horses were being led out and riders being given legs-up into the saddle. Everyone was saying good morning. They kidded Pop about being too old and then half seriously asked if he were trying to kill himself by reducing so hard. "Hey, Paddy," they called out, "when're you going to quit and let Little Paddy take over?" and, "Christ, Paddy, you'd better stop feeding your partner there; he's going to be bigger than you."

You could tell that some of the riders and trainers were giving us extra attention this morning because of Mom's fall a few days earlier. They'd kind of look at us a little longer than the usual, as if they wanted to say something about Mom but didn't know what to say, so they didn't say anything at all. Evan Jackson was outside his barn, bending over and feeling the tendons of a new filly he'd just gotten to train. He must've spotted us out of the corner of his eye. "Paddy, Little Paddy," he yelled out. He stood up, left the groom holding the filly, and jogged over to us. He walked out on the dirt path, and walked along, having to half jog to keep up with us. "Paddy — how's Suzie?"

"She's getting better, getting better all the time, Evan," Pop told him.

\* \* \*

We got another set of horses out fast. On the way back from the track, we took a slight detour, riding out to the end of a line of barns. "Maybe somebody'll be here today, Bud," Pop said. We rode up to a barn with no cars outside. We walked into the shed row. There were horses in only six of the forty stalls running the length of the shed row. There were no webbings or runners across the doorways. Instead, the bottoms of the Dutch doors were closed, and it didn't look as if anybody had been there all morning. Six horses immediately stuck their heads out over the doors, and two whinnied. "That's all right boys; whoa boys, we'll be back," Pop called out to them. He looked me in the eye, shook his head, and we headed back to our barn.

We'd met the young trainer of these horses in Esposito's. He told us how he had horses stabled at the track plus out at a farm on Long Island, and a few down in Pennsylvania. He couldn't get in to the track every day, but he had a groom called Dale who was "looking out" for the horses at Belmont. Pop and I had ridden over to the barn to see how the new trainer was doing. The barn had looked deserted. The stalls hadn't been mucked out. And the horses had no hay or water. Apparently, neither the trainer nor the groom was showing up. Emmett checked up on Dale, found out where his bunkhouse was, and told Pop that Dale was "lazy" and "no-account," but he'd try to get him to get up and go to work. Soon, Emmett had christened Dale, "Deadbeat Dale," and every morning we heard a story or two about just how "good for nothing" this deadbeat was.

When we returned to our barn on the second set, Emmett had a horse tacked up. It was getting hot. Pop walked into the tack room, stripped, and pulled on thermal underwear, rubber sweat suit, corduroys, turtleneck, wool sweater, and a jacket. Emmett gave him a leg up onto the horse. I stayed behind, grazing mine in the shade of a tree.

Tanza walked out to me carrying a stiff brush, a soft brush, and a rub rag. He started calmly working and talking. Unlike most of the men I met on the track, he'd had jobs and experiences that had nothing to do with horses. He often shared with me insights from his times away from the track. As he spoke, he brushed off the horse and switched to the rub rag, sweat running down his face.

"Come on, Tanza, what're you two doing out there? We don't have all day," yelled Emmett.

Tanza shook his head, didn't take the bait, and just kept rubbing. "Some mornings I don't know why I'm doing this, Little Paddy. I could have a nice job with all kinds of benefits working inside, in air-conditioning, all summer, and inside with central heating during the winter instead of being here shoveling shit, dodging heroin addicts ..." Just then the horse cow-kicked at a fly, the hoof coming up fast and just missing Tanza's hand. Tanza kept rubbing, not missing a beat. "... and trying to keep from being kicked — snatch on this bastard would you please, Little Paddy — or bitten by a bunch of crazy racehorses. But you see, here I am, and you know why?"

He caught me off guard. "No, why?" I asked.

"You honestly don't know?" he asked and stopped rubbing, giving me a disappointed look.

I strained but couldn't figure out this riddle.

"You need to wake up. Wake up and smell the coffee, son. I'm here for one reason ..." He was really rubbing now, over the horse's kidneys, right behind where the saddle goes, and the horse was bending down, lowering its back, enjoying the massage as the rub rag whipped back and forth.

"Emmett?" I said.

"No," he said, breathing hard. "Emmett did ask me. He did and he thinks I'm here because of him, but I'm here because of your father. That's the only reason I'm standing out here sweating with this horse that'd like to bite and kick and stomp on me." He stopped rubbing, stepped back from the horse, and gave him a look over. "Son, your father's special. Don't you get it? Don't you know that? Soon, he's going to be training full-time, and I want to be with him. I want to see his training career take off. He's going to be the best in the country, and he's the only trainer I'll work for." He stuffed the rub rag in his back pocket, picked up the two brushes, and headed back toward the shed row.

# 2

## Esposito's

The day before, the jumping race at Monmouth Park hadn't "filled"
— too few horses were entered, and the race was canceled. Pop and
I didn't have to rush off and race from Long Island down the New
Jersey Turnpike and the Garden State Parkway to Monmouth. We were
able to work late at the barn until all the horses were cleaned off, their
front legs bandaged, and they were fed. You couldn't buy alcohol on
the backside of the track back then, and a "bootlegger" — in that he
certainly did not have a permit or a license to sell his goods — came
around in a big old sedan. You could spot him a mile away. The car
drove a little funny, off balance — it sagged in the rear. Emmett had
told me the old man was going to get caught unless he put a set of
heavy-duty shocks in the rear. "You know why rednecks always drive
around with their hotrods jacked up, don't you?" No, I didn't. Emmett
explained that during Prohibition the bootleggers in Virginia would rig
their high-powered cars with extra shocks and springs in the back so
that the car would ride level and would look normal when loaded
down with hundreds of pounds of liquor. After they made their deliv-
eries and returned home, "they'd roar around like jackasses, showing
off, the rear ends of their cars all jacked up bouncing and leaping off

the road." Emmett wasn't too high on rednecks.

The bootlegger parked near the barn, slowly stepped out of the car, and looked around. He opened the trunk, revealing a custom-made, metal-lined ice chest taking up the entire space. He lifted the top. The cooler was filled with an array of loose beer bottles, their caps peeking up out of the ice. Pop handed some cash to the aging entrepreneur, who in turn pulled out a wet burlap feed bag, placed a few bottles in it one at a time, added a layer of newspapers and a few more bottles, and handed the wet feed bag to Pop.

Emmett, Tanza, Pop, a couple of grooms who worked on our shed row, and even the cantankerous Lenny sat on bales of straw under the shade outside the tack room and passed around Emmett's pocket knife to open the beers Pop had bought. They sipped the beer out of ice-cold bottles wrapped in newsprint and relaxed; it had been a long, hot morning. The numbers man had made the rounds earlier. Emmett had talked all morning, in a low voice, about his lucky number for the day — it was a combination of the month, day, and year of his birth (which he wouldn't tell us), the post position numbers of the horses that had won the last three races the day before, and a magical formula that included certain numbers from his Virginia license tags. Emmett and Tanza joked quietly about whose numerology theory would bring in the big bucks. Pop had his tan briefcase open, a cigarette in his mouth, and was writing on a yellow legal pad everything he had to organize for the horses that day: A vet was coming by later to check on a horse's tendon, the blacksmith had to shoe two horses, the feed man would stop by and ask for our order, and the hay man was supposed to make a delivery later in the day, but Emmett had to check to make sure it was fresh before it was unloaded. I was cleaning the tack. My mouth was watering as I thought of the beer, but I didn't want any until I was through work for the morning.

As I finished the tack, Pop reviewed with Emmett what he had written and handed Emmett the legal pad. Emmett wouldn't pay any atten-

## Chapter 2

tion to what was written but would remember every detail that Pop had gone over. Emmett would not admit it, and he was incredibly successful in hiding it — "Hey, Little Paddy, read me what the handicappers say about our entry today while I rub on this horse" — but he couldn't read. We all went along with the game. Pop closed his briefcase, stood up, put it under his left arm like a football, called me, and started walking fast toward the car. Then Tanza went over to Pop. They walked away from us, and I could see Pop nodding okay, and Tanza talking, and then Pop reaching into his back pocket, pulling out his wallet, and handing Tanza a few bills. Not too many or we might not see him the next morning.

Pop and I drove out the track gate and over the short distance to Esposito's Bar. We parked in the lot, alongside cars I recognized, cars belonging to trainers, riders, and hangers-on of the steeplechase set. The license tags were from South Carolina, North Carolina, Virginia, Maryland, and Pennsylvania, and the fenders and lower sides of the cars were streaked with layers of clay.

We got out. The sun and heat reflecting off the sidewalk made me squint. I was tired and felt sticky and sweaty. Inside Esposito's, the cool, dark air, soothing music, and humming voices relaxed me.

Pop knew all the Espositos well. There were the three sons — philosophic John, tall and taciturn Ralph, and fat, happy-go-lucky Junior — and old Mom and Pop Esposito, shorter versions of their children. As soon as we entered, John, who was tending bar, called out, "Paddy," in a low voice and nodded for him to come over to the empty bar stool.

"I'll get you a beer, Cowboy," Pop said to me. "Grab a table."

I sat at a little table by the wall. Pop and John had their heads close together. John's eyes were furrowed, and I could see his mouth shape the word "Suzie." I knew he was asking about Mom, and the others at the bar were listening to Pop's answer. While Pop was getting me a Heineken and himself a screwdriver, Mom Esposito handed me one of her special cold-cut sandwiches on thick, crusty bread and said, "Just because your father can't-a-eat don't mean that you can't-a-eat." To me, the Espositos were like family. This feeling was sparked by an odd catalyst. When I was little, I had in the back of my mind a memory of attending my parents' marriage, and in a vague way, I placed the marriage at Esposito's, none of which made any sense. Then, one night when I was eight years old, my best friend, Tom Voss, and I were sneaking around outside his house, spying on the adults having a party, when I overheard the phrase, "… back when Suzie and Paddy were divorced." With Tom there beside me, the concept of my parents once being divorced hit me like a bullet. A few years later, when I finally asked Mom about it, she explained that Pop's fast-paced life in those years led him to believe he'd be better off unmarried, and it led her to believe she and us kids would be better off unattached to this racing life. They'd gotten divorced, but their unmarried lifestyles did not pan out. They were unhappy apart. After a year of being divorced, they remarried in Elmont. A justice of the peace conducted the ceremony. Drinks and celebration followed at Esposito's, with me tagging along, Pop's best man. All I could remember was the celebration at Esposito's, and it was as if they had been married there with Mom and Pop Esposito, and John, Junior, and Ralph officiating.

We were later than usual, and some of Esposito's regulars were getting ready to leave. Tommy Walsh — one of my idols, a jumping rider a decade and a half younger than Pop — was sitting at the bar sipping a screwdriver. Whether on a bar stool or on a horse, Tommy sat slouched over, relaxed. He had longish, thin blond hair, large eyebrows, and sad eyes. He didn't have to worry about his weight much and always wore an Oxford shirt, rolled up at the sleeves, to work in the mornings. I much admired Tommy's don't-give-a-damn attitude. From a large Irish family of talented and successful horsemen, he had started riding races very young. And he had become one of the best, especially riding a finish. To me, he was like James Dean: *Rebel Without a Cause*. And when I was alone with him, driving somewhere to meet

## Chapter 2

Pop or go to the races, he'd let me have a beer and give me pep talks on just what I should be doing with my sex life and what kind of car I should get when I turned sixteen.

Evan Jackson, short and powerful and tan, and usually very excited about something, sat beside Tommy. Evan had just quit race-riding and had begun training, and Tommy was galloping for him in the mornings and riding races for him in the afternoons. Tommy and Evan loved Pop. They would do anything for him. Once a week, on the "dark day" — no racing — we'd drive to their favorite spot for hot roast beef sandwiches, a restaurant with a German name. Just Evan, Tommy, Pop, and me. It'd be an hour or two before the lunch crowd arrived, and we'd sit at the long bar, with a wall of glittering bottles and mirrors before us, and have the whole place to ourselves.

Evan had a hell of a temper and was frustrated with Pop's loyalty to Smithwick Stables. Almost all the earnings from the Smithwick Stables went back into the Hydes farm — a new paddock fence, a new shed, another tractor, buying twenty more acres from a neighboring farmer, repairing the vans, buying the materials for building more hurdles, adding stalls to the main barn. Evan had recently been urging Pop to quit race-riding, get away from his brother and his mother, and start training his own stable of horses. Pop had seriously considered retiring from race-riding the winter before, but there was this one exceptional horse — Bon Nouvel — who had been Steeplechase Horse of the Year and who had a shot of regaining the title. Pop had ridden him in most of his races last year and wanted to ride this champion one more season, at least this was what I thought at the time. Besides, the owner, Mrs. Randolph, wanted to run Bon Nouvel in one of the world's most prestigious steeplechase races, the Grand Steeple-Chase de Paris, and if Bon Nouvel went, she and Mikey wanted Pop to be the one in the tack. Lastly, I knew that Bon Nouvel was very difficult to ride. Tommy Walsh was the only other jockey to ride him successfully. When you left the tape, you had to drop the reins and let him go full blast, open up thirty lengths on the field. This took some extreme talent and nerve. He roared into every hurdle without any fear or respect of the fence; he'd tear right through a few of them. As Mikey explained to me, you had to be "fearless" and just let him go for the entire first mile, keep him from falling, before you could gather him in and control him.

Standing sideways between Evan and Tommy, leaning against the bar and laughing, was the un-ratable Billy "Turnpike" Turner. He was making motions to leave but being drawn into a heated conversation with John Esposito and perhaps being lured into having one more for the road. Billy had ridden races but had been way too big for it, over six feet tall. He had short, curly reddish-blond hair and had been nicknamed Turnpike Turner when he was making three-hour, one hundred mile an hour sprints in his powerful Oldsmobile up and down the New Jersey Turnpike to see his girlfriend. He was a lot of fun.

Our apartment mates, Scotty Schulhofer and Marvin Green, rarely frequented Esposito's after work in the morning, though they would stop by after the races in the afternoon. Scotty, once a very good jumping rider, had retired and was training an excellent stable of horses. Marvin was the biggest, fattest, happiest man I'd ever known. We often went out to dinner together, driving to the restaurant in his red convertible with the top down. A Long Island cop pulled us over for speeding one night, and Marvin gave him his license. The cop stood by Marvin's door, looked over the license, slid something from under the license into his pocket, and told Marvin to please slow down and to have a nice night. We drove away, Marvin laughing, me perplexed at what had transpired. Like everybody else, Scotty and Marvin loved and admired Pop. And they told me this. They told me incredible stories of his riding feats and of his generosity and his modesty. Women loved him, too, but this was never discussed with me until years later.

Pop brought the drinks over. Mom Esposito was just setting down my lunch. "What're you doing, Mom?" Pop asked, grinning. "How's he going to make any weight if you keep giving him those things?" Before me sat a big, beautiful sandwich. It was an Italian submarine, something I had just discovered.

Mom Esposito put a hand on each of her broad hips and gave Pop a stern look. "This boy, he's not-a-going to be a jockey. He's a-going to go to college and be a lawyer or a doctor, and he needs to eat so's he'll have strong bones."

"He can do that if he wants, Mom," Pop said in a serious tone. "That's fine with me." He set down his screwdriver and my Heineken.

"Good-t," she said, surprised at not having a fight on her hands. She started to walk away, stopped, and turned around, looking at us both. "And another thing, this boy should be having an Orange Crush not a Heineken with his sandwich."

Pop sat down opposite me. "She's probably right, Bud," he said, sipping his screwdriver. I hoped none of his admirers or friends would come over; I hoped we'd be left alone so we could talk. It seemed Pop knew everyone. Sometimes just the two of us would go out to dinner and halfway through the meal the restaurant owner would introduce a customer who was an admirer of Pop's and the rest of the meal would be ruined: We'd have to first talk to the customer, who would then introduce his wife, and then when they left, someone else who had overheard the conversation would approach our table, just to say hello, linger and linger, and finally, the restaurant owner would come back and have a drink with us and ask how we liked the couple he'd introduced.

I sipped the frosty beer from a glass. The taste of the Heineken, its dryness and coolness, made me so thirsty that I gulped down a few swallows. "First afternoon off for us in a long time," I said.

"You deserve it, Bud."

"When we leave I'm going back to the apartment, take a hot shower, and do some sleeping."

"That was a long morning, wasn't it?" He sipped his drink. "You know, you're doing well with that little black filly. You get along with her better than I do. I think I'll let you school her next time."

My heart leapt. I pictured the hurdles in the infield of Belmont Park's main track.

"When'll that be?"

"Oh, not till a few days after we've shipped to Saratoga."

My imagination shifted to envisioning the hurdles in the infield of Oklahoma, the training track at Saratoga. I leaned back against the chair. The beer was making me drowsy. I started thinking about Totem II and his poor jumping form. "Pop, are you going to ride Totem tomorrow?"

"I wish I didn't have to, Bud; he's not much account."

"Don't then."

"Well, I can't just do that … Wish you could stay for the race, but there's no way to get the horses shipped up unless you go with them."

"That's okay. I don't mind." I had to come back up from Monmouth Park, which was halfway down the Garden State Parkway, and go way out to Mrs. Phipps' farm on Long Island, with a load of horses on a nine-horse van. A three-hour ride. But it was all right; I hardly ever got to see Pop ride at Monmouth anyway unless Mom brought me to the backside and we watched from a little wooden stand by the half-mile pole. They didn't allow kids at the races there.

"I think I'm starting to get the knack of what you said the other day," I said.

"What was that?"

"About not pulling against a horse's mouth, about relaxing on a horse. But on a couple of them I just can't seem to do it."

"You have to give and take with them."

"It would work well on that filly."

"You're doing it now without even knowing it." He took a sip of his screwdriver. "I used to ride a horse called King Commander that was a lot like that little filly. He was rank as hell and would gallop into a hurdle with his head in the jock's lap. The riders were all fighting him, pulling against him, and he fought back. The first time I got on him I didn't touch his mouth once until I lined him up for the start. And when the man said, 'Go,' I dropped the reins, let him go to the front, and he galloped along quietly. Going into the last hurdle, I took a hold of him and we went about our business."

That meant they'd won. Pop always said King Commander was the best horse he'd ever ridden over hurdles, with Neji being the best he'd ever ridden over brush. Hurdle races were faster, shorter — one and a half miles to two and a half — and a horse could skip through the four-foot hurdles. Brush races were longer — two and a half miles to three and a half — and a horse had to jump higher and better to clear the five-foot brush fences. We had winning photographs of both King Commander and Neji all over the house. Tommy Walsh's uncle, the legendary M.G. Walsh, trained King Commander and stood grinning in the winner's circle along with a nephew or niece in every photo of King Commander. Uncle Mikey, Mrs. Phipps, and, sometimes, Ogden Phipps stood in all the photos of Neji.

Sitting in my chair at Esposito's, I waited while Pop walked up to the bar, ordered another beer and screwdriver, and sat back down with me. I tilted the glass and poured my beer down the clean sides of a fresh glass not quite tall enough to hold the whole bottle. "If I'm going to school this filly, I don't know," I said, the words not coming out the way I wanted them to. There seemed to be a lag between saying the thought and hearing the words I was pronouncing. "I feel confident going slow," I said to Pop, "but how can you make a horse jump right going fast?"

"When you start to get near a fence, don't slow down." Pop leaned forward and took a sip of his drink. "Squeeze with your legs, but at the same time have a good hold of the horse's mouth through your grip on the reins. With experience you learn how to time it. When you get near enough, you can tell whether you should push him to lengthen his stride — one, two, three, and take off — or just steady him and let him put in an extra one."

"What about toward the end of a race?"

"Well, that's a lot different today from how it used to be. When a horse starts getting tired, you've got to hold him together. But back when Scotty Riles was riding, every jock rode whipping and driving into that last fence like it wasn't there."

I took a quick drink of my beer. "You really think the riders back then were that much better?"

"On the average — yes. They were artists."

"Sometimes you act as though the riders now don't have as much heart."

"Listen, Bud, riders were real professionals then. They were out to win. I was riding at old Belmont one day, and Riles," he nodded to where Scotty was sitting down at the far end of the bar, "tried to come up on my inside. He was one of my best friends. He kept on yelling at me to let him through. Finally, I thought the hell with it. I let him through just enough so he had to jump off my quarters. He stood on his head — meaning he fell — and I won the race."

"Damn, did he stay a friend?"

"Oh, yeah. He was a little banged up and wouldn't talk to me for a day or two, but then we were all right."

I looked up and saw Tommy Walsh and Billy Turner head out the door. Evan Jackson walked over to our table, grabbed a chair from another table, turned it backward, and sat down, his arms folded across the back of the chair.

"How you doing, Little Paddy?"

"Good."

"Your dad taking good care of you?"

"Yes," I glanced over at Pop, "Yes, he is."

Pop grinned.

"You looked good on that filly this morning."

"Thanks," I said, a little embarrassed.

"You ready to head up to the Spa?"

## Chapter 2

"I sure am."

"What're you looking forward to the most?"

My mind lit up like a pinball machine, jammed with fast-blinking images — bicycling, fishing, lying around with the McFarlane sisters, schooling the little filly, betting with Elmer Delmer at the races, galloping around Oklahoma head-and-head with Pop. The images bounced and zinged off one another and then down a chute and back up, and it was all too fast. I couldn't slow them down, couldn't articulate a description of even one of the activities I'd been looking forward to for more than a month.

Evan turned to Pop and began asking him a series of questions at Gatling gun speed about a horse he had in training. Pop attempted to answer, but Evan continually interrupted him by either answering his own question or throwing in another question.

While they went back and forth, I steadied my mind and thought about what I'd be doing in Saratoga. Instead of racing my show pony, Twinkle, around "the pony track" of Horse Haven, I'd be galloping horses alongside my father on the Oklahoma training track. Maybe I'd get to gallop a horse around the main track. Plus, I had the little filly to school over hurdles. I couldn't wait to see my great friends Mike White and Willie Dixon, and I had been writing lavish love letters to one of the McFarlane sisters in preparation of Mike's and my plan to take them to our secret fishing hole at Yaddo. I was kind of stuck on this picture of Mike and me lying in the shade, fishing with the McFarlane sisters, when I heard Evan say, "All right, I see what you mean. Thank you, Paddy. Got to go." He looked over at me, "See you, Little Paddy." He bounced up out of his chair, swung it back over to the table where he'd gotten it, and walked out.

I looked around. The bar was thinning out. Pop and I got organized and decided to ship the horses up to Saratoga in a week. We'd drive up a day before the vans made the two-hour trip and make sure the barn was ready. We had rented a house in Saratoga for August, as we did every summer, and we'd originally planned for Mom, and my two sisters — Sue Sue, thirteen, and Sallie, seven — to come up just after we arrived. But now that Mom was in the hospital and might be there a few weeks, we'd had to cancel the house and get a small apartment. We were hoping Mom and the girls could come up at least for a few days at the end of the meet.

"We'd better get going, Bud," Pop said.

We stood up, pushed our chairs under the table. As we walked down the length of the room, John and Junior Esposito called out, "See you, Paddy. See you, Little Paddy," from behind the bar. Opening the door and stepping out onto the parking lot, I felt like I was entering a desert. The glare from the sunlight reflecting off the asphalt and off the cars at first blinded me, then made me squint. I was dizzy. Pop dropped me off at the apartment. He had to find the van man and go over to the racing secretary's office at the main track to see about some "papers" — the official identifying documents — for a new horse he was running on the flat the next day. I couldn't tell if he knew I was tipsy or not. I concentrated on every step as I walked down the bright, white cement sidewalk to the front door. Once up the narrow stairway and into the apartment, I turned on the air-conditioner full blast, took a hot shower, and slept into the afternoon.

# 3

# Hitting the Road in a Hot Car

"**H**ot horse! Hot horse!" yelled Emmett. "Hey boy — get your mind off that girlfriend of yours and wake up. Here comes a hot horse!" Grazing my horse, I looked up from the grass and saw Pop returning. His horse was jigging from one side of the path to the other, bumping into fences and trees, its neck covered with a soapy lather, its head shaking and held high.

While most jocks would be nervous — making the horse even worse — Pop was calm and relaxed, his stirrups down long. He rode longer than most jocks. With his long legs and the bulky sweat clothes, he looked big on the horse. As it sidled closer, you could see the redness of Pop's face and hands. You could smell the sweat trapped by the rubber suit mixing with the steaming coat of the horse. I knew Pop was in hell. It was the last week of July and the sun was blazing. I was hot without any extra clothes on.

"Little Paddy — put him in the hole! Put him in the hole!" yelled Emmett. I led my horse into the covered shed row, down the aisle, and into his stall. I gave him a rub between the eyes as he pushed his nose against my hip. I unsnapped the shank and came back outside. Pop's face was drawn, but he grinned at me and hopped off, landing with a splash inside the suit.

"We've gotta get cracking if we want to get to the races on time," he said, pulling the saddle off, streams of sweat running down into his eyes and mouth. He pulled the bridle off. Emmett buckled a halter behind the horse's ears. He unsnapped the brass chain of the leather shank from the bottom fastening of the halter and looped the chain through the fastening and around the noseband of the halter. He handed me the leather end of the shank. I gave it a snatch to show the horse I meant business. Emmett began to wash the horse with a thick, brown, irregular-shaped sponge — a real ocean sponge that soaked up the water and suds — starting between the ears, as the horse snapped at us and stomped his front feet and whipped his wet tail from side to side.

Holding the saddle over his arm, Pop bent over and stretched the tight rubber bands around his ankles, allowing a pool of sweat to flow out. He straightened and did the same with his wrists.

A short, fat trainer on a pony had come by earlier and asked Pop to jump his horse over a few hurdles. Pop also had two of our own to school. It was getting late, and we had to be at Monmouth in time for the third race, the steeplechase race, always held right after the "daily double," a favorite of gamblers, who liked to bet on the first two races as a unit.

We rode out. The sun was blazing and Pop still had his sweat suit on. He kidded me only once as we jogged our horses around the training track on the way to the main track. "Well, Partner, pretty soon I can let you take over." Jogging along, side-by-side, I could see that he kept opening and closing, and occasionally rubbing, his eye. I asked how it felt.

"Could be better."

We came off the training track, hacked around to an entrance to the main track, and jogged to the three-quarters pole. The main track of Belmont Park is huge. Every track I'd been on had been a mile or less. This track is a mile and a half, and it is twice as wide as most. I had originally learned to gallop on the "pony track" at Belmont, a lightly used quarter-mile track in the woods. Often I'd jog a green horse on it one mile and then canter a mile and a half, which meant I'd have to go around and around ten times. Sometimes I was the only one on the track. At the time, I was reading *Valley of the Dolls* by Jacqueline Susann, given to me by a woman of about thirty who went by the nickname of Kelly — she used to work with the great racehorse Kelso. She had met me at Esposito's, treated me to an extra Heineken or two, and then brought me back to her cramped apartment to give me, as she told Tommy Walsh, who was watching over me that day, "a good school" and to find out if I could "go the distance." Between daydreaming about the latest adventures and sex scenes I'd read in *Valley of the Dolls* and wondering when Kelly would invite me back to her apartment for some more "schooling," I sometimes lost count of how many times I'd circled the track. My method for staying focused was to count aloud in French — which Mom attempted to teach us at the dinner table when Pop was away. Finally, I'd moved up to the mile training track, which I knew my way around. No time for daydreaming on this track. It was crowded with horses breezing on the inside rail, galloping in the middle of the track, and jogging around backward on the outside rail, and the riders all singing and calling out to each other and sometimes yelling and cussing each other out. The one time I might relax, I'd look up and there'd be a loose horse — nostrils flared, reins broken and dragging, stirrups flapping madly — galloping full tilt straight at me.

This was my first day on the main track at Belmont Park, one of the greatest tracks in America. The sky was gigantic above us. The grandstand to our left loomed like the *Titanic*. The dirt track ahead looked as though it stretched into infinity. Only a few horses were still galloping on it this late in the morning. All the activity was inside the dirt track, on the turf course, and in the infield.

A Pinkerton waited for a horse to gallop by, and then magically pulled out an inside rail, and we stepped off the dampened, dark brown dirt track and onto the lush green turf of the infield crowded with owners, trainers, and spectators milling around on foot, and with horses warming up. There were six hurdles set up for schooling, three down the frontside, three down the backside. Each hurdle was about three-and-a-half-feet high, with five-foot-high white wooden "wings" extending out from the ends. The wings, looking similar to three-paneled board fences, were to keep the horses from "running out" or "ducking out." At the core of each hurdle was a two-foot-high "box," the hurdle's wooden frame, which you couldn't see. In front of the box was "the roll," a pile of green brush from a pine tree. And into the top of the box, a foot and a half of brush was stiffly stuffed. Horses hurdled over the roll and the box and through the top six inches of the brush.

Pop jogged his horse around looking for "company" — another horse and rider — to school with. He hooked up with Bobby McDonald, who was on a big chestnut, and he and Bobby went head-and-head, about a mile, over the six hurdles. They were clipping right along.

Pop galloped back to where I was waiting, hopped off his horse, and while holding it, grabbed the reins of mine. I got off, and he gave me a leg up onto the one he had just schooled and then hopped on mine. He schooled this one a turn of the field by himself, then galloped back to the trainer on the pony. The trainer was holding a nervous, big gray colt with an ornery-looking white blaze that ran from between his eyes down to one nostril. Pop handed his horse to the trainer and hopped on the colt.

He hadn't gotten his feet in the stirrups before the horse reared up. Pop threw his arms around the gray's neck, leaned forward as the colt teetered on the brink of falling over backward. On the way down Pop thrust his feet through the irons. Before the horse had a chance to go up again, I saw Pop dig in with his spurs and I heard a low hoarse growl; simultaneously, he twirled his whip and cracked the horse hard, *whack* across his rump, still digging in with his spurs. The colt lunged forward.

The horse wasn't even a jumper. He was a well-bred flat horse whose stable name was Devil. He was supposedly descended from the Native Dancer line, and his formal name was something like Dancing Devil. Because of his breeding potential, the owner didn't want to have him "cut" — castrated — but everyone who worked with him was ready to call the vet. Devil had grabbed a man walking past his stall by the shoulder and dragged him over the webbing and into the stall. He had broken away from a hot walker and tried to mount a filly being washed outside the barn. Nobody could make Devil gallop around the track. He stopped or wheeled, usually losing the rider. They had tried a battery — illegal, of course — but when the exercise rider hit him with the electric shocker hidden in the handle of his stick, the horse jammed on the brakes and the rider went flying over his head, hit the inside rail, and didn't get back up. The trainer had asked Pop for some help. Pop had galloped him every morning for a week or two, and Devil had continued to act roguish one day, sulky the next, and had tried to rear or wheel and get Pop off at every opportunity. Finally, Pop told the trainer that maybe if he started jumping Devil over some logs and then schooled him over hurdles, it would give him something different to think about and might make him focus on doing something positive for a change — jumping the hurdles — rather than just always trying to bolt, wheel, or stop. It seemed to be working — the colt had been getting some good workouts. The trainer had no plan to run him over jumps, and Pop hadn't asked to be paid.

Pop galloped the thick-necked gray slowly around in a circle. The horse's wide eyes were looking at everything and everybody except what was straight in front of him. Pop shortened his hold on the reins, dug in with the spurs, and gave a low growl.

Going into the first hurdle, Devil tried to put on the brakes. The stick flashed up and down three times, with three loud successive cracks.

Inside the wings, Devil dived for the fence, dragging his hind end through. His nose skimmed along the ground on the other side. Pop was sitting far back with a long hold. He pulled the colt's head up with the reins, shortened his hold, gathering the colt together for the next hurdle.

They were flying. They were inside the wings and they sailed over the hurdle. Devil landed, galloping fast with Pop sitting more forward. They jumped the next two down the back side and finished over three down the front side, going at what would be a fast pace for most horses, but for this big colt, with those long sweeping close-to-the-ground strides, it looked like he was just loafing along. Pop cantered over to the trainer on the pony and switched horses. We jogged to the gap where the Pinkerton pulled a rail out and let us through. We jogged the horses hurriedly down the main track, took the path to the training track, jogged backward around part of it, and walked-jigged down the broad path to the barn, Pop occasionally rubbing his eye.

As we approached the barn, I saw a long black car, and my spirits rose: It had to be Jack Dempsey. We hopped off our horses, handed them to Emmett and Tanza.

I started to walk toward the tack room when I heard all kinds of cussing and yelling. "Hold on, Paddy," Pop said. "Emmett, what the hell's going on in there?"

Emmett snatched on the horse, "I don't know. Tanza, do you know?"

"Sounds like a fight to me," Tanza said.

Pop started to head toward the barn. Just then the heroin addict Emmett thought was the devil incarnate walked out of the men's room of the bunkhouse, probably after giving himself an injection. "Here, man," Emmett said, holding out the shank. "Give this horse a couple of turns, would you please?"

"No problem," said the hot-walker, taking the shank.

I looked at Tanza. He smiled, shook his head, and turned to walk his horse away from all the excitement.

## Chapter 3

I followed Emmett into the barn and was greeted by the sight of Lenny's groom, in a tight white T-shirt that showed off his wide shoulders and thin waist, cussing out Lenny and threatening to knock the living hell out of him, run him through with a pitch fork, stick him on the wall, and leave him there to die. I looked for the massive form of Jack Dempsey but didn't see him. All I saw was his short roly-poly friend, leaning against the doorway of the tack room. The groom started pushing and shoving Lenny. Emmett was telling me, "I told you. I told you this would happen one day." Emmett used to box as an amateur, and it looked like he was getting ready to step in and try to break it up when all of a sudden Dempsey's roly-poly friend, five-foot-three or -four, pulled off his double-breasted jacket, tossed it on a bale of straw, and stepped between the two men, all in one surprisingly fluid motion. Rolling up his sleeves, he looked up at the six-foot-two groom, and said, "Come on. You want to fight someone. Fight me." The groom looked down at the short, squat challenger as if he were crazy and put his left hand out to brush him aside. Lightning struck. The little man danced and jabbed and shadow boxed, wading in toward the big man and ducking back out, wading in again, warning him, bobbing and weaving and fists flying, saying, "Come on, buddy, why don't you pick on somebody your own size." It was obvious he was an ex-professional boxer. By this time a cluster of grooms, galloping boys, and hot-walkers had circled around the ruckus — most of the spectators urging on the two fighters. Lenny was yelling, "Okay, okay, that's enough." Finally, the young groom turned and walked away; we never saw him again. I wasn't too sad; he was an angry man — scowled all morning and never had a nice word to say.

Pop and I jumped in the car, and we were off. But first, instead of taking a right and heading toward the back gate, we took a left. I didn't ask any questions. We drove out to the barn with the uncared for horses. Pop approached the first stall, rubbed the horse between his eyes, and opened the door. He unsnapped an empty water bucket, set it outside the stall. "Okay, Bud, I'll get the buckets out, and you start filling them." Then, as I was filling them, he got a bale of hay out of the feed room, opened it, and walked down the line of stalls, tossing a flake in each, patting the horses on their necks. We hung the water buckets up and left.

Pop took a shower and changed at the apartment. We made a quick stop at Esposito's. He had a drink standing at the bar but couldn't relax. Mom and Pop Esposito, and John and Junior, were all giving him hell and telling him he shouldn't ride that afternoon because of his eye. They made another patch and put it over his eye. I got a sandwich. We hit the road.

* * *

A few weeks before, on the first day of the steeplechase meeting at Monmouth Park, I'd hopped in the car beside Pop and he'd said, "Sorry about this heat, Partner." The air in the car had been stifling — the loud whirr from the heater even sounded hot. "I tried to get all the weight off this morning but just couldn't do it. Maybe you could take a sip out of the thermos when you get hot." Between us was a small thermos of ice-cold screwdriver mix Junior Esposito had made for the trip. Pop would just take a sip now and then. Liquor is good for sweating; it opens up your pores. Since Pop ate only steak and salad at night, and rarely had any salt, the vodka would speed through his system and back out through either his sweat or urine. Liquor also numbed the wrenching intensity of Pop's body losing so much water weight day after day, and it killed the hunger, as did cigarettes.

I could feel the sun baking the outside metal, its heat beating down, penetrating the windows. The faster Pop drove, the hotter it got. It was tough on Pop — training the string of horses all morning at Belmont and then having to race down the Garden State Parkway to ride in the jumping race, with a 2:30 post time, at Monmouth Park. He was supposed to be in the jocks' room by noon and on an average morning we didn't finish up at the barn until 10:30. On the highways we switched from lane to lane. Once we were on the single-lane roads, it was constant acceleration, then braking. We'd pull out to pass a line of cars and have to squeeze back in just when it looked like we'd collide with an oncoming car. I was petrified. I watched the speedometer climb the crescent-shaped dial, over the top, and back down to a hundred, trying not to let Pop see me. I thought of what would happen if he made a mistake or if someone pulled out in front of us.

Since it was the first day of the Monmouth Park meeting, and I'd never been in the jocks' room at Monmouth Park, Pop had snuck me in. Instead of meeting a calm, gentlemanly, reassuring valet such as Dick Dwyer, as I always did in New York jocks' rooms, I met a raging, cussing, big, heavy, pockmarked valet called Lacey who, upon seeing Pop enter the jocks' room in his sweating outfit, started bellowing, "Jesus fucking Christ, and here comes the great Paddy Smithwick trying to kill himself. When the fuck are you going to hang it up, Paddy? You can't keep up this shit at your age! Look at you! You look terrible!" All eyes in the jocks' room were on us now. Pop, grinning and shaking his head, kept walking toward Lacey. "Paddy, you've won every goddamn silly shit-ass head-rocker, bush-hopper, timber-topper steeple-fucking race in the country. Enough's enough." Everyone was staring at us. I was confused. A jumping rider, I think it was Jimmy Murphy, a great friend of Pop's, came up behind me and put his hands on my shoulders. "It's okay, Little Paddy. He does this with your father every year." And then I heard the wild man holler, "And who the hell is this? Are you fucking old enough to be in here, son? Is this what you're going to be doing when you grow up?" he asked, shaking, pumping, my hand. "Boy, you're going to be too big," he said, putting his huge face right up in front of mine, spit flying into my eyes. "Your father's too big, and he'd better just cut it out."

Pop was grinning and looking at us both. "How you been, Lacey?" he asked. "Got any good riders?"

They shook hands. "Paddy, I got me a bug boy who thinks he's the hottest thing in town and is about as useless as tits on a bull. And then I got a couple of journeyman jocks who have lost their nerve and couldn't outride my grandmother. And then, I got you, Paddy. The Master. You're going to make me some money this meet, right Paddy? Ah, Paddy," he put his huge hands on Pop's shoulders and looked him in the eye, "You're my man. You're my man. We're going to make some money this meet! Who you got to ride? Blackmail, Bon Nouvel, Mako, The Sport?" He then looked down at me. "Is he going to make a jumping rider?"

"Oh, he's going to be too big."

Lacey grabbed me by the thigh and squeezed so hard it hurt. "God damn, he might make a football player. Boy, you think you want to do this for a living?"

"I might."

Lacey looked over at Pop.

"It's his decision, Lacey. There's no pressure …"

"Yeah, well, what the hell, is he any fucking good?"

"Yes, and he's getting better every day. Might just take over when I hang it up."

"Boy, you go to college. You get an education. I don't want to ever fucking see you again in this goddamn jocks' room."

* * *

On the morning that Pop was wearing the eye patch, he'd already lost enough weight so we didn't have the heater blasting. He drove for a short while, wearing the patch, and then suddenly pulled over to the side of the highway, cars whooshing by a foot away. He pulled the patch off, tossed it in the back, and asked me to drive. At fifteen, I had no license, but I'd been helping him with the driving for a while. "You've got to step on it, Bud. We're running a little late." He slid over to the passenger side, I sidled over him, and in seconds we were bumping along the shoulder, building up speed to get back on the highway. He lay on his side, putting his head in my lap. We'd done this before, but never at high speed on the turnpike with heavy traffic. His head was heavy, surprisingly heavy, as it always was. He fell asleep.

I made it off Long Island, over and through the matrix of bridges and entrance and exit ramps, and was on the New Jersey Turnpike, hitting seventy, seventy-five. But this wasn't fast enough. Soon I was on the Garden State Parkway going eighty, cruising at ninety in the fast lane, in a long line of cars, with a black Lincoln Continental on my tail, pushing me. I was just able to keep the car in control at this speed. We hurtled down the highway, my grip tight on the steering wheel, Pop's head heavy in my lap. Finally, at the exit ramp for Monmouth Park, I woke him. We pulled over, switched places. He drove into the backside, the barn area, and dropped me off at our Monmouth Park stable.

I had to go in a nine-horse van all the way back up the route we'd just come down, and then it was another hour out to Mrs. Phipps' farm in Westbury, where we were unloading the horses. Someone has to ride in the back of the van to keep an eye on the horses, to settle them down, and, in case of an emergency, to pound on the wall so the van driver will pull over.

I was looking forward to a late dinner with Pop. He was going to drive out to the farm, pick me up, and we'd eat out near Westbury at a restaurant we both liked before going back to our apartment in Elmont. I knew he'd be able to relax and eat more than usual because the next jumping race was a week away at Saratoga.

# 4

## At the Hospital

Ten days later I was allowed to see him. The earliest stories I had heard were that he wouldn't live. Then I was told he would live but that he would be paralyzed for life. Totem II had fallen over a hurdle at Monmouth Park, catapulting Pop forward. The ground had been hard and dry and Pop's neck had taken all the pressure of the fall. His spinal cord had snapped.

For five long days I had been out at the Phipps' farm on Long Island. Lillian Phipps owned many of the great horses that Pop rode and he and Mikey trained, and they kept a dozen horses out on the farm, usually ones that needed "to freshen up" or just to get away from the fast pace of the racetrack. I had been walking hots and grazing horses and cleaning tack, living with my Aunt Dot, Uncle Mikey's wife, who before I arrived already had her hands full training twelve to fifteen horses on the farm. Mikey was off trying to keep up with running the string of eight horses at Belmont Park, where Pop and I had been, the twenty or so at Delaware Park racetrack, near Wilmington, and another fifteen at the racing farm in Maryland. Plus, he was preparing to ship two van-loads to Saratoga. Mikey and Dot's two young sons were at the home base in Maryland, being taken care of by Cat-Cat (Catherine), Emmett's wife.

## Chapter 4

I was wondering what was going to become of me, and I was living with this nervous tension that I didn't have anyone to tell about and that followed me around every second of my waking time. When I did laugh, or for a few moments forgot about Pop's condition, I'd suddenly remember and feel guilty about my lapse of worry and anxiety. Some mornings I worked on the farm; some mornings I shipped in to Belmont and worked. I always returned to the farm on Long Island where Dot had a good, hot dinner for me. She was very patient and let me be quiet. The grooms tried to cheer me up. They treated me differently. They were more gentle with me now. Most thoughtful of all was Speedy Kiniel, Mikey and Dot's top groom out at the farm.

One afternoon after Speedy and I had shipped in to Belmont from the farm with a load of horses, he took me out to lunch. He walked me all around, showed me where the whorehouses and rough bars were, might've even bought me a beer. Walking down the sidewalk at one point, I was staring gloomily down at the concrete, and Speedy started to sing, first in a slow, high whisper, then raising his voice, picking it up, and finally belting out "Amazing Grace." He told me of his gospel singing, and when I started to lag again, he zeroed in on my interest in boxing, put his fists up, danced around on the sidewalk, talking nonstop, telling me why when he was in the ring he led with this fist and followed with the other, showing me how he kept his elbows up to protect his face, and jabbed, jabbed, jabbed, telling me to watch his footwork, until he had me laughing and circling, fists up and feet dancing.

Early the next morning, the sun barely up and the grass soaked with dew, Speedy taught me a new strengthening exercise. More and more often, especially when I was still sleepy and first got to work, I had a stiffness in my blue jeans, and I'd have to struggle a bit, pushing it this way and that to get comfortable. Speedy caught me making these maneuvers one morning and started raising hell. "What's wrong with you, boy? What're you thinking about, boy? Goddamn, you got a bone-a, a bone-a?"

"What?" I said, embarrassed and perplexed, trying to comprehend his South Carolinian accent.

"You got a bone-a, you know, a hard-on!" he sang out in his highest pitch, my Aunt Dot standing just five or six horse lengths away.

"Bring that horse over here," he said.

I led the horse over and Speedy started brushing him off, his hands a flurry of activity. "Now you listen to me, son. Do you wake up like that every morning?"

"Like what?"

"God damn, you know what I mean. Like that!" he said, staring at my crotch.

"Yes, I do," I said.

"That's nothing to worry about son. That's good." He set the two brushes, side by side, handles down, on the wet ground, pulled a rub-rag out of his back pocket and started rubbing and massaging the horse.

"Now listen to me," he said in an unusually low, quiet voice. "You get yourself a Coke bottle. An empty Coke bottle."

He suddenly stopped rubbing and stared at me. "You listening!"

"Yes, yes."

He looked me over. "You just want to start off with one Coke bottle. Now, by the time I was a young man I was doing two bottles, but you'd better start off with one."

"Okay," I said, giving the horse a little snatch he really didn't need.

"You get yourself some big, thick rubber bands — even one of those bands kids use to put around their books."

I knew what that was. Galloping boys wrapped them around the caps on their helmets.

"You attach the rubber band to the bottle and then every morning, as soon as you wake up, and before you take a leak, you hang that Coke bottle from your cock and do cock-lifts, one-two, one-two — just like you were lifting weights ..."

## Chapter 4

One afternoon, I was left at the track by myself, waiting to hitch a ride back to the farm on Long Island after a horse ran in the last race. I went to the movies and froze. I don't think there was another soul in the overly air-conditioned theater. The movie was *Dr. Zhivago*. That night out on the farm I drank a fifth of Jack Daniels (the rectangular-shaped bottle seemed to make it look like it contained less than it really did) with a country sort of girl who lived in a tenant house. We had quite a night. I awoke the next morning to an awful surprise — feeling sick and miserable and listless, not knowing what the hell was wrong until the men at the barn, Speedy in particular, explained to me the ramifications of heavy late-night drinking. I experienced my first of many blackouts. I was not sure what the farm girl and I had done past the halfway mark of the bottle or how I had gotten back to the house attached to the barn, or if my Aunt Dot had seen me coming in.

Pop was in a hospital. Mom was in a hospital. I hadn't talked to either of my sisters. Dot told me I was being a big help with the horses. I kept working. I had been demoted to hot-walker, mucker-out, tack-cleaner, and worst of all, I became the specialist at holding crazy, kicking, stomping, tail-swishing, sore-legged horses in the whirlpool tub for forty-five minutes at a time. At the last minute, after five days on the farm, I rode with a load of horses from the Long Island farm down the New Jersey Turnpike to Delaware Park, thinking I would end up at home in Maryland with my mother and sisters. But I got stuck at Delaware Park for four days — with three dollars in quarters in my pocket, living in the bunk house with the grooms and hot-walkers, and working for some slave driver of a woman who was in charge of the Delaware branch of Mikey and Pop's operation. I got on no horses. I was back at the bottom of the ladder. I was the chief hot-walker. I took the horses from the hotshot jocks when they came in from the track. I held each horse as the groom washed him, getting more soapy suds and water on me than on the horse, and then walked each around and around the shed row — most of them leaning on me the entire time —

until the horse was cool and dry. I then grazed him, put him in the stall, and grabbed the next horse coming in from the track. At the end of the morning, after I'd cleaned all the tack, and when the men had finished up in the shade of the shed row and were heading back to the coolness of their bunk houses for a cold bootlegged bottle of beer or up to the cafeteria for a cold soda and lunch, the slave-driving woman would send me out under the broiling sun to rake up an acre around the barn, the parking area, and the manure pile.

After I finished raking one morning, I was informed by this assistant trainer that the doctors now predicted that Mom would have to remain in traction at Union Memorial Hospital for the entire month of August. I was dumbfounded when she told me this. Disoriented. I was standing there leaning on the hot aluminum shaft of the big rake. I was tired and hot, and on hearing this, the trainer and the walking ring and the barn and the horses started going into a spin. To pull myself back, I sat down on a foot-locker in the shade and stared at a pebble in the dirt. The assistant trainer then added that my sisters, Sue Sue and Sallie, were staying with my grandmother Whitman, and that she'd known all this since I'd arrived in Delaware but had decided it would be good for me to "rest and recuperate" from the news of Pop's fall before telling me of the seriousness of Mom's injury. The dizziness left and I looked up at her. It was noon, and I'd been working non-stop since six. I thanked her for relaying the information but not for the rest and recuperation. I pictured Sue Sue and Sallie a world away, living in the big white house of my grandparents, up on top of Chattalonee Hill in the Green Spring Valley. They'd be sleeping late, having seated breakfasts served by Louise Parker, and then going to swim and play tennis at the Green Spring Valley Club where Granny — Suzanne Voss White Whitman — was somewhat of a legend, first, for having beaten the club's number one grass court player, in her bare feet at the age of fourteen, and then going on to intimidate the great Bill Tilden when he approached the net in a renowned mixed doubles match at the Philadelphia Cricket

Club, and becoming one of the top women players of the 1920s before she started having children.

I was feeling doomed. I pictured a few of my classmates from Gilman School, wondered what they were doing at that moment, then remembered that they were up at a summer camp with an Indian-sounding name in Canada. I wondered how I would ever get my summer reading books for Gilman. I needed to put Kelly's selections of Jacqueline Susann and Harold Robbins paperbacks away and start turning the pages of the Gilman classics. A short book by Herman Melville was on the list, and suddenly I thought of a class I'd had last spring in which the English teacher, Mr. Armstrong, read and acted out several sections of *Moby Dick* to stimulate our interest. This is it, I thought, sitting there on the foot locker: I will be spending the rest of the summer working for this Ahab of a trainer who will never find her white whale. At that moment Ahab started to walk away. A six-horse van pulled up in front of the barn. Jim Rutherford, youthful and sandy-haired, shot me a grin from the driver's seat, waved, and hopped out, leaving the engine running. I knew Jim from working down at Hydes over the winters; he gave me valuable pointers — such as how to hop up onto a horse without having to put your foot in the stirrup — and helped me out when I got in a tight spot. Ahab walked toward him. They spoke for a few minutes. I couldn't hear a thing because of the roar of the van's engine. Jim and Ahab approached. I stood to shake hands with Jim. Ahab flatly told me it was time to pack up my stuff. I didn't bother to tell her that I had nothing to pack. She explained that I'd return to Long Island in the van with a load of horses, and the next day I'd catch a van up to Saratoga Springs. I'd stay with Evan Jackson through August. Evan had sent word for me to be ready: I'd be galloping horses for him, alongside steeplechase jockey Tommy Walsh.

I helped load the six horses onto the van late that afternoon. Once we were out of Delaware Park, I rode only a few miles in the back with the horses snorting all over me and the hay and straw blowing into my hair and one of the horses kicking the hell out of the side of the van when Jim pulled over, got out, unlocked the door, tightened the chain-ties on the misbehaving horse's halter, and let me sit up in the roar of the cab. He taught me the basics of driving a nine-horse van as I watched him smoothly maneuver through the ten forward gears and in and out of traffic for the rest of the trip up to Long Island.

On reaching the farm in Westbury, I helped Jim unload the horses, and then Jim and I rode the stable's tandem bike over to Mrs. Phipps' mansion, where he dropped me off. I took a bath and spent the night in a room that my friends back at the bunkhouse at Delaware Park would not believe. The mattress was soft and not sway-backed and didn't smell as if it'd been stored in a hay loft for a decade. The sheets were white and clean and had creases from being starched and ironed and didn't give way to buttons and scratchy horse-hair. I had a fluffy pillow with a clean white pillowcase. Instead of a heavy, itchy, wool-and-leather horse blanket to pull over me in the middle of the night, I had a big, light, fluffy down-filled comforter, and I wore a pair of silk pajamas — albeit a bit large — that the housekeeper had found for me.

The next morning I waited with the chauffeur by the white Rolls-Royce for Mrs. Phipps. I had an interesting time talking to him about the car. He wiped it off with a chamois cloth as we waited and explained to me that it was easier to keep a white Rolls clean than a black one. Mrs. Phipps came out and we drove to New York City in the white Rolls-Royce, the chauffeur now sitting stiffly at attention in the front, Mrs. Phipps and me in the back seat. I felt small in the back of that quiet smooth-sailing yacht and everyone stared at us as we whooshed by on the way to see my father. I don't know if I have ever felt more alone.

Mrs. Phipps took me out to lunch at a crowded restaurant, where we had a nice time. She seemed old to me, though I guess she was only about sixty. It was a strain having to act so polite and watch my manners while deep inside I was preparing to see my father.

## Chapter 4

"Would you like to go to the theater or to Brooks Brothers?" Mrs. Phipps asked, and then she looked me directly in the eye, "before we go to see your *fa-ther?*" She stretched out the words "your *fa-ther,*" giving them a sort of regal dignity.

"What do you mean?" I asked.

"We could go shopping at Brooks Brothers, get you outfitted for Saratoga, or we could see a play."

"I think I'd rather go to Brooks Brothers," I said.

The next thing I knew, we were in Brooks Brothers. I had three older butler-types, who all seemed to know Mrs. Phipps very well, waiting on me at one time. I was trying on tennis shorts, blue blazers, corduroy jackets, tweed jackets, cashmere sweaters, khakis, corduroy pants, argyle socks, polo shirts, Oxford shirts, ties. At one point Mrs. Phipps asked the salesman over in sweaters, "Could you find us a cable-knit, cashmere V-neck — something to wear to the races with a tie, and under a jacket?"

"Yes, Mrs. Phipps, I'll be right with you. Could you wait just a moment?"

She replied, "No." Someone else immediately came to our side, and within seconds I was pulling on a lightweight, beautiful green sweater of fine cashmere.

Then we were over in shoes where Mrs. Phipps explained to me that I needed one pair of tennis shoes for the grass courts at the Saratoga Golf Club, one pair of loafers for the evenings — "Your *fa-ther* takes such good care of his shoes. They're always shined, and I'm sure you're just the same way ..." — one pair of crepe-soled shoes for rainy days at Saratoga, and one pair of wing tips for going to the races. Soon we were out of Brooks Brothers, carrying nothing — the jackets, one a golden corduroy and the other a blue wool blazer with gold buttons, and pants and shirts were being altered to fit me just right and the clothing would all be delivered to me at Saratoga. Then we were in the Rolls and telling the chauffeur to take us to the hospital, and Mrs. Phipps and I were walking down a hospital hall, our leather-heeled footsteps echoing off the dreary, gray walls, and she was leaving me, alone, at a huge open doorway.

I walked into a large hospital room with four bedridden patients, the beds parallel to one another and facing two sets of televisions. I didn't see Pop. I looked at the patients and they stared back at me. I noticed a partition over by the window. I squeezed between the foot of the beds and the two television sets, each on a different station, the first on a soap opera playing depressing, syrupy organ music; the second on a game show with loud, cackling laughter. Blocking the vision of each of the patients for a moment, I walked past them and around the partition.

Instantly a lump formed in my throat, my eyes blurred, and I struggled to hold the tears in. Pop's head was shaved bare and two wire cables came out of the top of his skull. He was lying flat on his back with no pillow under his head. He couldn't see me.

I walked around to the opposite side of the partition, between the bed and the cluttered table along the wall, to his head. His weak eyes peered up at me. There was nothing I could do. The lump was growing in my throat. I read the embarrassment in his eyes. I strained to keep mine on his and not to look elsewhere. I had to bend over him so he could see me. "Hey, Pop."

"Hi, Partner." He forced a grin.

My eyes glanced above his head. The wires stretched to a pulley behind and on the same level as his head, straight up to a pulley about five feet above the bed, and then hung down with several weights on the end. Small screws protruded from his skull to which the wires were attached.

Across the bed was a tray of food on a swinging table. "Want anything to eat or drink?" I asked.

"A little something to drink."

I reached across to the top of the table projecting over the bed and

## Chapter 4

picked up a large paper cup full of liquid with the top on it. I wondered how he drank.

"You have to use a straw," he said.

I got a straw, stuck it in the hole at the top, bent it. I leaned forward, holding the cup with one hand, and placed the straw in his mouth with the other. He sucked down the liquid.

I sat there the rest of the afternoon with my father. His left side was completely paralyzed but according to the doctors he had 20 percent feeling in his right side. His hands were still and cold. He tried to open and close his fingers a fraction of an inch for exercise. I rubbed his hands to warm them and to get the blood circulating.

He was emaciated. His limbs were shriveled. He was much thinner than he had ever been, even when doing his lightest.

"Christ, Pop, I'll have to start coming here every day and make you eat," I said awkwardly, immediately feeling bad about the profanity. He always looked at me with a disappointed expression when I cussed, making me feel immature and show-offy. But he didn't do it this time. "What's the food like?" I asked.

"Haven't been able to eat much."

"Why didn't you eat any lunch?"

"Too cold."

"I'd think now that you can eat that you would eat."

His face looked hurt, worried. I wished I'd stopped. Later, when he'd gotten out, he told me that the nurses used to set the food on the table and leave. They'd come back in an hour and ask why he had not eaten.

I knew it hurt him to have me see him like that. Talking exhausted him.

"How are things out on Long Island?" he asked.

"They're all right." I didn't know if telling him about the horses and the men would cheer him up or depress him further. "Speedy showed me all around Elmont one day," I said.

He just smiled so I decided not to tell the story.

"Looking forward to Saratoga?" he asked.

"I guess so."

"You'll have a good time staying with Evan. Listen to him, all right, Bud."

"I will."

"He'll put you on a horse or two to gallop."

"That'll be good."

"Tommy's riding for Evan now. Watch him and you'll learn something."

The televisions in the room droned relentlessly, and I felt like walking around the partition and smashing both of the sets into little bits of glass and metal.

"You know, Whitey Ford owns one of Evan's horses, a hurdle horse, a good horse. Maybe you'll ride him." He knew Mom had turned me away from the Orioles and into a Yankees fan. In traction at Union Memorial Hospital, Mom had taken up watching baseball and winning money gambling on the Yankees, or so I'd heard.

"Have you talked to your mother?" he asked.

"No, I haven't," I said.

"When you get to Evan's, tell him you want to talk to her, and he'll call."

"Okay."

"Bud, I'm sorry about all this."

I didn't say anything. I held myself together.

"I heard your mother's getting a lot better."

"That's good," I said. "I'm glad to hear that."

"Been meeting any interesting girls?" He grinned.

"No, not really," I said, feeling a dark tinge of guilt about the country girl and the Jack Daniels and the hangover and the blackout, though I didn't know the term blackout then, and just thought of the experience as some kind of murky, mysterious event.

We continued to talk awkwardly, but soon I had to meet Mrs. Phipps and go back in the Rolls-Royce, and Pop was getting tired. I wished I didn't have to leave. I rubbed his cold hand. A nurse put her head around the partition. I looked at her questioningly and she nodded.

"Pop, I'll be back to see you soon," I said, rubbing his cold, still hand.

"Please do." His eyes were starting to tear up. "But don't worry about coming too often. It's a long ways from Saratoga."

"Okay, see you soon." I put his hand down on the bed. I didn't know what to do. I couldn't shake hands with him, even if I wanted to. Kissing him would have felt funny, though as I started to walk out I thought of the feeling of his face — his cheeks sandpapery by late afternoon — against mine, and I wished that was what I had done. I waved.

Walking through the room, I felt awkward, clumsy. The bed-ridden patients stared at me as I passed in front of their television sets. I had forgotten the outside world. I felt out of place, dizzy. I focused straight ahead and marched on. Walking down the hall to the elevator, I gritted my teeth, tightened the muscles of both arms. I made a fist with my right hand and cupped it over with my left. My eyes blurred. I wanted to hit something, even the wall. Then a feeling rushed into my chest. It was my time to stand up, to work for the family — for my father, for my mother, for my sisters — to pick up my father's whip, helmet, and tack, for him, and for the family, and to ride. It filled me, overwhelmed me, shocked me, but at the same time I wanted to get down on my knees and cry.

# PART II

# BEFORE THE FALL

# 5

## Nappy and Queenie

**M**y childhood riding started with lead-line classes on my first pony, Nappy. Mom would lead me most of the time. Her mother, Granny Whitman, would lead me sometimes. Pop might have led me once or twice. My grandmother Um (Emma Warner Smithwick — she loathed titles, and my youthful pronunciation of "Emma" gradually became "Um") would also be there watching. I wanted to lose weight and be thin and ride steeplechase races like my father. But Granny — probably as part of her ongoing effort to deflect me from becoming a jockey — told me it was great to have a little protruding stomach and to sit up perfectly straight on my pony, keep my heels down, have my hands in just the right place, and then I would do well in the lead-line class.

As Nappy and I graduated from lead-line class, Granny taught me how to ride in pony shows. She could be strict. She knew her stuff. And she gave rewards. I now was used to riding cross-country, through the woods and fields and across streams and rivers and up and down hills with Mom, and this going around a little circle, keeping the pony in perfect control in preparation for the show ring was not my cup of tea. Hack classes, where you entered the ring along with thirty others and followed the orders of the judges in the middle — "Walk, please." "Trot, please." "Reverse and canter, please." — were the absolute worst. The training for the show ring seemed a little sissified and could become boring very quickly, but Granny would place a quarter between one of my knees and the saddle, another quarter between the other knee and the saddle, and if I could walk around, and then trot around and not drop the quarters — they would be mine.

At this time I also began noticing the differences between my two primary teachers in sports and in life. Granny — whether in tennis or riding or living — was calm, understated, and in control, as you must be in the show ring, and a teetotaler. Mom took the opposite tack: She liked free-moving, flamboyant, flashy horses; she liked to ride them cross-country, where there were no rules or regulations; and she was not a teetotaler. In tennis Granny was all tactics and consistency, and she would rarely make an unforced error. She gradually ground her opponents down. Mom would die of boredom trying to play, or live, like that, and would get more joy out of slapping one risky winning backhand down the line than winning an entire game by being consistent and playing safe. When Mom taught me how to sail, she loved to go out in a strong wind and have the boat fully heeled over, the tip of the boom tracing a line through the waves and the two of us, side by side, holding the sheet to the mainsail and leaning back, far out over the side, our stomach muscles quivering, to keep the sailboat from capsizing as it soared across the tops of the waves. When Granny taught me carpentry, she drove me to the hardware store introduced me to her longtime associates there; bought nails, boards, a hammer, and saw for me; and then, patiently, guided me through building a shelf, showing me along the way how to hammer correctly and safely, how to measure, how to saw, and then how to clean up.

Both my grandmothers were devoted Christian Scientists — they didn't drink or smoke; they read their lesson from Mary Baker Eddy's *Key to the Scriptures*, along with the corresponding lesson from the

Bible, every single morning, then called one another to discuss the lesson. They did not believe in doctors. They did not believe in medicine. If you became sick, you most likely had "an error in your thinking" or you could have been having "bad thoughts." Either way you didn't go to see a doctor; you did your lesson, practiced your Christian Science, and through your faith and God's will — "mind over matter" — you got better. If you were ill, you called a practitioner and had her pray for you. It worked for them; both lived extremely healthy lives and just missed making it to one hundred. They were far ahead of their times in many ways. Yet, they did put Mom under enormous pressure to be the perfect Christian Scientist. This caused difficulties when one of us got really sick or had something like appendicitis. But most of the time we just accepted it as the way to live. We had no medicine in the house. No pills. None of us had ever taken an aspirin or anything like it. Pop and Mikey didn't worry too much about the philosophic and religious principles behind Christian Science, but they had a basic faith in its power: If Neji came up a little unsound two days before a big race, Mikey would call his mother immediately, "Mom, can you do a little work for us on Neji? His tendon is acting up." And she would do it — enlisting the aid of a practitioner. Neji's tendon would get better and he'd win the race.

My grandmothers had been best friends since childhood, and it was really through them — and riding — that Mom and Pop met. As teenagers, Mom and Pop would see each other out hunting and at horse shows, and occasionally the two families would get together for dinner. Mikey had told me that as soon as he and Pop got their first car, they'd hop in it at night and rush over to Chattalonee Hill, in the Green Spring Valley, to take out my mother and her best friend. "I had a terrible crush on your mother," Uncle Mikey said. "But she wouldn't even look at me. I'd always get stuck with her friend, who wasn't half as good looking." Then — he told me this in his tack room at Hydes one morning — "Your mother was the hottest thing in the Green

Spring Valley. Everyone was after her. She was the wildest, best-riding, best-looking girl in that valley. And your poor father had a rough time. We'd rush over there, running that old jalopy as hard as it could go, and we'd have all sorts of high expectations of what the night would bring. On arriving, we'd go in and shake hands with Mr. and Mrs. Whitman. Now Mr. Whitman, he was all right. He'd just tell us to be good and what time to be back, but then Mrs. Whitman would give us a talk that might drag on a little. Of course, she would have just gotten off the phone with Mom. Back then, you know, Suzie was never allowed out by herself with Paddy. Suzie always had to have at least one friend along."

Mom always said that the best time she had with Pop and Mikey was when Granny would bring her and a few friends down to Hydes. As soon as it got dark, Mikey would throw a bridle on a huge old work-horse and jog him over to the house. Mom, Pop, and a couple of Mom's friends would all hop up on the horse's back. Then, as Mikey, who always loved looking back on his childhood, told us one night, "Paddy and I would ride him over to the top of the steepest hill on the place. Then, we'd point him downhill, kick him in the belly and see who could stay on the longest. He'd go galloping down the hill and the girls would have their arms wrapped around us. Paddy never fell off a horse in his life, but on these nights we'd time it so we'd both fall off, and, you know, as soon as we hit the ground, we'd try to get a kiss, do some good."

My grandfather Whitman, whom we called Hi-ee, foxhunted occasionally, yet preferred rowing a scull (as he had at Princeton), skiing, and, most of all, golf. Tall, fit, and vigorous, he was not a Christian Scientist but had a quiet way of going along with it. He was a great reader and urged me to study history. I never met my grandfather Smithwick, a staunch Catholic, whom we called Alfred, but I had been to Prospect Park, his farm in Ireland, where he'd been raised. We had several photos of him, all looking very much like Pop, and quite a few elegant silver trophies from polo matches. Most interesting of our memorabilia was the framed certificate for gallant and distinguished military service, dated July 1, 1919, and signed by Winston Churchill, secretary of state for war, which we had on the wall in our living room.

Upon returning home to Ireland after the war, Captain Alfred Smithwick of the Royal Army Service Corps survived several attempts on his life by the Sinn Feiners, who didn't approve of his English affiliations and his growing friendship with Churchill. His farm manager woke him late one night, telling him he "was a marked man" and must leave that night or he would "soon be napping in a coffin." He was smuggled out of the country and boarded a ship headed for the United States, forced to start his life over. First, Alfred started up a stable at the Elkridge-Harford Hunt Club — twenty-five miles north of Baltimore and just a forty-five minute cross-country ride north from our farm — using his contacts in Ireland to buy Irish horses and have them shipped over. He'd school and train the horses, then sell them to Americans. Soon, he became honorary huntsman for the club, guiding it through the Depression. He met and married my grandmother, Emma Warner, and they lived on the club grounds. At this time, Winston Churchill, during a tour of the United States, stopped in Maryland to see how Alfred was doing and shared a picnic lunch with my grandparents at the club.

Alfred and Emma had two children, Mikey and Pop, and the club grounds were the boys' Eden. There were dozens of little "hunt boxes" — small, one-story accommodations for the foxhunters when they came into town for two or three weeks. There were barns filled with horses needing to be ridden, kennels overflowing with yapping and barking hounds needing to be trained, ponies whose owners wanted them schooled, and hundreds of men and women working there — including more than forty just for the acclaimed millionaire sportsman, art collector, and socialite Harvey Ladew, who employed them to rebuild his house, work in his topiary gardens, and care for his barn of foxhunters. Pop and Mikey played with the children of the employees and could ride their ponies for hours through the surrounding countryside. On hot summer nights they'd have friends over to sleep under the stars along with the children of club employees. During the day they followed their father through his rounds and rode and schooled their ponies beside him.

Alfred's business grew, and when the boys were about five and six years old, he and Um bought the farm at Hydes and moved his stable there. By the time the boys were in the fourth grade, they were working alongside their father after school, on the weekends, and during the summers.

Alfred would have liked the pony his sons found me. Nappy was a beautiful dark bay and competed in the small-pony division. He had a handsome head, like a little Thoroughbred's, and I rode him in a saddle with a leather handle I was proud to use only on rare occasions. Instead of iron stirrups, in which it was possible to get your feet stuck, I rode in wooden "box" stirrups that were enclosed in a leather sheath. There was no way my foot could go through the stirrup or get stuck in the stirrup, and thus if I had a fall I would not be dragged.

Early in the morning before shows Mom would groom Nappy and braid his mane. We'd put him on the trailer alongside a towering Thoroughbred Mom would ride in the show and off we would go. Nappy would do well in the lead-line class, and Mom would gallop around in all her classes on Fini or Crag and would "clean up" as she sometimes said, and we'd go home with a string of ribbons — blues and reds and yellows — flapping from the car's visor. Sometimes Mom would win the championship, receiving the blue-, red-, and yellow-banded ribbon for that highest honor.

By the time I was five or six, I'd had Nappy for a long time in my short life. He was like a brother to me. It seemed he was my size, though more plump, and looked at the world from the same vantage point, which was different from the way adults and horses looked at life. On Sunday, January 18, 1953, Mom wrote an entry in her diary about Nappy. She called Nappy by his full name, which was Adaptable. She, Pop, Sue Sue, and I were living at the club. It was just before we bought and moved to our farm, which Mom named Prospect Farm, partly after the farm on which Alfred Smithwick had grown up in Ireland.

*Took Sue in carriage and Patrick down to stable in the afternoon. Paddy on Patricia led Patrick around on Adaptable, his pony. He's the most perfect pony. He will walk into the house with Patrick on him. One day he came into my bedroom and then went up into the club. He will walk up into the tack room, up four or five steep steps all alone, without being led. George Smoot spoils him to death feeding him sugar and lots of feed.*

*Rode Clown all around by Harvey Ladew's.*

\* \* \*

I was graduating out of lead line and just starting to ride Nappy in classes where we walked and jogged around by ourselves and where we sometimes jumped one- or two-foot fences. One summer day I walked by the front paddock and saw that Nappy was lying down. It was in the middle of the day, and there Nappy was lying down, and I didn't see his rib cage going up and down or his tail swishing. He was still. He was terrifyingly still. Mom was suddenly behind me. Her strong hands were squeezing my shoulders, and she was pulling me into the house, and she was calling Pop on the phone, calling him at the racing farm, at Hydes, "I don't care what he is doing. Get him and tell him to come home right now. Right now!"

I had an ache inside. It couldn't be true. It could not be true. Mom made another couple of phone calls, keeping me there with her. Then she started pacing around the kitchen and made us both tomato sandwiches and glasses of milk, which sat untouched. She got out the dog bowls, fed the dogs, and started straightening the kitchen up. We heard the squeal of tires as Pop turned into our driveway and the crush of gravel as he stopped in front of the house. Mom walked me upstairs, into the back bedroom. She told me to wait there. She had to talk to my father and she would be right back.

She left and I wanted to run to the front of the house and look out the bathroom window to the front paddock, but I didn't budge. When Mom returned, she sat down on the edge of the bed and started crying. I wasn't sure what was going on. She told me that Nappy, my beautiful black little Nappy, had been kicked in the head by a horse in the field and killed. The horse had hind shoes on and had been turned out with Nappy by a man who was boarding the horse on the place. You never turned a horse with hind shoes out with a pony. This was something we never did, something you shouldn't do, something she wished had never happened.

Pop called a couple of friends over, strong-backed friends —Tiger Bennett and Jack Graybeal — and the threesome dug the hard-baked summer ground throughout the entire afternoon. I stayed with Mom. We didn't go out to where they were digging, but I could see them from the second-story windows. They buried Nappy right there, in the front paddock, just thirty steps from the front porch, under the locust tree. I could never pat him, ride him, again.

* * *

The summer passed without a pony. It took a long time for grass and weeds to grow over the hump of dirt in the front field. Finally, fall was arriving and with it, foxhunting with Mom. I was riding well enough to go now. I was out of the lead-line class, and I needed a good, strong pony to hunt, a pony that would gallop across fields and down paths in woods keeping up with Thoroughbred horses, a pony that could jump the three-foot and even four-foot post and rail, and board fences that divided up the pastureland all through the Elkridge-Harford Hunt country. I knew Mom and Pop were looking. I knew Uncle Mikey was looking.

Then came one hot Indian summer Sunday afternoon when the

leaves were beginning to fall from the trees all around our lawn, and the grass on the lawn was still green — but we had stopped letting the horses loose on the lawn to "mow" it. It had been a normal day except when Mom had taken Sue Sue, Sallie, and me to Gunpowder Falls for a swim we'd gone in Pop's car. I asked Mom why we were using his car, and she just replied, "Don't be so nosey." When we got back from the swim, Mom parked in the garage, pulling the car all the way in, and it was then that I noticed the trailer was missing. I asked about it, and she replied, "Curiosity killed the cat."

Standing there in front of the garage in my shorts and sneakers, I felt impatient. Then, Mom's gray-blue station wagon towing our gray-blue Rice trailer rumbled into the driveway. The car and trailer passed us before coming to a stop. I heard the unshod feet of a pony step forward and backward on the wooden floorboards of the trailer.

My father got out of the driver's seat and my Uncle Mikey got out the other side, both shutting their doors softly. This was an important event. You never saw Pop or Mikey hauling a trailer. All their horses were shipped in vans and a van driver drove. And you rarely saw Mikey up on our farm — he was always working day and night on the racing farm at Hydes. They walked to the back of the trailer. Pop pulled the bolt out of its socket at the top of the ramp and unlocked one side while Mikey simultaneously pulled the other bolt. Without looking at one another, they quietly lowered the heavy wooden ramp.

I could see the dark bay rump, and I knew this was my new and big pony. Pop went in the little side door of the trailer, untied the shank, rubbed the pony between her eyes, and spoke soothingly to her. Mikey unhooked the strap behind her rump and then stood on the near side, driver's side, just off the ramp with his hand placed gently on her hind quarters, guiding her. Then she was backing up straight off the ramp with Pop holding the leather shank, following her out. Her hind feet off the ramp, her front feet on it, she stopped, and Pop — in his fedora cocked at a jaunty angle and with a cigarette hanging out of his mouth

— relaxed his hold on the shank, letting it loop. She had a thick mane and a long neck with a slight crest, a fluffy bay coat, and two white stockings in front. Mom was standing beside me. Mom and Mikey and Pop were talking to one another and saying "Whoa, girl," and "How does she look?" and "Isn't she well-behaved?"

I watched as she pricked her big ears and stretched her neck and looked all around, up at the fields, back at the barn, and then down at me. Pop and Mikey let her stand there, and then she was off the ramp and Pop was walking her up onto the lawn and she was looking at everything and up on her toes and pulling Pop around and whinnying to the horses on the place. They were whinnying back as she reached down and took a mouthful of grass, picked her head back up, and chewed. Pop held her still, and I walked up to her — she looked huge to me, towering, like a horse out of King Arthur's stable. She had a long back and well-rounded rump and a white stripe down the center of her face.

Pop made her stand still. I reached up and patted her on the neck. She is mine and this will do for now, this patting, I thought. She is big, and her brown coat feels so thick between my fingers — and then I was in the air, flying, up high, Pop's hands under my armpits, and I heard Mom's voice, "Paddy, Paddy …" and I was on her, my legs around her, the feel of her soft coat against my bare thighs and calves, my hands gripping her thick mane. I was high up and Pop and Mikey were laughing, and Pop was leading me across the lawn and around the house and back to the barn, the pony pulling against him, and he was asking, "How's she feel, Bud? How's she feel?"

She was my pony, and there was no way in the world she could feel any better. We named her Queenie. I would learn to ride on her, learn to jump. In the autumn Mom and I would foxhunt and ride cross-country through miles of fields and pastures and woods. I used Queenie's ears the same way I used the sight of my BB gun. They'd be pricked, and I'd focus on the rump of Mom's horse between those little ears. Directly behind Mom, up and over the fences we'd go. Queenie would keep up with any horse, and many a time we galloped across a field behind Mom, jumping post-and-rail fences taller than Queenie, as horses refused and ran out around us.

After the hunts we'd hack home, sometimes in the dark. The temperature would be dropping. It might be drizzling. We might have miles to go. Close to home we'd be walking on Manor Road, the asphalt slick from the drizzle. Mom would be in front of me on our broodmare, Fini, who would be wearing four steel shoes. Queenie would be barefoot behind and would have to take two softer-sounding clip-clops to every cling-clang of Fini's. I'd have my hunting cap pulled down to keep the rain out of my eyes, my wool jacket buttoned up to my Adam's apple, and be leaning forward into the drizzle. The chill would be in my bones, especially my feet, and I'd feel stiff, squeezing my legs, shoulders, and arms inward, as if I couldn't possibly make a quick movement.

Arriving home, we'd kick our feet out of the irons, duck our heads, and ride straight into the barn, into the stalls, and stiffly lower ourselves out of the saddles. We'd pull off the clammy tack, and I'd twist up a handful of fresh straw and rub Queenie's thick, tangled bay coat with it, trying to dry her. I'd make sure she had fresh hay in her stall, and I'd let her have only a few gulps at a time out of the water bucket. Pop would come out with a hot mash — crushed oats and sweet feed boiled in water, much like oatmeal cereal — for the two hunters and tell me to go in and get warm. I'd feel short and awkward as I hobbled on numb feet, my legs remaining spread apart as if I still had a saddle between them, to the house, up the stairs. I'd turn on the hot water, strip off my clothes. I'd set one bare, blue-white foot, then the other, into the hot water of our bathtub and slowly, achingly, lower my butt, my back, my arms, my shoulders, into the steaming water, right to my chin.

# 6

## Winter

In December of 1960, I was in the fourth grade at Gilman School, twenty-five miles south of us in Baltimore. It was snowing hard, and Mom and I were listening to the school closings on the radio in the kitchen. It seemed that every school in the state was closed except for one, my school, Gilman. This was the norm. Mom hadn't even bothered to wake Sue Sue. I know because I kept a detailed account of all we did during this snowstorm, as well as another that hit later in the month, on the small pages of my leather-bound, lock-and-key diary.

"It's not fair that I have to go to school and Sue Sue doesn't," I told Mom.

"That's tough," Mom answered.

"Well, I might just not go," I asserted, standing by the kitchen door with my blue denim book bag — made by Granny — slung over my shoulder. I immediately regretted my impudence.

"Listen, young man, you'd better straighten out or I'll tell your father." I loved the way she said the word father. I listened to the flow of the sound of the word, letting down my guard for a moment. She looked up from lacing her boots. She was getting ready to go out to the barn and turn the horses out, and she was all business. I opened the door to walk out to the end of the driveway, and probably wait ten minutes or so, freezing, until Ronnie Maher picked me up in his little black Volkswagen Beetle with no heater — but packed with his own three warm-bodied kids — joking and calling me "Potstick" (for stirring up trouble), and dropped the four of us off at our schools on the way to his law office.

"Hold on a minute," Mom said. "While you're going out, climb up into the top of the garage and get your skis out for Sue Sue to use today. Set them by the station wagon, would you please? We might go up to Mount Bennett this afternoon."

I had a falling feeling. This was pushing the limit. What in the world was she up to? They were going skiing up at Tiger Bennett's, our great friend and neighbor, and I certainly did not want my little sister using, and thus ruining, my pair of blue wooden Northland skis, which had brand-new bindings Tiger and I had screwed in last winter by the living-room fire. I pushed the door.

"Ohhh, you better watch out … you better not cry … and now you know I'm telling you why … San-ta Claus is coming to town …" Mom sang out, holding her voice down in a low range, grinning, showing off a bit — she'd been trained in classical music at Westminster Choir College and had sung at Madison Square Garden and at Carnegie Hall. "I wonder," she said, "if you don't have any skis, whether Santa might think you need a new pair for Christmas."

I danced out of there into the snow. It was really coming down now. I climbed the ladder up into the top of the garage, got my skis down, and then tromped out through the six inches of powder to the end of the driveway. No cars came by, only an occasional truck. I waited and waited, and got colder and colder. I paced back and forth across the driveway, hopping up and down, clapping my hands. Then, I heard Mom calling, "Patrick, Patrick." Cold in my bones, I jogged stiffly up the driveway to the house, kicking through the fluffy flakes, perfect for skiing. What now? I thought. What now?

I came inside to the warmth of the kitchen and the smell of bacon sizzling in one frying pan and French toast in another. Mom was standing over the stove. "Want a slice?" she asked.

I stamped my feet, set my book bag down, and stared at her. She laughed. "Ronnie just called. Sally and Jamie's school is closed. He can't get the car started, and he's not going into town unless you really have to. He could take the pick-up truck …"

I jumped a foot off the floor and let out a holler that must've woken both Sue Sue and Sallie in the beds above us.

After Mom and I finished with the horses that morning, Mom drove around and picked up a whole pack of our friends and took us skiing in the freshly fallen powder up at Tiger Bennett's. This was especially satisfying as I kept imagining where I was supposed to be, which was in town at Gilman with a class full of city boys, or so I thought of them. Not one, as far as I could deduce, had ever witnessed his parents throwing wild parties that went on late into the night, had ever danced arm-in-arm with his mother, had ever lain in bed at one in the morning listening to his mother playing long, slow, tunes on the piano while his father was away at the track. Not one had ever ridden a pony, built a tree fort, seen a stallion mount a mare and drive himself deep into her, slipped his finger through the ring of a too-heavy earthenware gallon jug, flipped the jug back onto his arm, lifted his elbow high, and sipped hard eye-popping cider from the wide cool mouth of the jug. Who were these kids? Well, they could fight, and they knew their stuff on the sports field and in the classroom. I had to struggle to keep up.

While my classmates were staring out the windows at the snow falling on the football field and wondering when the bell would ever ring for recess so they could rush out and have a huge snowball fight, I was taking a long drink of Tiger's cider and then flying on my skis down through the trees in his woods, hitting the two narrow boards over the creek at the bottom just right, racing the ten feet across them, and not being quite able to put on the brakes quickly enough, crashing into the snow-covered bush as others piled into it from behind me. The adrenaline and the cider pounding through me, I hopped up, skated on my skis over to the field and grabbed the thick rope that Tiger had wrapped around the big steel tractor wheel — with the tire taken off — at the bottom of the hill. Laughing and the world spinning, I was jet-propelled to the top of the hill where Tiger, leprechaun-like, in a fur-lined overcoat that went to his knees, was standing between the jug of cider and the spinning pulley in a tree, calling to us to hurry. Tiger served the cider to each of us, and then, like the starter of a steeple-chase race, he lined us up in a row, raised his hand, flashed it down and off we raced again, back down through the trees and unpacked snow, vying for position to get across the narrow bridge over the stream first. Soon, all of us except Mom — she was our ski instructor and almost never fell — were soaking wet and covered with snow. Too cold to continue, we piled into the back of Tiger's World War II army jeep. I sat on Tiger's lap and grasped the lurching steering wheel, while he manned the accelerator, clutch, two gear shifts, and brakes, and we crashed over saplings and bushes, through streams, out of the woods, up the steep hill, to Tiger's house. We piled out, ran into his living room, stripped off layers of wet clothes, hung them from the furniture, and warmed ourselves by the crackling, popping, hopping wood stove.

Late that afternoon, waiting for Pop to come home, I was up in my room, seated in my swivel office chair, at my corner desk positioned between two windows. My grandmother Um had given me the desk as a birthday present and the chair as a Christmas present. Sometimes the way Um spoiled me was slightly embarrassing, but most of the time we just laughed about it. The same Christmas she'd given me the chair, she'd given each of my sisters a very nice calendar. Um liked boys.

As I sat at my desk, I looked out the window to my right. I could see the contour of the frozen stream that bisected our big back field. My other window faced west, over our side lawn, where the driveway con-tinued past our house to a line of buildings that started with a barn-size brown-shingled garage, continued with a little log-cabin smoke

## Chapter 6

house and a red corn crib, and ended with the huge red barn. I was supposed to be doing my math homework, and, boy, did they pile it on at my new school, but I was really just staring out the window at the white flakes coming down in front of our barn — and waiting.

A great deal of my life with Pop consisted of waiting — standing under the shade of trees outside the jocks' room at Saratoga after he had just ridden, waiting for him to shower and change. Or outside a doctor's office, outside a hospital door, outside a circle of reporters. Or seated beside him in a bar, or across the table from him in a restaurant. Or, in the winter, waiting for him to come home in the late afternoon from the racing farm at Hydes.

I heard his Ford Fairlane rumble in the driveway. Tippy, my Norwich terrier, jumped from my bed and ran out of the room and down the steps. Throughout the house, terriers and Labradors and basset hounds started bustling, barking, and yapping and scurrying to the kitchen.

I looked outside as his car, snow billowing up behind it, passed the house. I heard the kitchen door slam shut and then the dogs scrambling down the steps of the back porch, barking and yelping, and I watched as they chased Pop's car through the foot-deep snow toward the barn. The car turned sharply to the left, going up the hill — rear wheels spinning and throwing out two funnels of white spray. Then it circled back down to the walkway that led to our back porch.

Pop stepped out into the cold, into the pack of dogs wagging their tails and jumping and leaping on him. He was wearing the deerskin jacket he liked because it was long — coming down over his hips — and fit as if tapered to his torso, and a heavy canvas cap that Mom disliked, thick tan corduroy pants, and the old leather work boots he rode and worked in all winter. He reached into the car, pulled out his tan briefcase. Holding it under his arm and bending over to pat the dogs, he walked in fast, short strides, beneath my window, disappearing out of view. I heard his footsteps as he climbed the steep wooden steps to the back porch. I felt each step as it reverberated through the logs of the back part of the house and up through the hand-hewn timbers of the newer section, through the wooden floor and up the legs of the chair and desk, and into my body. I left my pencil and pad and mathematical calculations and was up and away from the desk and down the steps.

When I reached the den, Pop was setting down his briefcase beside his big yellow chair. Leaving his jacket and hat on, he walked up to Mom, put his arm around her waist, and grinning, pulled her to him and gave her a kiss on the cheek. She kiddingly pulled away, saying, "Go on now, Paddy. Not in front of the children. Better get those groceries in before they freeze."

"Hey, Cowboy, can you give me a hand?"

"Sure," I said. I ducked in the cold pantry beside the kitchen and grabbed a parka and a wool hat. Out into the snow we went, making several trips. Soon the old drop-leaf table in the center of the kitchen was covered with a week's supply of groceries. Mom had called Carroll's Store in Jacksonville, ordered them, and Pop had picked them up on the way back from Hydes. A winter or two before we'd been snowed in for two weeks, and Mom wanted to be prepared just in case. We'd had no electricity, and the only way you could get to the store five miles away was by horse or skis. We'd cooked all our dinners in the fireplace. Friends of my parents rode and skied over and we had big parties with Mom playing the piano and everyone dancing. All these people were involved in some form of the horse business, most of them in racing, some in showing or hunting, some in all three. At night, when they filled our living room and kitchen with laughter, all metaphors came from the world of horses. "Take a deep seat and a long hold ..." "Can he go the distance ...?" "He broke bad last night ..." "She has her tongue over the bit ..." "He's acting a little studdish tonight ..." "She was in season ..." They had been dancing together since childhood — most of them having grown up together in the heart of Thoroughbred horse country twenty miles north of Baltimore on My Lady's Manor — a ten thousand-acre plot that still retained the name Lord Baltimore bestowed upon it in the 1700s after he made it a gift to his fourth wife.

As children, this group had used ponies as a primary means of transportation, work, and play. They had been raised to be horsemen and horsewomen, they were pursuing this career, and they enjoyed their drinking and smoking and dancing and skiing and riding and flirting and "running around," as they called it. I'd loved being snowed in with no electricity. And, from sneaking some reading in Mom's diary, I'd learned that she had, too.

Pop set the last bag of groceries on the table. He pulled off his cap and deerskin jacket and dropped them on the old wooden trunk piled high with our puffy down parkas and wool ski hats and scarves. The cap and jacket and the wool sweater he was wearing smelled of dry, dusty straw, the sweetness of timothy and alfalfa, the scent of his own spent energy, the sweet friendliness of a horse's thick winter coat. He rubbed the top of my head with his strong, calloused hands, and said, "Thanks, Partner." He pulled up a chair to the table and sat down. Mom was bustling around, unpacking groceries, heating up some water for tea, telling Pop first how the horses and ponies on our farm were doing and then what a great time we'd all had up at Tiger's. Pop briefly told her how the horses were going at the racing farm at Hydes, looked over at me, and said, "How 'bout a little drink before we go out to the barn, Cowboy? And remember about the drought." I made Pop a bourbon and water — easy on the water — and handed it to him as he was telling Mom how the horses were going at the racing farm in Hydes.

The kitchen had windows on three sides. Like Sue Sue's and Sallie's rooms above, the kitchen was in the more narrow two hundred-year-old section of the house, built with logs. A set of steep stairs climbed, turning sharply, from the kitchen, directly up into Sue Sue's room. Down the stairs she came, carrying a music book. She'd changed out of her ski clothes and was in a nightgown and robe. She gave Pop a kiss, asked Mom a question about her French homework — Mom loved

French, had studied German, and soon would be learning Spanish — and walked through the kitchen, through the den — her thick brown hair swinging across the belt of her robe — to the living room to begin her piano practice. I fixed Pop an Old Grand Dad, easy on the water, and walked back up to my room listening to Sue Sue, a year younger than I, practicing her chords directly beneath me. I pulled on some boots and a couple of sweaters. Back downstairs Pop had his briefcase filled with papers open on the chair beside him, the bourbon by his side, an ashtray — some old silver trophy — with a lit cigarette leaning against its raised edge, the smoke spiraling upward, and he and Mom were discussing a couple of owners who owed them money.

"Owners" were the people who owned the horses that Mom and Pop trained on a small scale on our thirteen-acre farm, located "on the Manor." Pop trained the horses on a large scale with Mikey on East Coast racetracks and on the three-hundred-acre racing farm in Hydes, twenty-five miles northeast of Baltimore in the Long Green Valley, where they both grew up. Owners were the people who owned the Thoroughbred horses that Pop rode in steeplechase races — one and a half to three-mile races over fences held at "hunt meets" in the countryside, as in England and Ireland, during the fall and spring and at racetracks during the spring, summer, and fall. Owners were the people Pop risked his life for every afternoon when he went out to ride their horses at a nerve-wracking and dangerous pace, alongside a dozen other horses, over the four-foot hurdles made of brush, or the five-foot brush fences, set up on turf courses inside the dirt ovals of Pimlico, Laurel, Delaware Park, Monmouth Park, Aqueduct, Belmont Park, and Saratoga. Owners were the people for whom Pop literally stooped over: When standing beside an owner, say in the paddock at Saratoga, Pop bent his legs at the knee and leaned slightly forward, trying to make himself appear less tall. (They worried about how a jockey who was almost six feet tall could possibly make the weight.) Owners wanted to get their picture taken with Pop and Mikey in the winner's circle and then wanted a big check from the purse of the race mailed to them.

Owners were not normal people. They called you late at night, they asked questions about their horses, some of them not very intelligent questions. They paid their bills late; they threatened to take their horses away and have someone else train them. They always managed to show up at the barn at the wrong time — just the moment a vet leaned over and gently ran his hand down a horse's tendon to see if it was "bowed," or overly strained, and to determine whether the horse could stay in training for the season. In general, I did not think an owner could be trusted. Neither did Mom. Owners were kind of another species of humans, a subspecies with lots of money.

I also had to work with owners. I rode their ponies, training them to become foxhunters and show ponies. You had to be polite around owners, and you almost always told them their ponies were just wonderful, even if one of them had kicked you the day before. Even if the pony had spooked at a piece of paper outside the ring of a show and run off through a labyrinth of trailers and cars as you, riding bareback, struggled to hang on. Even if the pony had refused for ten torturous minutes to be loaded onto a trailer and then suddenly, crazily, when you least expected it, bolted over top of you into the stall.

But Pop trusted his owners. He and Mikey did have some very good owners. In general, he had faith in people; he trusted people. In general, Mom did not. He and Mom frequently discussed payments owed by an old friend, Johnnie Merryman, for whom they were boarding and training a couple of horses right on our place. That night Mom was more worried than Pop about us getting paid. Pop noted that Johnnie had brought by a truckload of corn just last week, along with a basket of good Pennsylvania mushrooms, and two gallons of fresh, healthy untreated milk right out of one of his cows, and that Johnnie had promised us a load of alfalfa next week.

This line of reasoning did not go far with Mom. She pointed out that the children couldn't live on promises, mushrooms, alfalfa, and milk —

especially milk that came with a smear of cow manure on the bottle neck, that was chokingly thick with cream, that contained a stalk or two of hay or straw, and that, in actuality, we kids wouldn't drink. Mom noted that Pop's so-called old friend also came into the house after unloading the corn and drank half a bottle of Pop's Old Grand Dad before Mom, finally, with my help — and this was after he'd chased her around the kitchen table — sent him home.

Pop laughed, finished his drink, took a last drag of his Pall Mall, and tapped it out in the old trophy, the wisp of smoke trailing off toward the ceiling.

"What's Ed doing tonight?" Pop asked Mom. Edward was Tiger's real name.

"Let's have him over," I butted in, before Mom could reply.

"Why don't you give him a call, Bud?" Pop said, winking at me.

I picked up the telephone, dialed the number, and invited Tiger over for dinner, which meant he'd end up sleeping in my room and most likely get snowed in with us.

Pop and I pulled on our coats and hats. Standing by the door, Pop hesitated and looked over at Mom, "Suzie, if it's still snowing tomorrow, I might have to take Paddy to Hydes with me. We'll be down a man or two," and out we went.

Kicking through the drifting snow, we walked up to the top part of the "bank barn." The barn was built into a bank so that trucks and tractors could back directly into the loft, with almost no incline, to load and unload hay and straw. The stalls below were protected from the wind and elements by the bank in the winter; in the summer, the bank kept the stalls cool.

I stood high up in the hay loft, pried the fifty-pound bales loose, and dragged and pushed and wrestled them down to Pop, the strands of tightly wrapped baling twine biting into my fingers. Pop lifted each bale by the two strands of baling twine and flung it across the floor, forming a pile. Then, with just one hand, he tossed each down the chute. We did the same with the bales of straw, noticeably lighter, on the other side of the barn, and I looked forward to the day I'd be as strong as he. The freshness of the timothy and alfalfa mixed well with the sweet smell of the Old Grand Dad, and Pop looked strong and healthy and like he'd be that way forever.

We walked outside, down through the snow, into the bottom of the barn where the stalls were, and stacked the bales of hay in one neat pile and the straw in another. Patting and talking to the horses, we ducked in and out of their stalls with a pitchfork, culling through the straw and flipping any droppings we found into a wheelbarrow. We tossed two flakes of timothy — each flake a four-inch thick square of compressed hay from the bale — and one flake of rich, green alfalfa in the corner of each stall, and we fed each horse his or her precise amount of oats, sweet feed, and supplements. We talked to each other as we worked, and Pop gave Fini, who was in foal, the special treatment, speaking soothingly to her, rubbing her between her eyes, checking her over. I threw some flakes of hay into the shed where the ponies were crowding together, and Pop spoiled Queenie, who was already plump, by giving her a quart of sweet feed.

Pop stood just inside the barn door and flicked off the lights. It was dark where we stood, but as we walked toward the house the outside light of the back porch fanned out over the snow-covered lawn and into the falling snowflakes. We walked carefully up the slippery snow-covered steps to the back porch and stamped our feet. Inside the door, the thick warmth of the kitchen enveloped us, the scent of roast lamb wafting through the room in almost visible currents. I went upstairs to Tippy, who was lying on my bed. He'd been given to me by Um, who was one of the first to breed Norwich terriers (we called them Jones terriers) in Maryland. Light brown, with a thick coat, bushy eyebrows, strong shoulders, and a tapered torso, he jumped up on all fours, looked me in the eye, and wagged his short tail as I entered. I gave him a pat, wrestled with him, and then, praying that the snow would continue and school would be called off the next day, I sat down at my desk. I opened my loose-leaf notebook to the math section, stared at a mimeographed sheet crowded with a faded, sickly blue matrix of twenty-five multiplication and division problems to do, each written by hand and involving huge numbers. I looked out the window at the snow slanting down and listened to the wind and shut the notebook. I put it aside and pulled out *PT 109*, my most recent arrival in the mail from the Book-of-the-Month Club. Outside my room, I heard Pop turn on the water to the bathtub. As I entered the world of war, PT boats, John F. Kennedy, and heroism, I knew Pop was pulling off his winter work clothes, and neatly setting on the steps to the attic his sweaters and long underwear to be put back on in the morning.

I was halfway through a chapter when Mom starting calling us. I heard Pop walking around in his leather-soled loafers on the hardwood floor of his and Mom's bedroom, and then he was out in the hallway. I kept reading, one more sentence, then one more sentence again. I was on *USS PT-109*, in the Pacific, with John F. Kennedy. I was in a rhythm. Pop cracked open my door, "Hey, Bud, you coming down?"

"I'll be right there," I said.

I finished the page, rushed down the steps, and sat at the table. We were all there, the whole family — Sallie in her tall baby chair. There was one empty seat — Tiger's. It was getting late so Pop went ahead and carved the leg of lamb and Mom prepared our plates of lamb and potatoes and onions and carrots and brussel sprouts. Just as Mom was setting the plates down before us, Tiger stepped into the kitchen, stamped his feet, slung off his heavy coat, apologized for being late — the roads were bad — and sat down with us. "How about a drink, Ed?" Pop said.

"Ay, you're a good man now, Paddy; you're a good man. A little nip might help take the edge off the cold."

Pop looked across the table at me. I hopped up, fixed Tiger a drink, and soon we were eating. Pop sipped on his bourbon and nodded in agreement to Mom's points on good manners as she insisted that Sue

# Chapter 6

Sue hold her fork correctly and that I sit up straight and that Tiger take his elbow off the table. No doubt knowing he would draw her wrath, Pop put his fork in his left hand, knife in his right, cut a piece of lamb, pushed a few vegetables on top of the lamb (as many of the Irish had done the winter before when we'd lived in Ireland) and started, with a grin, to raise his fork when Mom told him to stop, it just wasn't funny, and how were the children going to learn good table manners.

That night Tiger slept in my room in the extra bed, which he had nicknamed "the Grand Canyon," after the hammock-like condition of the mattress, which rested not on box springs but on a swaybacked wire mesh. We talked in low voices late into the night. Tiger fell asleep. I took my diary and flashlight out of the drawer of the bedside table, flipped the covers over my head, turned on the flashlight, and recorded all of the day's activities.

In the morning I arose with Pop in the quiet and the dark. Tiger continued to snore. Pop and I checked on the horses, fed and hayed them, and then drove slowly down the barely plowed Manor Road to the farm at Hydes. As the sun rose, we were bareback on a big chestnut horse, heading up the steep driveway to the gate to the hundred-acre field, on our way to check on the horses that had weathered the storm in the big run-in shed on the property. Then, we were cantering across the hundred-acre field, my arms wrapped tightly around Pop's chest, my face pressed against the deerskin of his jacket. "Hold on, Buddy," Pop hollered, and he clucked to the horse and the speed at which we were suddenly moving seemed unbelievable as the whiteness of the ground beneath us flashed by and the crystals of snow splashing up around us caught the reddish-yellow glow of the early morning sunlight creating a shimmering, golden wake and making it feel as if we might take off into flight. My arms ached as they gripped tighter and tighter around my father's hard torso and my groin and inside-the-thigh muscles felt on fire from squeezing against the horse's sides, and I could hear Pop laughing as we went faster and faster. I held on.

# 7

## Spring

Every spring, in early March, there would come an afternoon when I'd arrive home from Gilman School and find a pile of insulated, waffle-patterned underwear — top and bottom — old turtlenecks, wool sweaters, Irish wool cap, and yellow rain pants and yellow rain jacket balled up on the worn steps to the attic, and they'd be soaked with sweat. There'd be a rich, lively, gamey scent to the sweaty clothes, spiced with a hot rubbery smell given off by the heated rain suit, and there'd be the barnyard aroma of hot, steamy wool. As the spring lengthened, the sweat-soaked clothes would appear more often, signaling the beginning of another steeplechase season.

The carefree having-my-father-at-home of the winter, the watching him slice the lamb and ladle out the potatoes at dinner, the playing checkers with him by the fire at night while Mom played the piano, the joking around and bringing the miniature pony my sister Sue Sue was riding and training into the house or into the back seat of the car, would be over. So would the early morning drive on Saturday and Sunday down to Hydes with him, just the two of us, talking, then working with the horses and ponies in the vast fields. The driving home with him and the talking about our day's work were winding

# Chapter 7

down; winter was ending. His full Irish face would begin to narrow as he stoked the fires deep inside that drove him. He'd stop eating. He'd work in layers of clothes, melting off the muscle on his neck, shoulders, thighs and calves, honing the 165-pound body of a middleweight fighter down to 155, 150, 145, 140 — to his limit, 136.

The lightest he could rig up his racing boots, britches, stirrups, girths, and saddle was four pounds. Four pounds of gear added to his 136 meant that the lightest he'd be listed to ride was 140. The steeplechase horses he rode were assigned weights ranging from 130 pounds for three-year-old maidens to 165 for older horses. The handicappers were putting up to 170, even 175 pounds, on the great Neji the year before, which is why Sue Sue and I got to skip school for three months and spend that winter of my third grade with our cousins in Ireland. Pop and Neji went to Ireland, where Neji could run in races without being assigned so much weight and where he could train for the Cheltenham Gold Cup.

By late March my father would be off early Monday morning at eighty miles an hour to Belmont Park for the week. And everything in our lives got hotter, sharper, and more brilliant, as Pop fought his weight, as his nerves got touchier, as we read about him on the front pages of the sports section of the *New York Times* and the *Herald Tribune*, saw his picture in the *Morning Telegraph* and *The Chronicle of the Horse*, as he drifted away from us to his other love, to his gift, race-riding.

When he could, he drove home to Maryland. He drove fast, dodging cops, arriving in the evening. No more playing checkers at night. He had to arise at three in the morning to make it to the barn at Belmont Park by six. Sometimes I'd hear him start the car, in the dark, outside my window, and I'd wish I were going with him. Mom grew more tense. She worried about his driving. One night he pushed his new car too hard when making a turn two miles from our house. I saw the car the next day, lying there on its back like a turtle, its dark underbelly of pipes and metal parts oddly exposed, vulnerable. No one said much about it. It was a mystery to me, what had happened. For no reason I felt a tinge of guilt about it. He had his cars rigged so that the engine was set to idle at a higher speed than normal; you'd better have your foot on the brake when you put his car in gear.

Only a wall separated Mom and Pop's room from mine, and we shared a small bathroom with a wide-planked floor; the window beside the sink looked out over our front paddock where my ponies, first Nappy, then Queenie, and later Twinkle, were often turned out. When Pop was home, I could hear him and Mom through our adjoining wall late at night. I couldn't distinguish the words; I could just hear the tone of he tone of what they were saying. And I could tell from the pitch who was speaking. Sometimes they talked into the night, and sometimes there were no words, just rocking sounds. Other times, I could tell they were arguing about a woman.

Another controversial topic was how the Smithwick Stables — including the three-hundred-acre racing farm and all its facilities at Hydes — was conducting business, and especially how my father and his earnings and his talents were being treated by the other two-thirds of the corporation — my grandmother and my uncle. Pop was off winning the big races; as a rider, he received 10 percent of every purse, and most of these winnings he plowed back into the racing farm at Hydes. Mom wasn't sure of the wisdom of this.

One late spring afternoon, a Sunday, I walked right into my parents' room. Pop hadn't been home much and I wanted to ask Mom something. I opened the door and there they were with no clothes on, all tangled up into some kind of knot. I closed the door and went out to the barn, took a few unsuccessful shots at some pigeons with my new BB gun, and swung on the Tarzan rope that my grandmother Whitman had hung from a high beam for us. Soon Pop was out in the barn checking on the horses, and he came up into the loft, threw down a bale or two, and said, "Sorry, Cowboy. Guess sometimes you get caught in embarrassing positions," and that was it. I continued swinging on the rope and the whole thing slid off me like cold water does after you swim naked across a muddy, mucky pond.

Pop spotted my BB gun lying on a bale of hay. "Hey, Bud, how're you doing with the new gun?"

"My aim's not too great," I said.

"Then let's have a little target practice." We set up a couple of empty Budweiser cans on a stump in front of the meat house. "Now here's how they taught me to do it in the army," he said. We kneeled on the lawn above the meat house. He put his arms around me, corrected my stance, and then looking down the barrel of the gun through the sight, with his scratchy cheek pressed against mine, his right arm around my shoulder, his left hand under mine, I squeezed the trigger. There was a very satisfying popping sound and an empty can of Budweiser suddenly had a hole in it and Pop was saying, "Nice shot, Cowboy, nice shot."

**\* \* \***

On the weekends the spring race meets would commence, featuring steeplechase races over hurdles, brush, and timber. The season started with a couple of what Emmett Grayson called "Pint to Pints," more formally termed "Point to Points." These were the unsanctioned race meets sponsored by local foxhunting clubs in South Carolina, North Carolina, Kentucky, Tennessee, Virginia, Maryland, Pennsylvania, New Jersey, and New York. Pop and Mikey usually skipped most of these, and perhaps went to a few of the ones in Virginia — Casanova, Rappahannock, and Piedmont - just to school the horses. Soon, as the afternoon sun brightened and the ice and snow melted, the hunt meets sanctioned by the National Steeplechase and Hunt Association (NSHA) began. These races were for professional jockeys and had purses and bookies with chalkboards. Elmer Delmer the bookmaker would be there, and he'd ask me what my father and uncle said about their horses before he put his odds up on his blackboard. There would be big crowds and shiny Rolls Royces and old Packards from the 1930s and

'40s and picnicking tailgaters.

The NSHA races started down in the Carolinas in March, at Camden and Aiken in South Carolina, at Tryon in North Carolina, and then, following the warming of spring, moved up into Virginia, to Middleburg, to Warrenton, where the races were called the Gold Cup, to Richmond where they were called Deep Run, and finished up at Fair Hill in Maryland, the fanciest hunt meet in America, owned by the du Ponts, and the only hunt meet that featured pari-mutuel betting. In later years Mrs. Richard C. du Pont would sometimes have her great racehorse Kelso, who had been five times Horse of the Year with Pop's colleague Eddie Arcaro in the tack for several of those years, led out in front of the stands and paraded around before the races.

I'd met Arcaro a couple of times. And, sitting with Pop at home in front of our little black-and-white television, I'd watched Arcaro ride Kelso. I'd always be worried during the early part of the race.

"He's so far back, Pop. He's way back."

"Don't worry, Bud; Eddie knows what he's doing."

Arcaro and Kelso would be galloping along five or six lengths off the lead.

"You sit tight and watch. Maybe you'll learn something."

We'd be quiet, and gradually, without Arcaro making any visible change in his classic riding form, they'd start gaining on the leaders; they'd start reeling them in. Kelso's stride would look as if it were lengthening as he'd pick off one, then another, until he passed the front-runner just a length or two from the finish.

* * *

I made a lot of money at Fair Hill, for a kid. I was too young to place a bet at the windows, but adult friends in the hunt-and-jump set, usually retired race-riders, were only too happy to place my bets and learn whom I was putting my money on. I was a conservative gambler at this stage — having discovered the "across the board" bet of putting down six dollars — two to win, two to place, and two to show.

Pop would've been going down to the Carolina race meets in late March, but the first big race meet we'd attend as a family was the Middleburg hunt meet, in Virginia, and I couldn't wait to go. I loved helping Pop carry his tack bag from the car to the jocks' room — a private dressing space covered by a tin roof nailed onto some tall posts with rough-hewn fence boards fastened to the sides. The jocks' room was the inner sanctum. Only the riders were allowed in, and, of course, no women.

On the morning of April 15, 1961, Mom and I went for a cross-country school before we headed to Middleburg. Mom was on Fini; I was on Queenie; and Mom and Fini led, trotting, cantering, and galloping through the woods, over logs, and across creeks. We jumped one chicken coop after another, but I envisioned each as one of the fences over which Pop would be riding a horse called Valley Hart that afternoon. The three-foot chicken coops were built in trappy places without much room to maneuver: You'd come around a sharp turn, headed out of the woods, and there the jump suddenly was. Each was about twelve feet long and looked like a steeply gabled roof top, or an actual coop for chickens, with one side made of horizontal fence boards nailed closely together, leaning against another side of horizontal fence boards. Heading home, we jumped panels in board fences where the top rail had been lowered, and small post and rail fences. Queenie was my timber horse, my Valley Hart, and I was the jockey.

Soon I was up in my room changing into clean khakis, a clean blue long-sleeve shirt, and pulling a wool sports jacket out of the gigantic, towering armoire Pop, Tiger, and Jack Graybeal had recently carried up a ladder and muscled into my room through the space made by the empty window frame, out of which they had first pried and crowbarred the entire window. Tippy was perched nervously on the edge of my bed watching me, able to tell I would be leaving soon. Sue Sue was all dressed to go and practicing the piano in the living room. Mom was downstairs in the kitchen talking to the baby-sitter, Mrs. Pearce, who would be watching one-year-old Sallie while we were gone. (Pop kidded that Sallie was "Irish-bred." "It was cold over there, and … not much to do at night.") I looked down at my lace-up shoes, battered and scuffed from wearing them to school. I wanted a pair of Weejun loafers like Pop's, but Mom wouldn't let me get them yet. She said they wore out too fast. I pulled out my shoe-shine kit and was sitting in the swivel chair, starting to work on the shoes, when I heard the sound of a car slowing as it came through the tunnel of trees on Manor Road and then the wheels crunching and skidding on the gravel of the driveway. With a newspaper spread across my lap, as Pop had taught me, and a shoe wedged between my legs, I stretched forward, looked out the window, and watched the car as it neared the house. I looked carefully to see whether Pop had all the windows up and was in his sweating outfit, which meant he'd drive down in a "hot car" and we'd go with Mom; or, if he had the windows open and the air was flowing through, which meant his weight was good and we would all drive down together.

The car continued past, the passenger window all the way down and Pop's elbow sticking out. I felt a lift of excitement. Tippy jumped off the bed and ran down the steps. Sue Sue stopped practicing the piano. Alfred of Monkton, Pop's basset hound; Wo Wo, Sue Sue's black Labrador; Wug the Pug, Mom's pug dog; and a couple of young Jack Russells started scampering around in the kitchen and on the back porch, barking and yelping. As Pop's car coasted to a stop, his door was open, his foot skidding on the ground, and he was out. He walked fast to the kitchen. I could hear him talking to Mom, and then he was trotting up the front steps. He looked in my doorway at me. "Hey, Bud, you ready?"

"Just about," I said.

"You have time to knock the dust off my loafers?"

"Sure."

He went into his bedroom, got his loafers, and brought them in to me. I finished up my lace-ups and polished his loafers while he shaved and dressed.

Then, we were off to the races, Pop at the wheel, a little on edge, pushing it, passing cars, accelerating, judging the passing of long lines of cars just right, down to a hairline. He had a ride on a maiden in the first race, post time for which was 1:30.

Mom was in the front seat. "Remember, the kids are in the back," she told him. Mom asked Pop about the upcoming races, but he didn't really like talking about races before he rode them. "Murph will win most of them. Tommy'll gallop in the Skinner. I should do all right in the timber race." That meant that his great friend Jimmy Murphy, whom I sometimes shot pool with and who could clear the table, would win most of the races. (Jimmy rode for Sidney Watters, Sue Sue's godfather. Although Sidney did most of his training in Virginia and New York, his family farm was right next to ours and was where the Hunter Trials were held early each fall.) Tommy Walsh would win the William Skinner Memorial, and Pop, if everything went all right, would win the timber race. My adrenalin shot up, for two reasons. First, I knew Jimmy Murphy and Tommy Walsh very well, which meant I would know the winner of every race; second, this would be simple to tell Elmer Delmer, the bookmaker, and it would enable me to make some money on the side.

Mom asked Pop why he wasn't riding Bampton Castle, a good horse, in the first race. He explained that he had to ride Alezan because the horse was owned by Mrs. Randolph, one of his and Mikey's top own-ers. Mom didn't like this much. Then he would be riding Blackmail in the second race — but he and Mikey just wanted "to give him a race." Pop didn't have a ride in the third race. Then, he was riding Valley Hart in the feature race of the day, the timber race. Valley Hart was trained by Jamie Hruska, a close friend of the family who had just stopped rid-ing races — he'd had some bad falls and kept breaking too many bones, especially collarbones — and started training. Mom and Pop talked about Valley Hart. I could tell they both wanted to win this one for Jamie, who was a unique horseman. He was a finesse rider, more of a show-ring rider with an artistic temperament; he was especially good with young horses and loved bringing them along. At night, after a few drinks, he'd sit at the piano at Goldberg's, as we called it (or Four Corners Corral), in nearby Jacksonville. He'd maintain total focus on the piano keys and play song after song, beautifully, into the night. Mom especially appreciated his gifts as a musician.

Twenty miles outside of Middleburg we got in a traffic jam. It was getting a little late, and the needle on the speedometer was creeping higher and higher on the crescent dial of the Ford and then down and to the right as Pop pulled the car into the lane of on-coming traffic and flew by the long line of race-going cars.

Mom grabbed the dashboard with both hands and gritted her teeth. "Paddy, remember the children are in the back." Sue Sue ducked down behind the front seat. I watched as miles and miles of stark Virginia fields, the sites of bloody Civil War battles, unraveled outside the window — hilly, rocky, coarse, with cattle and horses grazing, and historic markers stuck seemingly in the middle of nowhere. We slowed and drove through the village of Middleburg, and soon we were at the gates of the Glenwood Park Course for the Middleburg races and bumping across the cattle guard, and the tires accustomed to speeds of seventy and eighty miles per hour on asphalt were rolling quietly over a smooth dirt path worn through the grass that morning, a blood-red snow fence to our left. A big country boy in khaki work shirt and overalls waved us into his parking area, which was way too far from the paddock. Pop had the window down, held out our sticker saying "Owners, Trainers, and Riders Parking," and drove on. Another parking attendant, who didn't know any better, stood directly in our way, waving us into his area. Old and grumpy, he was there every year, and he did the same thing every year. "Paddy ... Paddy ...," Mom said. Pop didn't slow. Sue Sue was on the floor. The attendant furiously waved his flag, which he had on a long cane, as we rumbled toward him and still Pop didn't slow. Pop muttered a few rare cuss words, and just as it looked like we would run right over the crazy old coot, the attendant stepped out of the way, slapping his cane loudly across our hood as we passed. "Par for the course," Mom mumbled, her hand over her mouth.

We rumbled past the large bowl of a racecourse on the left. There were actually three courses, ovals within ovals, set inside the bowl. The timber course was the uppermost oval — a mile and a half once around the perimeter. Each timber fence consisted of half a dozen panels, some of which had recently been reinforced with new rails, freshly cut and light colored, that stood out from the older weather-beaten rails. Inside the timber course was the hurdle course — a mile and a quarter once around the oval — each hurdle made up of fresh green brush. And inside the hurdle course was the "flat" course — a mile once around — with no jumps, the dark-red snow fence making up the inside rail of the last turn. The grass on all three courses was so green and thick, it made you feel like hopping on a horse and galloping across it.

As we passed the course, spectators were setting up picnic tables, pouring drinks, and organizing ice chests and bottles of bourbon and flutes of mint on the tailgates of station wagons that overflowed with plates of fried chicken and roast beef and deviled eggs and biscuits and ham. We drove up a hill into a stand of trees and parked alongside other cars with "Owners, Trainers, and Riders Parking" stickers in the windshields.

* * *

The sun shone brightly. The air shimmered with energy. Pop opened the trunk. "Suzie — do you and Suedy Sue want your jackets?" he asked.

"No thanks," Mom said, "Just leave them there for now."

"How about the binoculars?"

"Yes, take them out, please."

Pop reached in and pulled out two pairs of binoculars, both enclosed in leather cases. Pop's were big and had especially wide lenses so you could take in the whole field of horses when watching a race. Mom's were smaller and lighter. "Hand these to your mother, would you, Bud?" Pop said, handing me the smaller pair.

A young country boy, a few inches taller and a few years older than I and dressed in blue jeans and a heavy, checkered work shirt rolled up at the sleeves, approached the car; he was holding a fistful of programs. Mom got some cash, bought a couple of programs, and handed one to me. I walked back to Pop, behind the car. Our tweed jackets lay across the top of his tack bag. He handed me mine and I slipped it on. He pulled his on. He and I both were wearing shined shoes, clean pants, shirt and tie, and a jacket. Pop always dressed well at the races, even if just to walk to the jocks' room. He reached into the trunk with one hand, grabbed the two handles of his worn leather tack bag — a duffle bag filled with his saddles and gear and ten pounds of thin, dollar bill-sized slivers of lead — lifted the bag out and set it on the ground. The boy with the programs was now awkwardly hovering around us. He was wearing a stiff new pair of lace-up riding boots. The light tan leather was darkened with dirt and sweat on the inside of the ankles, and the inside of the calves of his blue jeans was frayed and sweat stained. He stepped forward, holding a program open to the first race. "Mr. Smithwick, would you autograph my program, please, sir?" he asked, pronouncing our name correctly, the Irish way, without the "w," so that it sounded like "Smith-ick."

"Sure, jock," Pop said, looking the boy in the eye.

The boy beamed at Pop's recognition of his riding ambition.

"Where'd you like me to sign it?" Pop asked, taking the pen. The boy pointed to the spot where Pop was listed to ride Alezan in the first race. Pop bent forward, signed his name, and handed back the program and pen. "Nice-looking boots. How many did you get on this morning?"

"Three," the boy said, grinning.

## Chapter 7

"Keep it up. Maybe I'll see you here in a pair of silks in a year or two."

The boy looked up at him. "I hope so, Mr. Smithwick. Do you think you'll win many today?"

Pop stood on one side of the tack bag, me on the other. Pop leaned forward and gripped the handle on his side of the bag; I leaned forward, gripped my handle, and we both lifted up. "No, won't win many today," he told the boy, "but I might do all right in the fourth."

The boy flipped the pages of his program to the fourth race, the timber race. Pop gave me a wink, and we carried the bag along a tractor path through the trees on top of the hill toward the jocks' room. I almost had to jog to keep up with his long steps. Halfway there, seeing I was slowing, Pop asked, "You okay, Cowboy?" We stopped, took a breather, and switched sides.

We made our way into the jocks' room. This wasn't Belmont Park. There was a rusty tin roof over our heads, and worn, weathered fence boards made up the walls. No Dick Dwyer here. There was a confusion of greetings: "How ya doing, Paddy" … "Good afternoon, Little Paddy — you got any good rides today?" … "Hey, Little Paddy, when're you going to take over? Getting a little hard for your old man to make the weight, don't you think?"

About a dozen riders were packed under the tin roof. Some were shirtless, pulling off pants, pulling on nylon britches, exposing their veined, sinewy, muscled torsos. They were organizing their spots from which to operate for the rest of the day — setting two or three saddles on the fence, hanging their elastic overgirths and undergirths over the saddles, laying the rubber pads and brightly colored wool pommel pads, and the freshly cleaned-and-saddle-soaped yokes across the two-to eight-pound saddles.

They were pulling their racing silks out of tack bags, holding them up high, and snapping them to get the wrinkles out, then neatly stretching them across hangers and hooking the hangers over nails. A few of the younger, lighter riders were organizing their lead pads. We set our tack bag down in a corner.

Jimmy Murphy, already dressed in his boots, britches, and silks, walked over to me, looked me in the eye, and shook my hand. "How're you doing, Patrick?" he asked. He was the only rider who called me by my actual name.

"Fine, thank you," I said. I didn't know whether to call him Mr. Murphy, or Jimmy, so I didn't say either.

"Did your mother come down with you?"

"Yes, she's here."

"And Sue Sue?"

"She's here, too."

"You coming over after the races?" he asked me. I looked hopefully at Pop.

"If all goes well, we'll be there, Jimmy," said Pop.

Jimmy walked outside. Pop said to me in a low voice, "He's one of my best friends, Bud. He's like a brother. You can call him Jimmy."

Tommy Walsh, long blond hair combed back, stepped into the room, carrying a small tack bag. He had driven all the way down from Belmont Park to ride one race, which meant he'd be doing well in that race. He walked over and set his tack bag down beside ours. "Hey, Little Paddy," he said, barely moving his lips, in a low, muffled voice. He mussed my hair, which had been neatly combed.

"Hi, Tommy," I said, feeling a shot of adrenalin from the contact with him.

"I see you didn't come down in a hot car. Your old man must be light today."

"Hey, Tommy," Pop said, "still working on it." He winked at me. "The Mrs. wouldn't allow a hot car today, but I ought to be all right after I ride a few." He lost a couple of pounds each time he rode a race.

"Got any juice?" Tommy asked.

"No, you got anything?"

"I got a thermos in the bag." I knew this would not be run-of-the-mill fruit juice. I'd made the mistake of taking a swig out of Tommy's thermos the spring before, and I'd walked around on six inches of air for about forty-five minutes afterward.

Pop started changing into his britches, T-shirt, and stock — a compact, thickly woven, white cotton neck cover — and pulled on his boots. He asked me to rig up his middleweight saddle for the first race. He was doing 153. I took out a freshly saddle-soaped pair of stirrup leathers and sat down on the ground beside Joe Aitcheson.

Joe was focused on adjusting the straps to the shoulder pads he wore. He hadn't pulled on a T-shirt yet, and I snuck a look at the tattoo he had on his bicep. He didn't have long, sinewy muscles like Pop. His muscles were sharply delineated and accentuated. They popped and rippled as he moved the pads around. He looked up at me for a second, "You taking care of your dad's tack for him today?"

"Yes," I said. "I am."

"He's a lucky man to have you helping out. Wish I had a son to help me." This made me feel great. Joe always said something to me, in a calm and gentle voice, that made me feel good. Not only was Joe one of the top up-and-coming riders, I knew that he had also served a tour or two with the Navy and had been a champion Navy boxer. Joe was sincere. There was no small talk with him, no wasted movement. He was down to business. Just the way he rode a race: Get a good start, get on the inside, save ground every inch of the way, and then make your move. He was a mystery to many people, seeming to live totally in his own disciplined world.

I started lacing the stirrup leathers through the light aluminum stirrups, which were wrapped with a layer of rubber gauze to keep Pop's feet from sliding and to make the stirrups more comfortable in his thin-soled riding boots.

Pop had two pairs of race-riding boots. One had a thin slice of hard leather for soles and a band of leather, about an inch wide, sewn into the heels in the form of a horseshoe. They were custom-made, came all the way up his calves. There was a four-inch band of brown leather at the top, and the rest of the leather, paper thin, was black and supple. Round patches, the size of silver dollars, had been sewn on where the ankle rubs against the horse. The other pair were his "cheating boots," made — heel, sole, and leg — of soft, light leather. Riding in these light boots was like riding barefoot, and Pop was one of the few who did it. Most jockeys weighed out before a race wearing their cheating boots, then rushed back and pulled on their more supportive boots before the race.

I laced the thin, belt-like leathers into the feathery-light saddle, and set the lightest rubber pad, a wool pommel pad, the undergirth, overgirth, and yoke on the saddle, and set the saddle on the fence. Because the tack, boots, and britches weighed five pounds, Pop had to weigh 148 to make 153. This would be no problem. However, later in the afternoon he had to make lighter weights. He was depending on losing about two pounds of water weight in each early race in order to make the light weights later on.

Pop and I walked over to the scales. Carlyle Cameron — a big friendly man who knew in his bones how difficult it was for Pop to make weight — was standing behind the scales with the day's program in one hand, a pen in the other. Pop stepped up on the scales, holding his tack under his arm. Carlyle took his eye from the program, looked Pop in the eye, and glanced over the tack. Pop called out each piece of tack he had in his arms as Carlyle nudged the cube-shaped weight over to 153. The tip of the scale balanced perfectly. "Okay, Smithwicks," he said, giving me a wink.

Later in the day, when Pop was doing light, say, 144, I'd stand and watch as Carlyle pushed the little weight out with the tip of his finger — at 144, the pointer wouldn't waver; at 145, it wouldn't budge; he'd nudge it to 145 1/2, and it would just start to waver, meaning Pop was a pound and a half overweight. Carlyle would look down at his program, and say "Okay, Paddy," and mark Pop off, as Pop, not an extra ounce of flesh on him, all long bones and hanging silks and loose britches, stepped off the scales. There would be no announcement over the loudspeaker system before the race that number so and so, ridden by A.P. Smithwick, was two pounds overweight. Carlyle knew that no rider in America worked harder to make the weight than Pop. Later in the season, for the big races at the major tracks, making the exact weight was a point of honor for Pop.

We walked back to the jocks' room. Pop sat by his tack bag. He wrapped two specially cut half-inch wide rubber bands around the sleeves of the silks on each wrist. I got out two thin strips of gum, and he set them under the bands, beneath his left wrist. Later, right before the race, he'd chew them to keep his mouth from feeling dried out.

We relaxed for a moment while riders rushed in and out of the jocks' room, changing their equipment. Pop studied his program. I looked over mine. Then he closed his program and said, "You ready, Bud?"

"I'm ready," I said, and we both rose to go.

# 8

## "Riders Up!"

We walked from the jocks' room over to the fenced-in paddock. I was carrying the tack, and I had to stay on one side of Pop. He was superstitious about a few things before he rode and one was that when you walked to the paddock with him, you picked one side of him — I liked the right side — and you stayed there. He was carrying his whip. I held the saddle up high against my chest to keep the girths from dragging, and the buckles of the girths slapped against my legs with every stride.

A Pinkerton nodded to us as we neared the crowded entrance to the paddock. At the gate another Pinkerton asked a few people to step aside and we marched right in, not breaking our stride, Pop grinning and nodding to the owners and trainers and their spouses as he headed for a spot in a corner, where his brother Mikey, tall, thin, and dressed in a coat and tie, was standing.

You never knew whom you might meet at the races. On this day everyone was buzzing around talking about how the Kennedys were there. We knew that Jacqueline Kennedy foxhunted with the Middleburg Hunt and had gone out with the Elkridge-Harford Hunt up where we lived, so this all seemed pretty natural to us. Dot — Uncle

## Chapter 8

Mikey's wife — had gone to Vassar with Jacqueline and knew her well.

All the riders were in the paddock, a fenced-in area the size of a show ring. Each was in black boots with brown tops, white britches, brightly colored silks, and a helmet with a matching silk cap over it. I knew Mrs. Theodora A. Randolph would soon be approaching us because Pop was in her silks, which were a light, faded blue with a pinkish cross sash. Pop was riding half of an "entry," meaning his horse was "coupled" with another because both of them were trained by the same man, namely Mikey. They were listed in the program as numbers "4" and "4a."

Mikey spent most of his time talking to the other rider, a young "bug boy" — so-called because of the bug-like stars printed beside his name in the program. A steeplechase jockey who had never ridden a winner and was allowed a ten-pound advantage had three bugs by his name. (If the horse would normally carry 150 pounds, it would carry only 140 with the bug boy aboard.) The advantage in weights helped novice riders get started.

As more and more people streamed into the paddock, I wondered how the horses would fit in. Men wore Irish wool caps and stylish fedoras with the brims pulled down low over their eyes. They were dressed in English-cut wool jackets, longish and tapered at the waists like riding coats, bright blue and pink and yellow shirts, intricately designed silk ties, and British ankle-high lace-up shoes shined to a high gloss that morning. A few wore mid-length, gray British Warms — like polo coats but heavier and made with more tightly woven wool — because there was still a chill coming off the damp ground. The women were in long, floppy dresses, and tight-fitting ankle and calf-high boots. A few wore colorful old-fashioned, wide-brimmed hats as if they were at Churchill Downs on Derby Day. There were little islands of people, each centered around a jockey.

Mrs. Randolph, from my grandparents' generation, walked out of one circle of friends and over to us. I didn't think much about clothes, but Mrs. Randolph always did wear a funny-looking hat. It was round, plopped down tight on her head, and had a two-inch brim. It reminded me of the World War I helmets worn by the English.

Pop stepped out, shook Mrs. Randolph's hand, and did a half-bow. I did the same. She was one of the great owners; she didn't bother Pop and Mikey one bit by asking them what the plan was or how the horse would run or whether they thought he would win.

The horses finally began parading in. Most of the crowd automatically went to the middle of the paddock, leaving the horses room to walk out on the perimeter. The Pinkertons, leading the line of horses, had to show a few people, who were overly engaged in their conversations, toward the middle. The grooms, some old, some young, some white, some black — all neatly dressed and strutting tall and proud — led the horses around. The horses — chestnuts, bays, blacks, a gray — danced and jigged and kicked out — their backs beautiful, glistening, and bare.

The jockeys stood, thin and tall and quiet, holding their whips, their arms crossed, eyeing their mounts, listening to instructions from their trainers, joking with the owners, looking over the long legs of the young women in short skirts. Some horses walked calmly. Others kicked and reared and threw their heads. Teenaged daughters of owners tossed their heads back to get their long straight hair out of their eyes.

Speedy Kiniel was leading Alezan; Junior Tibbs was leading Bampton Castle, and Jim Rutherford was following behind. Speedy and Junior were boxers and thus gods to me. At the tracks, once or twice a week, organized fights well held in well-kept rings, matching a groom of one stable against a groom of another. Speedy was tall, lanky, with lightning-fast reactions and a long reach; his hair was long, black, and swept-back into a style he called a "process." Junior was shorter, broad-backed, each shoulder like a cannon ball; his hair was cropped to the skull. He could look intimidating, but he was as gentle as could be with a horse. Jim was young, rode some races, and kept an eye on me, giving me tips on how to get through the long mornings at the track.

"Saddle 'em up!" the paddock judge called out. First, Mikey and Jim Rutherford saddled up Bampton Castle. The moment they finished, Speedy pulled Alezan over to our spot. Mikey stood on the left side, the "near side," of Alezan; Pop, on the right. I stood beside Pop and handed him each piece of tack in the correct order: first, the foam rubber pad, then the number cloth fully extended up over the horse's mane. They placed the pommel pad over the horse's withers and folded the number cloth back over it. Pop set the saddle down over the number cloth and grabbed hold of the saddle with one hand and pulled down on the elastic girth with the other. Mikey reached down, pulled the undergirth around and up to the saddle, pulled the billet through the buckle, leaned his full weight forward and up, and buckled it. Then came the long elastic overgirth, which went the full circumference of the horse's chest. Pop placed the mid-section of the girth on top of the saddle. He and Mikey pulled down simultaneously on each end, and bending down low — the horse snorting and kicking — Mikey pulled the leather billet through the buckle directly under the horse's chest, just behind his legs. Saddles can slip if they aren't on just right.

Speedy led Alezan around the paddock a couple of times with all the other horses. The paddock judge called out, "Riders Up!" Pop and Mikey walked out to the horse. Bending his left knee and holding his left calf at a right angle to his thigh, Pop stood by Alezan's side. Mikey cupped his hand around Pop's ankle and up Pop went, landing gently in the saddle, expression calm. Mikey set Pop's left foot in the stirrup. Pop stretched his long, rubber-sheathed reins out their full length to the buckle that connects them and tied the end into a knot. The procession of horses walked once around the paddock, their jockeys' silks a panoply of color and geometric forms — black cross sashes across yellow chests, blue triangles and chevrons set against red, red hearts on a pink background. As they walked out onto the course, the grooms looked up at the riders, wished them good luck, and unsnapped their shanks.

I headed out of the paddock with the crush of older, taller people. I jogged up to the spot on the hill where I knew Mom and Sue Sue would be. On the way I passed Elmer Delmer, fat and jocular, standing beside his chalkboard set up on an easel. On the chalkboard was a list of horses, riders, and their odds. He was politely taking a fistful of dollars from an eager, older Virginia gentleman in a wool suit with sharply creased pants. I wanted to get up the hill to our spot for watching the race, but I hadn't seen Elmer Delmer yet. "Well, hello there, young Smithwick," the older gentleman said. "Won't be long before we'll be watching you out there," he nodded toward the course.

We shook hands. "Yes, sir. I hope so."

"Are you by any chance placing a wager on your father in this race?" he asked.

"No, sir, I don't think so."

"Oh. Really?"

"Maybe later in the day."

A group of friends were waiting for this man. They were headed for one of the station wagons with a tailgate filled with food and drinks. A woman called out, "Come on, Bill, come on."

"All right," he yelled back at them. He put his hand out and we shook again. "See you in the saddle one day, young Smithwick."

I looked up at Elmer Delmer.

"Got anything?" he asked.

"Murphy, most of the day, and Pop said he 'might do all right' in the timber race."

"That's a good boy," he said, pulling out his thick wad of cash, peeling off four ones, taking a glance around, and handing them to me. I could always depend on Elmer for a few bucks at the races. "Check back later," he said.

"All right. Got to go." I turned to leave. I hadn't told him about Tommy. I could skip it …

I pivoted back toward Elmer Delmer. He looked at me questioningly.

"And Tommy. Tommy Walsh's horse should run very well."

I reached our spot under a tree. "Pa-trick," Mom said, enunciating my name as if it were made up of sharp, clashing edges, "who was that you were talking to on the way up?"

I knew she knew exactly who it was. "That was Elmer Delmer, Mom." Elmer Delmer was not a favorite of hers.

"And what did he want?" she asked, handing me Pop's heavy binoculars, which she had lugged over for me. I heard a "Not it!" and looked over to see Sue Sue, who was in her new dress, running in and out of the trees playing tag with some newly met friends. Her kneecaps were already embedded with dirt.

"Never mind," she said, putting her binoculars up to her eyes. "I know what he wanted, and I'm telling you now, you'd be better off staying away from him."

I adjusted the lenses of my field glasses and watched Pop circle around, getting ready to file in for the start. Pop's silks would be "old rose," or a faded pink, if Mrs. Phipps owned the horse; or dark green cross sashes set against light green if June McKnight owned the horse; or pale blue with pink cross sashes if Mrs. Randolph owned the horse. These were Pop's and Mikey's main owners. They were very good owners.

I watched Pop in the blue-and-pink silks glide away from the start, far off, half a mile across the bowl-like valley. Pop always got a good start, even in a long race. "A length at the start is a length at the finish," he'd say. By the third hurdle he was in second place, just a length off the leader. It was easy to follow Pop because he was taller than the other riders and he had a unique style. He stood up higher in the stirrups, in a more relaxed fashion, getting his horse to relax and not waste valuable energy early in the race. Jimmy Murphy was in front, and he was going easy.

The pack of horses rounded the curve on the rim of the bowl, barreled down the hill, and turning left, shot by the white wooden two-story stewards' stand and under what next time around would be the finish wire — Jimmy still in front, Pop second, the bug-boy on Bampton Castle third. They were going impossibly fast, riders leaning back, pulling against their horses' mouths. Descending the steep hill, they went out of our sight for ten seconds. They emerged and progressed up the hill. Turning to their left, they continued for a mile around the rim of the bowl, jumping the hurdles, the bright silks flashing in the sunlight. Bampton Castle moved into second place. Pop was third. Jimmy had opened up three lengths on the field. A quarter-mile from home, Pop was down lower now, galloping around the last turn, stick raised in right hand, in third place; Joe Aitcheson behind him, fourth.

The pack thundered under the wire, Jimmy Murphy winning easy, Bampton second, Pop third, the horses' hooves throwing divots and clods of turf and dirt into the air. The second the riders passed under the wire, they stood up, leaned back against their horses' mouths. The horses' legs got loose-jointed and their heads dropped down and the riders eased them up at the bottom of the hill, turned around, and cantered back up.

I handed the binoculars back to Mom and ran down to the stewards' stand. The riders waved their sticks at the stewards on the top floor, seeking permission to dismount. Pop slid off, unbuckled the girths, pulled off the saddle, pads, and yoke, and stepped on the scales beside the stewards' stand to have Carlyle check his weight. (An unscrupulous rider might weigh out before the race with a saddle and a heavy lead pad, switch to a lighter lead pad before saddling up, and ride the race with ten or twenty pounds less than what was written in the program. After the race the rider would untack and then "bump" into an accomplice on the way to "weigh in," and switch the light pad for the heavy lead pad. To prevent these sorts of shenanigans, jockeys and their tack are very closely monitored, and jockeys are weighed both before and immediately after a race. If a rider were caught cheating on his weight, the stewards would hand him a stiff fine and ban him from riding races for a year or more. He'd be "ruled off.")

Smiling and sweating and with dirt splattered over his face, silks, and britches, Pop handed me the armful of tack and we walked back to the jocks' room through the crowd of men and women — old and young, some dressed for the races at Ascot, England, others dressed for Charles Town, West Virginia — that parted before us. "Nice going, Paddy," a woman called out. "Good-ridin', Paddy. You can't win 'em all," said a gambler type who sounded as if he'd already had a few. "How do you think you'll do in the next race, Paddy?" asked the Virginia gentleman in the sharply creased suit. "Hey, Smithwick, that Bampton Castle looked good. Will you ride him when he runs again?"

Then we were through the crowd, out in the open, on our way to the jocks' room. Suddenly an old horseman who had done a little of everything around the track jogged up beside Pop. His face was flushed and his herringbone jacket tattered. I knew he'd been forced to quit race-riding after being ruled off the track for trying to fix a race. He started training on farms, but that hadn't gone well. He had returned to exercising horses, on farms, but he'd had a couple of falls and lost his nerve, so he had to stop that. He had the double curse of being hooked on alcohol and on gambling. He jigged along close to Pop, giving off a sweet, syrupy bourbon smell, mixed with the stench of old dried sweat. I could only hear scraps. "Not doing too well …" "… lost job as assistant to asshole-trainer … an ignorant, arrogant Virginia-bred sonofabitch …" "… plan to stop drinking and fly straight…" "… could put some money on Valley Hart…" "What do you think of your chances on Jamie's horse?"

"Put what you got on Valley Hart," Pop said. "And then hang it up, Danny. I don't want to see you here again."

"Okay. I got it. Thanks, Paddy. Thanks." His eyes swung embarrassingly across mine and he left us. I'd seen him operate before. He'd leave the hunt meet altogether, go to the nearest bar, call his bookmaker in New York, and start drinking. If he won one bet, then he'd take those winnings and bet it all back — parlay it — on another horse. One day at Delaware Park, he ruined himself for life. He bet every race, won every race, and parlayed it all back on the next. He'd been trying to do this again ever since.

We passed Elmer Delmer, erasing the old odds from his chalkboard and writing the list of the horses and riders for the next race. My tip might've helped him keep the odds low on Murphy. He waved to us both and gave me a wink. Pop glanced down questioningly at me, his forehead furrowed, right eyebrow raised, left eye squinting.

In the jocks' room I heard the riders' versions of what had happened out there. One fuming jockey was complaining about the assistant starter. "That old fart couldn't start a foxhunt. When are they going to retire him?" Two young riders I didn't know were in a corner, one badgering the other, looking like they might come to blows. "Why the hell wouldn't you let me through. I was on all kinds of horse. You were dying. Why the hell ..." Joe Aitcheson was seated nearby on a rubber pad, his face covered with mud. He was wiping the mud off his goggles and trying to relax. The young riders began pushing each other, encroaching on his spot; he looked up, "Okay, boys, that's about enough," he said in a quiet voice. They gave each other terrible looks and went back to their tack bags.

The next race was another hurdle race, and Pop was riding Blackmail, who got in light with 144. I organized a lighter set of tack, using Pop's smallest saddle. Pop tucked in his silks, and then we were walking to the scales beside the jocks' room. One of the stewards was standing by the scales. I had overheard Pop talking to Mom about him last year: He just stirred up trouble; he had never worked a day in his life. When Mom was not around, Pop referred to such wealthy mink-and-manure types as "the pale-faced bastards." Carlyle set the weight on 144, Pop stood on the scales, and the bar didn't budge.

"Paddy, is there anything you can lose?" Carlyle asked.

"Here, Bud." He handed me his pommel pad and yoke.

# Chapter 8

The steward stood there. He was tall, thin, and still wearing an English-cut wool overcoat and a fedora. As he watched Pop weigh in, a smirk spread across his lips. Carlyle inched the weight out, 145, 147, 149, 150 and the bar tipped. Pop looked down at me and back at the scales. Carlyle pushed the weight back to 149. The bar balanced.

"Looks like you're five pounds overweight, Paddy," the steward cheerfully pointed out.

"Yes, sir, that's what it looks like." Pop stepped off the scales.

We walked to the paddock, Pop none too pleased about this steward. I was sure to stay on one side of Pop, not to switch even if someone latched on and started walking with us. This sometimes created an awkwardly shaped phalanx forcing its way through the crowd. We were early and the horses had not yet arrived. I looked forward to Pop and me sitting up against the splintery red laths of the snow fence, tack beside us, and relaxing for a moment.

This did not happen. Before this race, and before each race for the rest of the day, every time Pop walked into the paddock he was greeted by a tall, strikingly beautiful woman in a tightly fitting dress that couldn't have been more impractical for a day at the races. She handed him an Irish cap and a new wool sports jacket to pull over his silks. Then, he stood around talking to her as a photographer circled, taking shots. I couldn't make heads or tails of this unusual behavior, and it wasn't until years later, when I was looking through one of the many scrapbooks Mom had put together and I saw a classy black-and-white photograph of Pop standing in his boots, britches, and new jacket with his hair perfectly parted and combed, that I understood.

The photo in the scrapbook was glued to the page and it was ripped down the middle. Pop was on the left side of the photo looking off into the ripped out section. Flipping through the scrapbook, I later found the right-hand half of the photo, the beautiful long-legged woman standing there in the paddock having eye contact with the ripped out left-hand section of the photograph. These were photo sessions for a clothes company, and the woman was a model. This all took place around the time our family lawyer, Ronnie Maher — who drove me to Gilman every morning — was dealing with Ford Motor Company's request to have Pop endorse Ford for producing not only the fastest and most reliable car for him to race up and down highways but also the best car for him to turn into a sauna on wheels because of the superiority of the heater. Everybody wanted a piece of Pop. A TV show, *What's My Line*, asked Pop to be a guest. He appeared, along with two other fit, athletic-looking men. A panel of three asked them questions, trying to figure out who was the champion steeplechase jockey. One panelist asked one of the phony jockeys, "What is a bat?" He answered, "A wooden stick that a baseball player uses to hit a baseball." The same question went to the next imposter, and the answer: "A bat is an animal that is black and flies ..." The same question went to Pop, and he was stuck. He had to tell the truth. "A bat is a whip that a jockey uses to hit his horse at the end of a race." It didn't take long for them to figure out who was the legendary steeplechase jockey who had won more races than any other in America.

\* \* \*

Jimmy Murphy won the second race on a horse with the boring name of Be Moderate; Joe was second; Pop was third on Blackmail. Mom and I walked down and watched as the trophy was presented. "Sidney's cleaning up this spring," Mom said to me as we watched Sidney Watters — tall and having the erect posture and stunning good looks of Cary Grant — and Jimmy receive the trophy. Sidney was a decade older than Pop, and I knew that Pop had won a lot of races for him before he'd teamed up with Mikey. "Whew," Mom said, "he's one good-looking man." She laughed and looked down at me. I didn't approve much of all this, so I didn't agree or laugh back. I had noticed that Sidney made Mom a little jumpy when he was around, and he had a polite, open way of flirting with her. Besides, I thought Pop was much better looking.

## Chapter 8

Pop didn't have a ride in the third race. I ran out after the second to buy us two Cokes. "With plenty of ice, okay, Bud?"

I brought them back. He was seated on a pad outside the jocks' room, discussing racing tactics with Tommy Walsh, who was tucking in his silks, getting ready to ride. "Thanks, Bud, I needed this," Pop said, sipping the still-fizzling Coke from the paper cup. "Mike White was just here," Pop said to me. "He said to meet him in the paddock. Why don't you watch the next race with him, and I'll meet you back here."

Mike was from Middleburg. I rarely saw him except during August at Saratoga Springs, where we were inseparable. I found Mike in the paddock. We were the same age, and I was shocked and a little disconcerted to see that he had grown another three or so inches since last August, and was now almost a head taller than I. Though I didn't bet much with bookmakers, and I didn't have time to bet when I was helping Pop with his tack, I told Mike what Pop had said about Tommy Walsh — that "he'd gallop." We watched Tommy's uncle, the great steeplechase trainer M.G. Walsh, give Tommy a leg up on Rythmn Master. This was the same M.G. Walsh whom we had photos of all over our house, standing in the winner's circle with Pop and King Commander in the early 1950s. We watched Tommy walk Rythmn Master around the paddock. Tommy was slouched over, all his muscles relaxed, his body synchronized with the horse. Rythmn Master spooked when a spectator raised her program and waved to a friend with it. Tommy didn't flinch. He sat there, perfectly centered on the horse's back, not touching the horse's mouth, the reins looped, letting the groom lead the horse. They walked out to the racecourse. Mike and I hurried out and jogged up to Elmer Delmer's chalkboard.

"Two-to-one odds!" Elmer Delmer called out.

"Ah, come on, that's no good," I said.

"Give us a break," Mike said. "He's got to jump all those stiff fences and there're four other good horses in the race. How about three to one?"

"Okay, boys. Five to two, five to two for you," Elmer Delmer sang

116

out, "that's all I can do."

We took every crumpled dollar bill and piece of change from our pockets. Mike piled it all in my hands. He counted it up. We had a bankroll of more than twelve dollars.

"Can you bet on a race ahead of time?" I asked Elmer Delmer.

"What do you mean?"

"Could we bet now on a race later in the day?" I knew you could do this. What I was really wondering was how we'd know what kind of odds we could get, and I couldn't figure out how to ask this question without sounding like we thought Elmer Delmer would take advantage of us and give us poor odds, which is exactly what we thought he might be tempted to do.

"Sure you can."

Mike and I drew away and conferred on this complex decision. We decided to place ten dollars on Tommy in the upcoming race and keep two dollars "in the bank." After Tommy — hopefully — won the Skinner, Mike would collect our winnings and parlay it, plus the two dollars, back on Pop. We walked up the hill to the precise spot where Mike liked to watch the races. This was not any old spot. Mike had walked all around one day with his binoculars and had figured out that you could see more of the races from this little knoll than any other viewing point. Mike liked to have everything perfect.

Tommy left the start in front, jumped the first in front, and led the field the entire race looking as if he were schooling around the outside course of a show ring. He won easily. Mike rushed off to collect our money on Tommy and parlay our winnings back on Pop in the big race of the day, the Middleburg Hunt Cup.

When I reached the jocks' room, Pop was sitting on the ground, lacing his stirrup leathers into his timber saddle, his largest saddle. Timber horses always carried more weight. His mount, Valley Hart, was carrying 165. You would think Pop could relax about his weight, but he couldn't because he had a ride in the following race, a flat race, that got in light. If he took a leak, rode this race, and didn't have anything to drink, he would make the weight on the dot. June McKnight, a very good owner, owned the horse, Palladio, in the last race, and Pop did not want any jackass, pale-faced bastard who had never done a day's work in his life announcing over the loudspeaker that Pop was overweight.

Tommy Walsh walked in, "phlegmatic" — as Mom would put it — after winning the race in such style. Everyone congratulated him, but he didn't pay any attention. Joe was seated quietly in his corner, fooling with his tack, but really meditating, rehearsing what he wanted to do in the next race.

"Did you know that the president was here?" Pop asked me.

"The president?"

"Yes, the president of the United States."

"I heard that the Kennedys are here, but I haven't seen any of them."

"Well, President Kennedy was here earlier." Pop explained that he had walked down to the rail, away from everybody, to watch Tommy's race. He had been leaning on the rail, watching the race, when he realized the man leaning on the rail beside him was President Kennedy. They watched the race together, JFK asking a question or two. After the race Pop asked the president if he was going to stay for the next race. JFK had sighed, said he'd love to. His wife could stay for the rest of the afternoon but he had to get back to the office; he had some work to do. Pop seemed to be pointing out to me that maybe it wasn't so bad having a career as a steeplechase jockey after all, for look, even the president of the United States couldn't get an afternoon away from work and the problems of the country to spend a day at the races. We got up, weighed out, and walked to the paddock.

Pop rode the hell out of Valley Hart that afternoon. It was a three-and-a-half-mile race. He galloped around in the front end of the pack of twelve horses for most of the way, biding his time. As usual for him, he gained ground on each of the seventeen four-foot post-and-rail fences by "setting" Valley Hart to take off and fly over the fence at just the right place and time. At the tenth fence, with four more to go, Pop eased Valley Hart past the third horse. Going into the twelfth, he was galloping along well, in second place, when Joe made his move, passing three horses, and pulling into the lead. Joe jumped the twelfth fence two lengths ahead of Pop, the thirteenth one length ahead. They went into the last, whipping and driving. Pop asked for a big one. Joe was still a nose ahead on taking off, but when they landed, Pop was ahead and pulling away, using the downhill slope to his advantage, galloping out and winning by one and a half lengths.

I stood outside a fenced-in area that doubled as the winner's circle and watched as Jacqueline Kennedy presented my father the trophy. She, young, black-haired, fit; he, young, black-haired, fit, both of them grinning and holding the huge, ornate silver trophy together and looking like they'd live forever.

We took a victorious walk back to the jocks' room. "You taught 'em a thing or two out there, Smithwick," "Hey, I had my money on you, Smithwick. You going to do the same in the next race?" "You're the master, Paddy! You're the master!"

Tommy Walsh, having changed into slacks and a jacket, stepped out of the crowd and walked along with us, looking down at the ground ahead of him. "Nice going, Paddy," he said in his muffled voice, his lips barely moving.

"Thanks, Tommy," Pop said. Tommy mussed my hair again and walked along with us. On reaching the jocks' room, I had a slight sinking feeling when I saw Tommy's tack bag, zipped up and ready to go, set outside.

"All right Paddy — good luck in the next race," Tommy said. "I'd better get up the road."

"Little Paddy, take care of your father. You hear me."

"I will," I said, standing between the two men.

Tommy stepped toward his tack bag, and Pop walked into the jocks' room. I stood there and watched as Tommy slung his bag over his shoulder and headed up the hill. He kept his head down and walked non-stop, lacing through the clumps of people and stands of trees, avoiding eye contact with anyone. He was focused — get to the car, fire up the engine, and hit the road home to Long Island.

I stepped into the jocks' room. Pop and I still had more work to do. We had to maintain our own focus. Pop was pulling on a new set of silks. "Hey, Bud, can you slip this cap cover on?" he asked.

I sat down, put his helmet between my knees, worked the cap on, and then the rubber band and the elastic strap of the goggles. I grabbed Pop's tack and we were out, heading for the paddock.

\* \* \*

During some springs, it could be hot and dry and the ground brick-hard at Middleburg. Or, it could be chilly and drizzling and the going deep and muddy and every time Pop walked back from riding a race he'd be splattered with mud — unless he were on a frontrunner that "stayed." He could rate a rank frontrunner better than anyone else; he could get him out there on the lead, drop the reins, and let the horse coast along. With another rider, the horse would be pulling, struggling to go faster, and using up all his energy.

I didn't care what the weather was — so long as I was out in it.

If the sun's beams were warming my face or sheets of rain were stinging my eyes, I loved it.

If I was hot and wearing a shirt and tie with my sleeves rolled up and the sweat rolling down my sides, or if I had on boots and a wool sweater and rain slicker and wool cap and smelled like a damn sheep yard, I loved it.

If Pop was winning race after race, and people were betting more and more on him, and he was smiling and happy and lucky and nothing could go wrong and men I barely knew would jog up alongside me and try to pick up a gambling tip, I loved it.

If the sun was blocked by clouds and the big horse — Mako or The

Sport or Bon Nouvel — didn't run like he was supposed to and we just didn't seem to get to the winner's circle, I loved it.

If Pop had lost too much weight too fast and was starting to get cramps, I still loved it. I would run out into the sea of cars and spectators to find a cup of hot bouillon or chicken soup with a spoonful of salt. He would have to have it right away, before the next race, and I would sprint among the cars with their tailgates down, stopping to ask the amply fleshed laughing, eating, and partying people I didn't know for bouillon or soup, looking at least for a few slices of ham or roast beef I could put some salt on. I knew what could happen if he didn't get the salt. My mind would flash back to the time at the Peninsula House hotel in New Jersey when Pop had been losing weight at the track all morning and had driven back to our rooms at the beach in a hot car. I'd walked in from swimming in the ocean to find him lying there unable to move, his legs, his arms, his body cramped from loss of salt and potassium. I ran across the street and into a busy restaurant in my swimming trunks. I told the manager what I needed, that I needed it instantly. Then I was out in the sticky ocean air, sprinting barefoot over the black asphalt through the traffic, causing cars to jam on their brakes and honk, the scalding-hot soup splashing on my wrists, the tar hot and soft between my toes. Back in the room I spooned the soup into Pop's mouth and then as the stiffness left his body I held the Styrofoam bowl to his lips. Finally, he sat up and I saw and felt the pain leave his face and a loosening go through his limbs and he sighed and said, "Thanks, Cowboy."

No matter what, I loved it. On the days when we were on a roll and in and out of the winner's circle and the cameras were clicking and we were smiling and the pile of trophies was mounting up and at the end of the afternoon, walking back to the jocks' room, we were exhausted, drained, and the spectators were sheepishly asking Pop for his autograph and he was stopping and signing a few of their programs, well, I thought, this was living, this was the good life, this is it.

## Chapter 8

Finally, the last race would be run and all the tension would be gone from the day. In the jocks' room, Pop would pull on a tweed jacket over his silks, and we'd bundle the tack into his leather tack bag. Carrying the bag together, we'd walk fast across the discarded betting tickets and chewed, saliva-stained half-smoked cigars and crushed paper cups and crumpled programs and flattened cigarette butts, past the drinking and laughing "tailgaters," to our car. We'd lift the bag into the trunk, slap the trunk shut, and then with Mom and Sue Sue, we'd leave the race-course as the last of the sun's rays receded behind its rim. Relaxed, drained, the race-riding over, Pop would ease the car across the mile or two of beaten-down red clay, along the tractor and pick-up-truck path-ways of the two thousand-acre farm of Mikey's father-in-law, Mr. Fred, from whom Jimmy Murphy rented an old farmhouse. Pop would carry a clean set of clothes on a hanger into the house, up the stairs, into a bedroom. He'd pull off his silks and T-shirt, sit on the edge of a bed, and stick one leg out. I'd straddle the boot, facing away from him, and he'd place his other foot on my rump and push hard. Gripping the heel of the boot and wiggling it, I'd loosen the boot just right, so as not to cause a cramp, and off it would come and across the room, laughingly, I'd go. We'd do the same with the other boot. Then he'd pull off his sweat-and-saddle-stained nylon britches and his jockey shorts. I'd stuff it all into his britches, tie the legs of the britches into a knot, carry the bundle downstairs, and toss it in the trunk of the car while he took a bath and put on fresh clothes.

Mom and Pop and Jimmy and his wife, Theresa, would have drinks, and the sun would go down and Sue Sue and I would go outside with Foxy, Jimmy and Theresa's daughter, and throw stones at the long thick black snake that was always there slithering slowly around in the gigan-tic stump left over from an ancient locust tree.

We'd have dinner, and soon Sue Sue and I would be collapsed in the back seat of the car. Pop would be driving and he and Mom would be talking about horses and people. We'd rumble out the bumpy clay-and-stone driveway, dipping down and rattling and thrumming over the metal poles of the cattle guard that crossed the culvert at the entrance, and then out onto the road. We'd fall asleep listening to the back roads of Virginia fly by beneath us and to Mom saying, "Paddy, please slow down. The children are in the back." Sometimes if they were arguing, he'd step on it and we'd feel like we were in a rocket as the asphalt unwound inches beneath our heads and the car flung us into its sides around the curves. Mom would insist on driving, and they'd pull over, switch seats, and Pop, leaning heavily against the passenger door, would fall instantly, heavily asleep.

Then, Sue Sue and I would awaken to Mom gently rubbing our shoulders and whispering that we were home. There we'd be, in the driveway. Safe. At home.

Sue Sue would go to her room. Mom would try to wake Pop but he wouldn't budge. About to cry, she'd go inside. I'd open the car door wide, try to pull his legs out. I'd get one leg outside the door. I'd pull and prod and coax him, "Come on, Pop, we're home. You've got to come up to bed." He'd seem unbelievably heavy. I'd grip his arm and pull and he might fling his arm. He would awaken, "Sorry, Cowboy. I'm just a little tired." Into the house he'd go — only to slump down in his favorite old easy chair, out of which I'd have to prod him. Finally, I would trudge up the stairs, my terrier Tippy, fit and trim, trotting excitedly alongside me. Tippy would leap onto my bed, stand tensely at attention, and watch my every move. I'd toss off my clothes, pull on pajamas, yank the covers down, and collapse onto the clean white sheets. I'd hear Tippy's soft breathing beside me as I drifted off into a night filled with dreams of race-riding and fast driving and working alongside my father.

# 9

## Summer

By the spring of my fifth-grade year at Gilman, I was schooling ponies during the week at home and riding in the show ring almost every weekend. It was Mom and I. Pop was away at the track. When Pop did attend a show, it was a special occasion.

Queenie was the best foxhunting pony I would ever have. She was built for going cross-country, hunting all day, jumping trappy fences, and never spooking or shying when we trotted through some old rough-looking barnyard and a couple of mangy mutts charged out barking and yelping around us, scaring up a flock of chickens and causing them to squawk and flap their wings. But Queenie was not the flashy-looking type that judges at pony shows preferred.

Mom found Twinkle for me to show. She was smaller than Queenie, but she was tougher to ride. Sometimes, at shows, we rode in "family classes," with both my grandmothers, and Mom and my sister Sue Sue, and even my baby sister, Sallie — three generations — participating. Sue Sue would be on Queenie and I'd ride Twinkle. Our picture would be in the paper the next day, and Mr. Menzies at Gilman would catch me in the hall and tease me about my little sister riding the big pony while I was on the little one. Graeme Menzies, who taught me one class in the fifth grade, was my favorite teacher at Gilman.He had been in Mikey's class during the few years Pop and Mikey had gone to Gilman before gas rationing forced them to commute to a school closer to home. Mr. Menzies had been a friend of Pop's at Gilman and had followed his career; he knew about horses and living in the country; and he looked out for a few of us country boys.

Twinkle had Arabian blood in her. She was black, with a white star between her eyes and a perfectly shaped, high cheek-boned face. She had the most beautiful conformation; she was very feminine; she was flashy. She had big brown eyes, three white stockings, and a well-rounded rump, and the judges at the shows loved her. She'd trot into the ring, high-stepping, on the bit. We'd do a circle and then start over the jumps — often all kinds of crazy-looking obstacles, very different from the normal fences you jump going cross-country. There'd be fences made of barrels, fences with flowers in pots in front of them, and there'd be spread fences — two or three jumps pushed together to make one wide fence. Twinkle would canter around, light on her toes, her feet barely touching the ground. She'd be eyeing every single fence. She'd try to slow, and prop, going into one fence. I'd have to squeeze with my legs as hard as I could and push her into it. Then she'd sail over it and on landing start to go too fast; I'd have to pull hard on the reins, slow her down — trying, for the judges, to make it look easy — regain control of her mouth, steer her around a sharp turn, then ride her, squeezing hard, into the next crazy-looking jump.

One afternoon I was riding home by myself, trotting and galloping Twinkle through the Griswolds' woods. Half a mile from home I pulled her up to a walk, gave her a good pat on the neck. We were lollygagging along the edge of a big field of clover. I kicked my feet out of the stirrups, tilted my hunting cap back, and slumped in the saddle, letting the reins flap. We ambled along without a care. I didn't pay any attention to the fresh dirt around a recently dug hole to my side. I was staring down at the clover, trying to find a four-leaf specimen, thinking about getting off and walking so I could count the individual leaves more accurately, when a groundhog scurried between Twinkle's front feet. It was as if the starting gate bell at the track had rung. Twinkle took off galloping across that vast field as fast as she could go.

My hunting cap went flying, and I was hanging on for dear life. I'd never been this fast. The clover flashed beneath Twinkle's feet. There was no loping rhythm to her stride — her head was down low and her legs were churning up the ground in a blur and I was scared as hell. Idiotically, I screamed, "Help! Help!" which only made her go faster. Out of the corner of my eye, I saw a farmer sitting on his stationary tractor at the top of the hill, both hands on the steering wheel, watching us fly by. I gathered the reins together and shortened my hold, but with my feet out of the stirrups — which were flapping and bouncing against Twinkle's sides, scaring her further — I couldn't pull hard on the reins without pulling myself up onto her neck. I grabbed the mane and hung on. We were approaching a post-and-rail fence and it looked as though she was going to either crash through it — I pictured the rails breaking and splintering and the two of us going into a somersault — or attempt to sail over it, when suddenly she ducked to the left. I slid down her right side but pulled myself back onto the saddle with my grip of mane. Squeezing as hard as I could with my legs and keeping my hands as low as possible — to keep me from sliding up onto her neck — I gave one all-out yank on the reins and brought her to a halt.

We turned around and went back to look for my hunting cap in the clover. I didn't kick Twinkle or snatch her or scold her. I patted her neck and spoke soothingly to her. It had been my fault. She was fit as a racehorse, on edge from all the showing, and the groundhog had scared her. I was the rider, and I had been sitting there "like a bump on a log," as Pop would have described it, feet out of the stirrups, reins slack, hunting cap cocked back in a useless position. I had not been paying attention. I had not been prepared for what could happen. At home I didn't tell a soul about being "run-off with."

*  *  *

Mom and I were a team. She bought green ponies. We'd "make" the ponies, turning them into good show ponies or foxhunting ponies, and then sell them. I'd help Mom teach riding to many of my friends. Catching the ponies, tacking them up, getting beginning riders up in the saddle, giving them pointers during the ride, and then after the ride, untacking the ponies, cooling them out, turning them out in the correct fields — it could be a lot of work, though I never thought of it that way. Mom made it fun. On Sundays she'd take us out on marathon rides cross-country. She'd be on Crag or Fini, in front. Sue Sue might have her friend Sass Small with her, and I'd have Tom Whedbee and Rob Deford with me. The six of us would ride half a mile over to the Griswolds, pick up Jay, ten years our senior and thus a big shot. Then we'd move through the countryside in an ever-growing and more powerful pack, picking up friends. Another mile or two and over to the Secors to pick up J.B. and Beth, then across the road to get Tom Voss, then over a hill to the Igleharts, pick up Tom or Frank, and soon we'd have a posse. We'd be trotting and cantering and galloping through the countryside together, laughing and hanging on and stopping by farms to see other friends and planning future rides, splashing through deep creeks as in the Westerns, and schooling over small fences.

Friday nights we'd be out in the barn late. If Pop were home, I'd hold the ponies and horses in the aisleway of the barn as he "pulled" or trimmed their manes, and Mom then wetted the manes down and braided them. We'd curry and brush their coats until they shined, and then we'd throw light blankets over them for the night to keep the dust off. Pop and I would hook the trailer up to Mom's car. We'd go into the kitchen, and Mom would have the tack spread out on chairs and hanging from doorknobs. There'd be a bucket of steaming water in the center of the kitchen, and Mom and I would clean the tack, washing it with hot water, rubbing saddle soap and Lexol into it, and then scouring the bits and stirrups with wiry metallic-smelling Brillo pads while we talked about the classes the horses and ponies would go in the next day. It'd be getting late, and I'd leave the unfinished tack all over the kitchen, go upstairs, and fall asleep.

What seemed like seconds later, Mom would awaken me. It would still be dark outside. I'd pull on my clean jodhpurs. I'd go downstairs and Mom would have cooked up either "eggs-in-the-middle" or French toast. The saddles and bridles would be shined and polished and neatly set by the door. We'd eat together and I'd slip on my well-shined paddock boots in which both my mother and grandmother had ridden. We'd carry the tack out, and put it in the back seat of the car, lead the horse and the pony outside, load them onto the trailer, and take off for a long day at a horse and pony show.

Sometimes Mom and I got tired of the show-ring schedule. We would take a break every August when she would pack up her station wagon and transfer our entire household, including the dogs, to Saratoga Springs, where the world's best racing was held for four solid weeks and where steeplechase races were held almost every day.

A couple of summers I was allowed to bring Twinkle. I'd go to the track early in the morning with Pop, and spend most of my time walking horses around and around a dirt ring, letting them "cool out" and "water off" for half an hour, then graze for fifteen minutes, after Pop or Mikey or Jim Rutherford or one of the other riders had galloped them on the track. Toward the end of the morning I'd pull Twinkle out of her stall, tack her up, and head over to the stable area called Horse Haven where Ridgely White, a close friend of Pop's and the father of my friend Mike White, was stabled. Mike would hop on his palomino and we'd gallop our ponies head and head, racing around the one-mile "pony track" that encircled Horse Haven, creating havoc, scaring and spooking racehorses held by grooms and hot-walkers, who laughed and yelled out, "Slow down, race-riders!" as we sped by.

Mike — tall, rangy, sinewy, freckled, a hot-tempered redhead — and I used to bicycle, often with my sister Sue Sue, everywhere in Saratoga

Springs. Sometimes we'd try to drop her off somewhere, but she would stick to us like glue. Mike and I both had hot-shot bikes — English bikes with three gears — and Sue Sue had her American bike, a heavy, clunky, wide-wheeled thing that looked like a Harley Davidson. At the time she looked pretty tough herself. She had bangs, was missing a couple of front teeth, and was as strong as a lightweight wrestler.

In the afternoons, if Mike's father was running a horse or my father was riding one, we'd shine our shoes (Mike would shine his twice, once the night before, and again the morning of the race), get dressed up, and go to the races with our families. We'd meet at the track by the jocks' room, and we might do a little gambling. We were too young to place a bet at the windows — but we had our system, and it revolved around Elmer Delmer. We never heard any grown-ups call him Elmer. And we never called him Mister Delmer. It was always Elmer Delmer.

We'd give Elmer Delmer our money to bet and not only would he place the bet for us, he'd also match whatever we bet. So, if we wanted to put one two-dollar ticket on Pop, Elmer Delmer would buy us two. If we lost a couple of races, Elmer Delmer would pull out a fistful of cash, lean back and peel off a few bills, just like James Cagney in the gangster movies, which impressed us very much, but which was also the problem.

One morning after work I overheard Mom and Pop talking in our kitchen. There'd been a two-paragraph story in the *Morning Telegraph*. Elmer Delmer had been found dead in a ditch. "It must've been the Mob," I heard Pop tell Mom. "He must've crossed the Mob." I felt sad, empty. There was no replacing Elmer Delmer. I thought of how Mom had always tried to keep me away from Elmer Delmer; maybe she'd had a point after all.

Hearing this made me jumpy and want to get out, go for a bike ride with Mike, for I knew that the summer before the Mob had approached Pop and tried to talk him into "pulling" a horse — that is, not permit his horse, the favorite, to win, and instead allow a longshot, on which the Mafia would bet lots of money, to gallop past him and finish first under the wire. Pop had told them he wanted no part of their plan. This all made Mom, who claimed to have had such a sheltered upbringing, very nervous. Not only did she have to put up with the owners pressuring Pop to win and win, to push himself to the limit, now she had to worry about the damn Mafia pressuring him, and perhaps threatening him, to lose.

The day we learned that Elmer Delmer had been murdered, Mike and I decided not to go to the races. We snuck away from Sue Sue and her fat-wheeled bicycle and her tendency to taunt local Saratoga gangs of bicyclers and get us into fights (she yelled "Hey, city slickers" at them, and told them I was "the boxing champion at Gilman School"). We took off to go fishing at Yaddo, a beautiful park with a mansion and studios and gardens.

First, we dropped our poles off over by our secret fishing spot. Then, we raced up and down the shaded drives — trees and ponds and waterfalls flashing by. We rode through the landscaped Italian gardens with their straight paths and little concrete walls, our fenders and chain guards jangling as we bumped down long flights of steps. We pedaled fast so no one could catch us, laughing and yelling at each other, branches of exotic plants and breasts of even more exotic statues flashing past. Finally, we rode to a spot in the woods where a steep path led into one of the series of connected ponds and we rattled full-tilt, the handlebars shaking and reverberating, down the bumpy, root-crossed path, hit the water, and sailed over the handlebars into the pond. That cooled us off, and also probably scared all the fish away for half a mile.

Dripping wet, we pushed our bikes back up the path, along the steep ridge with the pond below, over to our fishing spot, closer to the racetrack. We hid the bikes in the brush, walked down to the water, baited our lines, and cast. There was a huge fish in there. I had seen it magically, slowly, seductively swim away after it had broken my line, so easily, the week before.

We lay back, fished, and talked, mainly about sex and the McFarlane sisters. They had adopted us. They were local girls, and every morning after work we'd ride our bikes over to their house. Many mornings a big, black 1948 Packard would already be parked in the driveway — that was Willie Dixon's; he was a year or two older than us and already had his license. Yet, Mike and I had an advantage over him. Though he had this great car, and a license, and seemed to have hit puberty before he reached his teens, and though we were still on bicycles and had never shaved, he worked for his father, the trainer Billie Dixon, solely as a hot-walker; however, we were riders, or at least that's what we told Megan, Evonne, and Theresa McFarlane, and we were the ones who most needed the back massages.

So — Mike and I lay on the bank in the shade, trading ideas back and forth on the topics of drinking, reducing, driving fast, race-riding, and the mysteries of sex. Then, from the nearby racetrack, we heard the bugle, that sharp blow of the horn that would ripple up my spine and tingle the recesses of my brain, and the famous accent of the great race-caller Marshall Cassidy with his clipped, clear, and unique speech pattern: "The horses (slight pause) are on (slight pause) the track." And later, "It is now (slight pause) post time."

We listened carefully, forgetting our fishing lines, as Cassidy called the race. Mike's father had a horse entered, and my father was riding one that he and Mikey trained. Once the race was over, we heard coming from a round two-story-high stone tower across the pond the most beautiful piano playing, the tickling and tingling of keys, and magical melodies drifted across the pond to our fishing spot. We both relaxed, our backs against the cool dirt of the bank, stared up through the leaves at the sky, and snoozed off.

Bicycling out that afternoon, we recognized a groundsman who was working in a garden as someone who had once or twice waved to us as we had flown past him and the nude statues that summer. We stopped and asked what the story was with the piano playing.

## Chapter 9

He leaned on his rake, pulled the brim of his Yankees cap up, and looked us over. We had no fish on a string that day, but still, we looked pretty guilty holding two fishing poles.

"Boys, that fellow on the piano goes by the name of Aaron Copland. Ever heard of him?"

"No," we answered. A pick-up truck was speeding down the gravel driveway.

"We'd better get going," I said.

"Yeah. You come on back. I saw a big one in there the other day." He held his hands about two feet apart. "Just try to hide them poles a little better."

Showing off our bicycling skills, we accelerated — spinning our rear wheels on the gravel — and my chain hopped off its sprocket, got caught in the frame, and snapped. The pick-up with a couple of workmen pulled up beside us. Embarrassed, I got off and stared at the broken chain.

"Hey," said the driver. "What you need is a tow-line."

He hopped out, grabbed a coil of weathered rope in the back, unraveled one arm's span, and then another. He pulled a hawkbill out of his pocket, opened it, cut the line with one easy slice, and tossed it to us. We wrapped the mid-section of the rope two or three times around my handlebars. Mike tied the two ends around his waist, and we took off, Mike towing me home.

\* \* \*

That September, when Mom, Sue Sue, Sallie, and I returned to Maryland from Saratoga, I continued to ride the ponies, but Mom and Pop also added Crag to my list. He was a small, light-bay gelding with the biggest heart a horse ever had. Pop had ridden him in races over brush, hurdles, and timber, and he had won over all three.

I hunted Crag a few times, and Mom and Pop decided it was time for me to ride him in the Elkridge-Harford Hunter Trials held in early October. I was eleven and in Graeme Menzies' sixth-grade class at

Gilman. Crag was twelve, and retired from racing, but didn't know it — he pulled hard, and would take off at top speed whenever given the chance. Pop often called Crag, "The Old Man," or if speaking to him, "Old Man."

One hot October day, Crag and I went in class after class, and we pulled in ribbon after ribbon galloping around the mile and a half course over chicken coops, post-and-rails, in-and-outs, log fences, board-line fences, just about everything. I was wearing my grandmother's old riding boots and a pair of corduroy jodhpurs, and we were finishing in front of all kinds of fancy adults coming down from Pennsylvania in their swanky vans and dressed up in black boots, black coats, derbies, and top hats. I was enjoying the day, and at one point, getting ready to go in another class, when I couldn't find my hunting cap. Sue Sue handed me one and I pulled it on. "That's not mine," I said. "It's too small." Ann Merryman, sitting beside Sue Sue on the hood of Mom's car, said, "Maybe your head's getting too big." I let that remark sink in.

Toward the middle of the day, I was getting tired and thirsty. Pop, still in his work clothes, had just pulled up in his car after spending the morning riding at Hydes. I had a class coming up, an important one. I was standing on the ground, holding Crag. "Pop, can you hold him for a minute? I've got to run over and get a Coke."

Instead of taking the reins as I expected, Pop looked at me seriously, as if I'd just asked the most insulting question. "If you're thirsty," he said, and turned his eyes toward Crag, "how do you think The Old Man feels?" I didn't know what to do. We were standing out in the middle of a hundred-acre field, the class was coming up, and there was nowhere close to get Crag any water. Most of the other people had driven over in their vans and probably had their own water supplies, but we had ridden our horses over and Mom just had her car. Pop took the reins and led Crag around to the back of his car. He popped open the trunk. There was a big cooler of water, one empty bucket, and another bucket with a sponge and a few rub rags in it. We got the cooler and buckets out.

"Pour half the water in one bucket, half in the other," Pop said.

I did as told. Pop handed me the reins. He grabbed the handle of one bucket, held it up to Crag with one hand while he rubbed Crag's face with the other. Crag took a few good-sized gulps. "Okay, Old Man, that's enough for now," he said, rubbing Crag between his eyes, and put the bucket down. Then, he dunked the sponge in the other bucket. He wiped off Crag's face, all around his eyes, ears, and mouth; Crag seeming to enjoy it. Then, using plenty of the cold water, he wiped the sponge down each leg. Finally, he lifted Crag's tail and sponged him off between his legs.

"Okay, Bud, the class is not for another fifteen minutes and you're the eleventh to go …" A loud laugh coming from nearby broke Pop's train of thought. He glanced two cars over at a one-time amateur jockey we knew — now a middle-aged foxhunter — who would be going in our class. The foxhunter, from a wealthy family, had packed on the weight since he'd quit riding races, and he was sitting up in his heavy hunting saddle with both feet out of the stirrups and one leg crossed over the pommel of the saddle, talking to a friend seated on the hood of a car. It looked as though the buttons would pop off his hunting coat at any second. Beneath this rider was a classy old hurdle horse Pop and Mikey had trained, and Pop had won on many a time. The horse was dripping sweat under his belly and his back was bent under the unyielding pressure of the rider's weight.

Pop's eyes went from the rider to my eyes; his expression had completely changed. His eyes had that angry, piercing look. This rider was one of the "pale-faced bastards," as Pop called them, and I was worried Pop was about to lose his temper.

"Eleventh in the class. Okay," I said, "That means I won't be going for half an hour."

"Right, Bud," Pop said, holding Crag by the reins. "This is going to be a long day for the Old Man. I'm going to keep him moving, walk him around in the shade. You don't need to get on him until the last moment. Get yourself a soda. I'll be over there," he said, pointing to a quiet, shaded clearing in the nearby woods. "Come on over after you get a drink."

Crag did so well at the Hunter Trials and had gotten so fit and strong in preparation for them, that Pop decided to enter Crag in the upcoming Rochelle Tin Cup, a race set up by a few high-spirited and prank-loving horsemen who wanted to poke a little fun at the stuffy hunt meets — the Virginia Gold Cup, the Maryland Hunt Cup, the Pennsylvania Hunt Cup, and the rest. I galloped Crag every morning before going to Gilman, and Pop even let me breeze him three-quarters of a mile up a long hill head-and-head with a racehorse, who was ridden by Tiger Bennett.

The day of the race Mom held Crag as Pop gave me a leg up. My orders were to hold him back as long as I could, then let him run over the last two fences. The starter dropped his flag and we were off. I was right behind Bill Norris, the whip of the Elkridge-Harford Hunt, and he was kicking and urging his horse on and we were flying around the top of a hill jumping hurdles made of bales of straw, stacked two high, and staked into the ground. Bill's horse hurdled through the top of each bale, breaking the baling twine, and shooting the straw high up into the air just as Crag and I approached each jump. This happened the whole way around, Crag and I galloping into a jump we couldn't see because of the exploding straw. Then, I couldn't hold Crag back any longer. I pulled him out from behind Bill and he took off, on his own, sailing over the last three straw jumps. That was the first race I won, and it was on Crag, on whom Pop had won many a time. Over the years I came to know and trust and love Crag, like an older brother.

The next morning at Gilman, Mr. Menzies stood before our sixth-grade homeroom and said he had an important announcement to make before we began our studies of English history. Everybody groaned. I was sitting inattentively at my desk, waiting to hear about yet another glorious achievement of one of my scholar-athlete classmates. Who would it be? I glanced around the room. One of these twenty boys had no doubt starred in a football game, catching the game-clinching touchdown pass against the evil Calvert School, or was on the victorious side in a big debate held over the weekend at the State House in Annapolis, or had written an essay that had been published by the *Baltimore Sun*.

Standing before us, black-haired, fit, broad-shouldered, Mr. Menzies started talking about a boy at Gilman who had a famous steeplechase jockey for a father, then about a boy in the sixth grade who had ridden a full-sized horse in the Elkridge-Harford Hunter Trials the day before, and finally about a boy in our homeroom who, on that horse, had won the championship of the Hunter Trials. He never said my name once. I kind of sat there, heating up as if I were on a burner. Then, he said, "And that boy is Patrick Smithwick." The whole class suddenly applauded. I was shocked, stunned. I never thought they would have cared in the least. It made me feel good inside — not because I wanted applause and attention but because it seemed no one in the class knew anything of my life in the country. It was as if that part of me did not exist when I stepped on the campus of Gilman. But now, Mr. Menzies had shared this story with my classmates, and they were interested. Mr. Menzies knew what a kid needed.

# PART III

## AFTER THE FALL

# 10

## The Voss Filly

O n the morning of July 22, 1966, while Pop and I were galloping the horses at Belmont Park, Speedy Kiniel had loaded Totem II onto a van out at Mrs. Phipps' farm on Long Island and had ridden down to Monmouth Park in the van, standing beside the kicking, stomping, biting horse. Speedy was the only groom on the farm who could handle Totem, a gray Argentinian-bred with a deeply embedded "common streak" — if given the chance, he'd usually do the opposite of what you wanted him to do, but there was no pattern to his misbehavior. One morning you could be tacking up Totem, chatting away to Speedy in the next stall, and Totem would stand there just fine. The next morning when you were tacking him up, just the second you were using both hands to cinch up the girth and you couldn't protect yourself, he'd whip his head around quick as lightning and take a sharp bite out of your left tricep. Later in the day, you could walk right in the stall, snap a shank onto his halter, and walk him out.

Totem especially hated blacksmiths. If he so much as saw one, in leather chaps and carrying a hammer or rasp, walking down the shed row, he would try to break loose and savage him. No blacksmiths at Belmont Park or out at Westbury would go near the horse. Mikey and

Dot had to get Harvey Powell, the highly respected Maryland black-smith, to drive all the way up to shoe Totem. Harvey was strong, talent-ed, and took pride in being able to handle a rough horse; Mikey paid him well.

Totem was especially bad shipping down in the van that day. He threw his head all around, shaking the chains attached to his halter. He kicked the back of the stall. Speedy held him with a shank, sang to him, tried to calm him.

When Speedy led Totem into the paddock to be tacked up, Totem was wild-eyed, shaking his head, jigging, and in a lather. When Pop got on him, he was still acting crazy. At the start the horse refused to go. Pop had to crack him hard with the whip, and Totem then took off. Pop relaxed on him, but Totem wouldn't settle. The last time around, Totem jumping poorly, Pop picked up the stick, hit him a couple of times, and Totem started gaining fast on the other horses. Then, he didn't even take off going into the sixth fence. He slammed into the hurdle, tearing up his legs, and flipped — throwing Pop to the ground, breaking Pop's neck. Pop lay there motionless. The ambulance picked him up. Many thought he'd been killed. I was not there to witness any of this as I was on the van back to Westbury at this time; I know because Speedy relat-ed it to me, in detail, several times during the long month of August while Pop was in the hospital and we were both working at Saratoga. "There was nothing your daddy could do. He picked up the stick on that horse and drove him. That's what a race-rider's supposed to do, and your daddy was the gamest race-rider of them all; he'd let a horse run. Totem was gaining fast. I can remember the announcer saying, 'Here comes Totem II.' I was standing by the rail and I was totally focused on him. I was just watching the one horse, and he was easy to pick out because he was a gray. He was passing horses, and I thought we might end up in the winner's circle. Then, coming into that one hurdle down the backside, Totem didn't even take off. He hit that hurdle and flipped, and all I could see were legs and brush flying, and then your daddy lying on the ground."

Pop was taken to the nearby Monmouth Medical Center in Long Branch, New Jersey. He remained there for ten days but showed no improvement. Mrs. Phipps had him sent to New York Hospital, where specialists in spinal cord injuries treated him. I visited Pop twice, the one time with Mrs. Phipps about a week after Pop's fall and the other in mid-August while I was living with Evan Jackson at Saratoga and working for him in the mornings. I was one of Evan's two "galloping boys" — the other being Tommy Walsh. Evan, Tommy, Scotty Schulhofer, and I drove to the hospital to see Pop. At that point, four weeks after the fall, Pop was still in bed and in traction, but he had regained some use of his right arm.

By the time the Saratoga meet ended on the last day of August, Mom was out of Union Memorial Hospital. I returned home from Saratoga, and Sue Sue and Sallie returned home from our grandmother Whitman's.

We read articles about Pop in newspapers and racing publications.

An article on the front of the sports section of the *Baltimore Sun*, "Smithwick Ends Riding Career," described Pop's fall, and his injury, and quoted Pop: "For about three weeks I really didn't know what was going on. Then, when things cleared up, I just knew I wasn't going to ride again."

The article continued: "And just five days before the accident at Monmouth, a horse had rolled over his wife at a Maryland horse show and sent her to the hospital with a broken leg. Both Smithwicks are back home now with their three children, five hunt and show horses, and four ponies."

Later in the piece Pop said, "Actually, I had fewer spills than most jockeys. My brother's horses were well-schooled. But you just don't last too long because you break everything you've got."

At first Pop was barely able to walk, and he got exhausted quickly. He wasn't supposed to drive a car, but he did. He'd been given a thick, white spongy neck brace that he was supposed to wear every day; it made it so he had to turn his whole body to see sideways. He wore the brace for a few days, and one morning it mysteriously disappeared.

Partially paralyzed, emaciated, and having little strength in his left side, he had to start his working life completely over on two fronts. He could not make a gradual transition from full-time professional jockey to full-time professional trainer. He had to do it immediately — a near-impossible task, even with the best credentials in the world. First, trainers need a few prospective owners; then they need to find some horses for the owners to buy; then they need stalls in which to keep the horses and a good racetrack or farm on which to train them. If they have jumpers, they have to spend a couple of months schooling them over fences. Finally, whether they have flat horses or jumpers, they have to run them. And yet, they are still not working trainers. To make a living, they can't just run the horses; the horses have to win. If they don't, the trainers won't be able to pay their bills, and owners will drop them faster than a horse with a broken leg.

Plenty of people wanted Pop to train their horses — but it would take a while to develop the stable, and Pop was too weak and in too much pain to start one up right away. Of course, the big question for friends and family was why didn't he just continue training with his brother within the framework of the Smithwick family business, where he had already been training as well as riding. Besides — wasn't he one-third owner of the whole business? He could insist. This was a touchy subject, especially with Mom. It was one of those family issues that surfaced on and off for years. In essence, Mikey and Pop had been an ideal brother team for twenty years — but they did have their differences; their theories on how to train horses, school horses, sell horses, deal with owners, deal with "the help" sometimes led down divergent paths. They'd been compromising for twenty years. Mikey was always more of a dreamer — he thought he could train any horse to jump like a deer and run like the wind, and, indeed, he usually could and did. (Along this line, when Mikey first visited Pop in New York Hospital, he innocently asked him, "When do you think you'll be able to start riding again?" They'd been riding and training together for so long, Mikey couldn't see it any other way.) Pop was a little more of a worrier and a little more practical. Mikey was a country boy; he absolutely loved the Hydes farm; he loved training from there, working from sun up to sun down, even creating work to keep the help busy — he was notorious for having new riders go out and pick up rocks for several days before they got their first mount or for taking one horse out and schooling it over and over the same fences for hours until he had the horse jumping exactly as he wanted. And he didn't really like going to the track. Pop loved the track as the track loved him. He was not a proponent of completely changing a horse's jumping style. He had told me that when you're on a horse that's exhausted, and you're whipping and driving him alongside two others going into the last fence, your horse is going to resort to his natural way of jumping and you don't want him being mixed up on just what that is. Pop loved to work hard, to ride hard, and then to get out of the barn and see friends and family. When the time came to decide on Pop's future, my grandmother and Mikey did not invite Pop to become one of two full-time trainers in the corporation. Pop decided not to force himself into this family situation; he finally did what his great friends Evan Jackson and Scotty Schulhofer, both training their own stables now, and Mom, as well as our lawyer, Ronnie Maher, had been telling him to do for years: He went out on his own.

That October when Pop was fighting his way out of the paralysis, I had wanted to quit school, ride, help my father begin his training career. I was fifteen, in the ninth grade at Gilman, and the studying, going to classes, engaging in boyish pranks, playing linebacker on the football team, listening to sermons on serving the community — all seemed irrelevant. I wanted to serve my family. But Mom and Pop did not allow such a move.

By November, Pop was getting antsy. He drove down to Florida to work with Eddie Neloy, training the horses of Ogden Phipps, owner of one of the world's most renowned outfits. The doctors thought this was a good idea — plenty of exercise to strengthen him and the warm weather to help him heal faster. This was a demotion — to go from being the country's leading steeplechase jockey, one of the best in the world, to being the assistant of another trainer, not to mention what it must've felt like to go from being a natural athlete with God's gift of balance on a horse to someone who had a hard time lifting a bale of hay. Pop was gone all fall and all winter. At home money was now an issue. I'd never thought about it before. But now I sometimes overheard Mom talking long-distance over the telephone to Pop, and I heard her talking to her own mother, and it was about the lack of money.

All my life Pop had left his silver-dollar money clip out at night on the dresser in the hall, and it had always held a few fifties or a couple of hundred dollar bills. And beside it he'd left his change — a mound of quarters, dimes, and nickels. When we'd gone to bars and restaurants, it had always been Pop who treated his friends and colleagues. At the barn it had always been Pop whom old friends and current employees took aside late in the morning and asked for a loan to make it through the week or to get out of trouble. This generosity drove Mom wild. She viewed it less as his generosity and more as this large group of hangers-on taking advantage of him. Past winters, at night, I used to "borrow" a few of those quarters on Pop's dresser and ring them up in my little metal cash register. This winter there was no silver-dollar money clip heavily lying beside a mound of coins on the dresser. There were no pictures of Pop on the front of the sports section of the *New York Times*, on the back cover of *The Chronicle of the Horse*, or on the front page of the *Morning Telegraph*, flying over hurdles and standing happily in the winner's circle accepting trophies.

I heard Mom talking to Ronnie Maher about filling out financial aid forms for the schools my sisters and I attended. I came home and saw her coming in from the barn in the dark, having fed and hayed the ponies and the horses, and then begin to make us dinner. Sue Sue started to help more with the cooking. We didn't take the family ski trip to Ligonier, Pennsylvania.

Mom, Tom Voss, and I drove down to see Pop at the Florida track. Mom split the driving with Tom, who had just gotten his license, and she delighted in making the trip in record time. Pop showed us around the barn, around the track, introduced us to his new colleagues. His spirit was back. So was his smile. His left shoulder hung down, and he leaned to the left, but he had his quick step back and was getting stronger by the day.

That Christmas, Jack Graybeal, who was the number one whip for the Elkridge-Harford Hounds — meaning he was highly skilled at controlling the pack of hounds during the foxhunts — and who was our blacksmith, stopped by in his truck and left a fairly large box on the back porch. The box moved, a little this way, a little that way. We opened it and there was a piglet, soon to be named Sidney, with a ribbon around his neck, along with a gallon of Early Times. Sidney was so cute we let him run all over the house Christmas morning. We let him outside, and he fell asleep in a big pile of discarded red and green and white Christmas wrappings. I put the bottle of Early Times beside him so that it looked like he'd had a swig of bourbon and then gone to sleep. Mom took a Polaroid snapshot of him. We sent it to Pop in Florida, and we joked that we should send another photo to Early Times to use as an advertisement.

*  *  *

In the spring Pop came home and started his own stable of racehorses. I helped him mucking out, haying, feeding, and riding early in the mornings before school and in the late afternoons after school. Soon he took the stable to Belmont Park. I went up for spring break and worked for him.

Pop's only concession to pain was his occasional request for a massage. In the evening after he took a bath, he would sometimes ask,

"Bud, how about a back rub?" He would still be warm from his bath. He would have sprinkled Vitalis into his short black hair. It would be combed back with a perfect part revealing his clean scalp, and it would have that fresh, sharp Vitalis scent.

He'd lie face down on the bed with his boxers on. I would sit on his rump, place both hands on one shoulder, and rub and massage the muscles, and then I'd massage the muscles on the other shoulder. Gradually, the layer of tightened muscle directly beneath the skin would loosen and float over the underlying shoulder bone, shoulder blade, and collarbone. Then I would focus on the difficult part, his neck. It was thickened in the back. In the middle of his neck, at the spine, a hard spot protruded, like a knot in a tree limb. I would work both hands across the relaxed muscles in toward the neck. I'd try to loosen up the muscles all around that hard-as-an-apple area, and then I'd move directly in on it. He might be talking while I worked in from his shoulders to his collarbone to the neck, and when I started on that hard area, he would be still and quiet.

When my grip began to weaken, he'd say, "That's good, Bud."

I'd push myself up and off his back.

"You have no idea how much better that makes it feel," he'd say as he got up. "You're the only one who'll do it."

\* \* \*

Over the summer I worked hard alongside Pop, and that fall, again, I did not want to go back to school. I wanted to quit school altogether and work full time for my father, for my family, but Mom and Pop ushered me back to the classroom. Pop's stable was starting to come together; he had a few good owners and a mixture of flat and steeplechase horses. Our family was beginning to heal when one of the owners insisted that his horses go to Florida to train for the winter.

So, again, Pop had to go to Florida. He took a string of flat horses and left Mom to run the barn at home with the jumpers. It was a long, dark, cold winter without Pop at home making the fire in the living room at night, pouring himself a bourbon, and challenging any of us to a game of checkers. But his horses were running well, and this made life at home less tense. Late at night I sometimes awoke to Mom playing "Girl from Ipanema" and old Sinatra love songs on the piano directly beneath my room.

Pop did come home for Christmas. Mom and I drove to the airport near Baltimore, which had the wonderful name of Friendship, to pick him up. We got as close as we were allowed to where the passengers unloaded. I'd never seen Mom so excited. We stood behind a hip-high glass balustrade with a rail running across the top. Mom leaned on the rail, looking down the long aisle. A wave of people started flowing up the aisle toward us, and there was Pop, the brim of his fedora cocked upward. He was beaming. He walked fast, leaning slightly to the left, looking directly at Mom. I could feel her pushing against the balustrade and bouncing up and down on her toes. I glanced up into her face — she was looking directly at Pop. Her eyes were tearing up. She tapped her fingers on the rail as if she were playing piano keys. He barreled through the gateway and threw his arms around her.

* * *

Before Pop had left for Florida, around Thanksgiving, I was dropped off at the end of the driveway by the carpool one afternoon. I walked in, dragging my heels, carrying my heavy sack of books over my shoulder, feeling sorry for myself — having to go to this difficult school, Gilman, where the students were all so smart and where the teachers gave so damn much homework. The sun was going down and there was the beginning of a chill in the air. I was trudging along when I heard the sound of a horse trotting. It was that low, guttural, rhythmical sound a horse's stomach sometimes makes, an in-and-out, back-and-forth churning sound, with each step of a trot. I stopped dragging my feet. I could hear the sound of tack loosely flapping, maybe stirrup leathers flapping against the side of a saddle, and reins — not being held — gently slapping against a horse's neck.

## Chapter 10

My blue sack of books slung over my shoulder, I walked to the upper paddock. Pop was in the center, a lunge line — long shank — in his right hand, a buggy whip in his right and he was lunging a black, light-boned horse … a filly. He was wearing a fedora, the brim low over his eyes, a pair of corduroys, and his deerskin jacket. A cigarette hung from his mouth. His left shoulder drooped.

The filly attentively jogged around clockwise, the flaps of my favorite hunting saddle — which had once belonged to "Cousin Frank Voss," as Granny referred to the great sporting artist — slapping against her sides. Each time she made a full turn Pop extended his right arm, and the lunge line, up and over his head. This way he didn't have to keep twirling around and around like the centerpiece of a lazy Susan. When she slowed, he gently swished the end of the buggy whip near her hocks and rear ankles by swinging his left arm out from the shoulder. She moved nicely, light on her toes.

"How do you like her?" Pop asked, keeping his eye on her.

"I like her. Looks like a nice mover."

"Okay — why don't we see how she moves when you're on her. Get your boots on."

I plowed my way through the pack of dogs, plucked Tippy out from the melee, walked up onto the back porch, and was blocked from entering the kitchen door by the now formidably sized Sidney the pig (so-named because he often ran off to Sidney Watters' farm, where he loved to root and dig up the box bushes with his powerful nose. Sidney would then call Mom up, and as she put it, "raise hell with me and order me to come get the pig immediately before he became a ham sandwich." Of course, Mom knew that Sidney actually liked having her stop by. Mom started calling the pig "Sidney," and the name stuck.). Sidney had taken to lying right in front of the kitchen door. He grunted as Tippy and I stepped over him. I walked up to my room. While changing clothes, I looked out the window and watched Pop let the filly gradually go from a trot to a walk to a full stop. He walked toward her, coiling a length of the lunge line with each step, and then gently patted her on the neck.

Back outside I walked to the upper paddock. "You'd better get your skull cap," Pop said, referring to my hunting cap. I walked down to the barn, pulled my black hunting cap off a nail. It had a thin protective, helmet-like interior, covered with velvet, and a hard visor. I used it for showing, hunting, and even galloping horses on the racetrack. I hadn't bought a helmet yet.

I walked back up to the paddock. As I reached the gate, Pop said, "See the spurs?"

He had hung a pair of rowel spurs on the gate. I picked them up, the thin rowels — dime-sized disks with spokes — spinning. As I leaned down to buckle on the spurs, I noticed Pop's old race-riding stick leaning against the post.

"Bring the stick, too," he said.

I walked into the paddock, the rowels spinning and jingling. Pop had pulled the filly into the center of the ring. I walked up to her, rubbed her between the eyes, and patted her on the neck.

"She belongs to old Mrs. Voss," Pop said, referring to Tom's grandmother. "Wassie's been having some trouble with her. She's been freezing and then rearing up."

Wassie Ball ran the hunter operation at the Vosses. He was an old-time Maryland horseman who knew how to do things that the younger generation was forgetting such as "bone" a pair of boots. Wassie was meticulous and even a bit fussy in an old-maid kind of way about this sort of thing. I'd never "boned" boots with Wassie but Tom had. Wassie took full responsibility, especially after the sudden death of Tom's father, in teaching Tom everything he knew, first about ponies, then hunters, then racehorses. Tom said boning boots was more fun in the evening when Wassie had had a drink or two and would tell some good stories. Wassie would take a pair of full-length boots, slip wooden trees into them, and push the trees in snugly while pulling the top of the boot to get all of the wrinkles out. He'd wipe off the already-clean boots with a cloth dampened with rubbing alcohol to leach out any bit of horse sweat or dirt. He'd let that dry and then rub Kiwi boot cream vigorously into every square inch of leather with a brush that looked like the type barbers in old Westerns used to slap on shaving cream. Out would come the dry deer bone, and he'd start working it, back and forth, back and forth, across the leather, smoothing out any last cracks, rubbing the polish in deep. Finally, he'd brush the boots hard and fast, and then buff them with a cloth. Wassie boned my boots once or twice a year, and he often came over and did some specialized work for us, such as braiding manes and tails the night before a big show. He didn't use rubber bands when he braided. He did it with a needle and black thread, and after he finished, the horses looked sharp enough for the Hunt Ball.

A good horseman such as Wassie knew that sometimes a horse, especially a filly, needed a new approach, and that Pop was just the man to help.

"What I want to do is keep her moving. Not give her a chance to stop or freeze. Not give her a chance to rear. I'd rather not have a fight with her. Okay, Bud?"

"Okay."

We were walking in a circle now.

"If she does freeze, I'll be right behind you with the buggy whip and you use the spurs."

"All right."

He unsnapped the lunge line. I walked alongside her. I grabbed hold of the reins — Pop continued to lead her — and then he gave me a leg up into the saddle without letting her break her stride.

She moved light and free. Her step was springy. She felt small, but she had a nice long neck. Pop moved to the center of the paddock. She slowed.

"Keep her moving. Don't let her stop."

I stayed calm on her, walked her around. Pop swished the buggy whip behind her ankles. I moved her into a trot. Pulled up to a walk, turned her around, trotted her some more. Pulled her to a walk.

With a short hold on the reins, my legs squeezing tightly, the rowels just touching her sides, I rode her through the paddock gate, down the hill, past the barn on my left, the corn crib on my right, and out the gate into the big field — Pop following behind me with the buggy whip. "Keep her moving," Pop quietly said.

We had some old show fences, some barrel jumps, a little chicken coop, and some logs set up in the field. "Pop her over that log," Pop said. Sitting down in the saddle, I jogged her slowly into the log. Up and over she went.

"Now that one," Pop said, pointing to the last log in a line of four. I circled around, sitting down in the saddle, keeping a close hold of the reins, letting the rowels tickle her sides, and rode her into the two-foot log. Gracefully, smoothly, up she went, jumping an extra foot over the log. In the air, high over the log, I was thinking to myself, this is going to be a walk in the park. I relaxed for a split second, and when her front feet touched the ground, she let loose a fart, put her head down between her knees, and took off bucking like a bronco with me leaning back and gripping with my legs and having to let the reins slide all the way out through my fingers in an effort not to be flung over her head. I pulled her up on the other side of the field. Hmm ... not such an angel after all.

"Okay, bring her back, Bud."

I trotted back. The sun had gone down. The shapes of the fences were less distinct. I could see my cottony-looking exhalations, and hers, in the air.

"Now, make her go slowly over all four logs."

I rode her into the logs at a slow trot. The logs were placed about one horse length from each other so that as soon as you landed after jumping one, you had to take off to jump the next. I was touching the rowels against her sides and squeezing my legs, keeping her "up into the bit." I had a good hold on the reins and was moving my hands back and forth so that the bit jiggled in her mouth and she kept her head up.

Up and over the first log. On landing she tried to duck out to the left. I pulled on the right rein.

Up and over the next log. Not too pretty. A bit sideways.

We landed too close to the third log, but she took off the second her feet hit the ground, arched her back, and up and over we went.

We landed just right, she didn't try to duck out, and we sailed over the last and biggest log.

I let out a sigh of relief and pulled her up, my adrenaline pumping.

"Okay, do it again."

We jumped all four again. She was light and agile between my legs. She was quick.

I popped her over a few other small jumps in the paddock, and Pop said that was enough. We didn't want to overdo it. Besides, it was getting dark. I rode her in. We flicked on the barn lights, untacked her, put on her halter, and cross-tied her in the aisleway of the barn. He stood on one side with a rub rag, me on the other, and we rubbed the sweat out of her steaming coat.

"I've got to go to Florida in a week," Pop said. "Wassie sent this filly over for us to make into a hunter. We've got her on a deal. Think you could hunt her over the winter, get her going right?"

"Yes — I could do that."

"They want people to see her going well out in the hunting field and then to sell her in the spring when the hunting season ends."

"All right."

"She's going to take some work," he said, leaning his weight into her, trying to rub out the saddle mark.

"That's okay," I said, putting a little more elbow grease into my rubbing.

"She went well for you today, Bud. Just remember she has a history of freezing and rearing." He looked up and eyed me to be sure I was paying attention. "She's been getting away with it, so she'll try it sooner or later. You could hunt her on the weekends; then you'll have to ride her two or three times a week, before or after school, to keep her fit and going right."

* * *

For the next few days, as soon as I got home from school, I went into the house, changed, and came out to the barn where Pop waited for me, the Voss filly all tacked up. I had worked on many problem ponies with Mom, training them to go straight, to jump without trying to refuse or run out at the fence, but this was the first time we'd been sent a horse that I was supposed to straighten out.

On about the fifth afternoon Pop gave me a leg up on the filly, and we walked together out to the jumps. I'd gotten home later than usual, and it was darker and colder than the other afternoons. I rode out to the field, leaning into a blustery wind coming out of the northwest. Pop had put up a new set of fences. I couldn't figure out how he had moved them all around by himself, but he clearly had.

There were three jumps in a row. First, a log on the ground. Then, a little chicken coop. Then, a "spread fence" — consisting of two standards holding an eight-foot-long rail at a foot's height, then two more standards, holding a rail at two feet, and, finally, a set of standards holding a rail at three feet. Pop had also set up another new fence: a rail suspended from two standards and two barrels lay end to end beneath it.

I popped her over the regular logs and coops and show fences, Pop standing in the middle of the field with the buggy whip. My hands were cold on the reins and the wind was gusting, making her jittery. I was circling around, getting ready to jump the barrel fence, when I heard a car drive in our entrance behind me. Its lights swept across the field, and it stopped. I heard the back door to our house slam shut and our dogs running out, barking and yelping, and chasing the car. I could hear another whole ruckus of dogs in the car barking, and then our pack — dogs and pig — came flying out into the field, circling around me.

I pulled the Voss filly up to watch what was happening. The dogs yelped and wagged their tails. Sidney was doing his dog imitation, which was pretty good until he got into the vocal part and came out with a series of grunt-oinks. A horse in the barn whinnied. The dogs back in the car barked. The Voss filly whinnied to the horse in the barn. She backed up two steps down the hill, trying to head back to the barn. Pop was beside us. I let my body remain loose and relaxed, but inside I snapped to attention. I gave her a light squeeze to urge her forward. She pinned her ears back, thrust her front feet forward, and froze.

"Okay, Bud, you ready? We might have to teach her a lesson now."

This is what he had been waiting for; this is why he'd been working out here with me every night in the cold and dark even though he was aching and stiff and sore. This is why I'd been wearing the rowel spurs and carrying the whip.

"Okay now, just give her a little squeeze. Don't use the spurs yet."

I squeezed and she hunkered down, digging in her front hooves.

"All right now, Bud, get after her."

I squeezed with the spurs, digging them into her sides and walloped her across the rear end with the stick. She lowered her entire body and started scrambling backward, fast, uncontrollably fast down the hill. I'd never felt anything like it. I heard the swish of Pop's buggy whip and the snap as it stung her around her ankles. I pushed hard to get her going forward, and instead her front end went up, up, her head and neck up, and I was standing straight up in the stirrups, my hands high on her neck, trying to keep from flipping over. "Careful, Bud; careful, Bud," I heard from behind. When I landed, Pop let out a low, hoarse growl, and snapped the buggy whip across her hocks. I squeezed with the spurs and forward we went.

We cantered around a big circle, and when we came around to make our approach to the barrel jump, and to head slightly up the hill and away from the barn, she started to slow. Swish — went the buggy whip. I squeezed with the spurs, and up and over the barrels we flew. Around and around we cantered, turning sharply, jumping the barrels.

"Now, try the triple."

I headed for the spread combination. I'd been pushing and squeezing and having to hold myself down in the saddle as Granny had taught me in this same field years earlier; my legs were getting rubbery. I couldn't do everything I wanted to do on her. I just rode her headlong into that first log as hard as I could. Up and over the log we went, landed, took one stride, and up and over the chicken coop we went, landed, took one stride. Going into the spread, we were too close to take a stride. I asked her for a big one, and she took off, airing over the spread, and landed moving right along.

"You got her now, Bud. Let's head in."

# 11

## First Race

I started schooling the Voss filly cross-country. She could "jump the moon" — an expression Mom liked. The filly was light, agile, springy. She was my project. I was the trainer. I was the rider. To get her used to hounds, I usually took our whole pack of dogs and the fast-growing, toe-trotting Sidney with us.

I started taking her out foxhunting. At first she did freeze and she did rear up, but only a few times and always when I had allowed her to stand flat-footed. I learned to keep her moving. I always had to think ahead, watch where we were going, never let her get stuck in a spot where she felt trapped and couldn't move. After four or five hunts without freezing or rearing, she forgot all about the bad habit.

I'd get up early in the morning, before school, and exercise her two or three days a week. I hunted her with the Elkridge-Harford most Saturdays. Mr. and Mrs. Voss, Tom's grandparents, were often at the meet to greet us. Mr. Voss would walk up, ask me how she was going, and pat her on the neck.

By March, Pop was back from Florida, and he, Mom, and I decided to race the Voss filly in the Green Spring Valley Hounds Old Fashioned Point to Point. First, I rode her in a "drag" with the Green Spring Hunt.

It was held up in Black Rock, in a hilly area. We wouldn't be following the natural scent of a fox, as is done when out foxhunting. Instead, a fox's scent had been dragged cross-country, up and down hills, over rivers, through barnyards, and over some big fences.

About forty of us arrived at the Black Rock "meet," hung around and talked for a few minutes, and then the hounds took off and we were running and jumping. All around us, some horses were stopping at fences, their riders flying over their heads. Other horses were running out at huge fences, their riders hanging onto their necks. The core group just kept galloping through and past all the confusion. I felt like I was riding in a Confederate cavalry charge.

I was galloping along behind one pretty young girl I'd been chatting with at the start. She looked beautiful in her black hunting coat tailored perfectly to her hourglass figure. A group of us splashed into a swollen river. The current was strong, and when we reached the middle — the Voss filly being small — the water was up over my ankles. But my filly kept going. She didn't hesitate.

The pretty girl had made it across the deepest part of the river ahead of me and was headed for a narrow path up the bank, as were several other riders. Water sprayed and sloshed and the horses surged through the current and no one pulled back. When the group of riders reached the bank, they fell in line, except for the last two. A man on a big clunky "warmblood" (not a Thoroughbred) and the pretty girl started to scramble up the muddy slope head and head. The clunker came over, bumping into the girl, knocking her horse off stride, knocking the girl off balance. She tried to stay on as the horse went up onto two hind legs and over to the side, but to keep from falling off she gripped one of the reins and pulled the horse further off balance. Up, up they went and then over, flipping, splashing into the swollen current. For a split second I hesitated on what to do — but I didn't let the filly between my legs know it. Then I saw the girl's head bob up out of the water and her hunting cap floating down the current. She was all right.

# Chapter 11

By this time the Voss filly and I were at the bank and three or four hors-es were splashing up behind us. There could be no turning back or breaking my filly's rhythm. I threw my weight forward and she attacked the steep, slippery slope. Once up on the bank I saw the girl's horse climbing up the bank farther down stream. I touched the Voss filly with my spurs, and we galloped down along the creek, prepared to chase after the loose horse. Instead, he just stood there and shook all over like a big dog. I grabbed the reins, jogged him back to the girl. She had climbed out of the river, and I thought she'd probably call it a day. Dripping wet, she quickly tied her shoulder length hair in a knot, pulled herself up onto the horse, thanked me rather perfunctorily, and took off on the drag, leaving me three or four lengths behind. She did not look back.

* * *

Two weeks later Mom and I entered the filly in the Green Spring Old Fashioned. This was a pick-your-own course, a four-mile race across the Green Spring's best hunting country. There was a specific place from which we would all start. There were two checkpoints, from which we had to pick up a poker chip. And there was the finish. You raced a mile and a half to the first "chip," a mile and a half to the sec-ond "chip," and then a mile to the finish. You could get to these spots any way you wanted. If you were on a good jumper, you took the shortest route over the highest fences. If you were on a mediocre jumper that was fast, you sped around a longer route.

Mom had grown up in the Green Spring Valley, and she had me walk the course with her childhood friend Herman "Humpy" Stump, who had foxhunted and ridden across this land since he'd been a little boy. I explained to Humpy that my filly was a good jumper, especially over "trappy" fences, and we picked the shortest route, but one that includ-ed some difficult fences.

The night before the Old Fashioned, Pop and I cleaned out the trailer and hitched it to the pick-up he'd recently bought for his new stable.

The Old Fashioned was always held on a Saturday morning at the end of the foxhunting season. Pop couldn't attend. He had to be at Pimlico Racetrack, where he had seven horses in training.

The morning of the race, on March 30, 1968, I arose early and went to the barn to take a look. The filly's stall had been "picked up" and all the hay had been taken out. Pop had come out at 5:15 before he'd gone into Pimlico and fed her. I went back in the house and pulled on my most lightweight hunting clothes. Downstairs, Mom had four perfectly cooked slices of French toast ready for us to split. My saddle and bridle lay cleaned on a kitchen chair. We ate our French toast, and I headed out.

I cranked up the pick-up and pulled the trailer out of the garage. Then, I had a little trouble. Feeling that Mom was watching from the kitchen door and laughingly shaking her head, I attempted to back the trailer up to our loading spot, but the pick-up seemed to go one way and the trailer the other. I pulled the pick-up and trailer forward so they were in a straight line, and I started backing up again. This time I overcompensated so that the same thing happened but with the trailer going the opposite direction. I jammed the gearshift into first and pulled forward again. On this, the third try, I finally succeeded in backing the trailer up to our loading spot.

We drove over, Mom telling me stories of hunting with the Green Spring when she was a child. Wassie Ball was there when we arrived. The filly was acting up, kicking the hell out of the inside of the trailer. Wassie got down to business. He helped us unload her. He led her around, quieting her, talking soothingly to her, while I pulled on my spurs. I stepped behind the trailer to take a leak, and I overheard Wassie telling Mom that Sheila Jackson, the master of the Green Spring Hounds, was there "to see how the filly jumps." I didn't think much of this, walked back around the trailer, and Wassie gave me a leg up. He continued leading her until I had my feet in the stirrups and the end of the reins tied in a knot.

Then my filly and I were up on a hill, circling around with a few dozen other horses and riders. I rehearsed the course a couple of times in my head and relaxed. She felt great under me. We knew each other well. Some Green Spring riders came over and said hello, wished me luck, and asked if I knew a good course. I gave the filly a little squeeze and jigged away from them. And then we were off and running. Two riders who were too lazy to walk the countryside and figure out their own courses followed us. The Voss filly and I crossed a road, took three strides, and jumped into a paddock over a four-foot board fence. I heard one of the riders yell out, "No thanks!" and then his horse's hooves skidding on the asphalt. We went up a steep hill, and instead of going around the fenced-in barnyard, we jumped a board fence going into it, cantered through a clump of five or six startled cows, and jumped a stone wall going out. I could hear the horse directly behind me. I knew who it was, an older man who had once been a top jockey and who had heard I'd been out walking the course with Humpy. We flew down a steep hill toward a creek that was lined with a hedgerow of multiflora rose, thick and prickly. The bush had grown up all over a post-and-rail fence, and I was galloping right for it. I heard the rider behind me yell out, "Where're you going? Where're you going? You're crazy!" and then he pulled away. Out of the corner of my eye, I could see him galloping along the hedgerow, headed for the creek crossing, which I knew was about an eighth of a mile out of the way. I turned my eyes back to the oncoming five-foot bush in front of me and for a second almost panicked. Then I saw my gap. There was a spot Humpy and I had found where the multiflora rose was thinner than anywhere else, and you could see the top rail of the fence. I slowed, ran the bit back and through her mouth. We cantered in toward the gap, popped up and over the fence, and pulled to a trot. We skidded down a bank, splashed across the creek, and scrambled up a steep bank on the other side. It had been a little risky, but this sort of thing was her cup of tea. We'd saved a lot of ground.

I let her catch her breath as we cantered down a path in the woods. I didn't want to hurt her. I waited until I felt her swell her chest and take that deep breath, as Pop had taught me. We came out of the woods into a pasture. Out of the corner of my eye, I saw one other rider charge out of the woods just a hundred yards to my right. It was that same rider. He must've been flying.

The finish was a quarter of a mile away on the other side of the hill. Separating us from the finish was a long asphalt driveway at the top of the hill lined with a three-board paddock fence on either side. Foxhunters normally go out of their way to gallop over to where there is an inset, a lowered panel of the fence, slow to a trot, pop over it, cross the asphalt driveway at a trot, and then jump out over the other inset. I could see the other rider heading for the inset — which would take him off his most direct route to the finish.

I kept riding my filly at a steady gallop straight into the four-foot board fence. She sailed over it, landed on the thin strip of grass, skidded and skated across the asphalt driveway, and the split second she touched the next grass strip, she took off and jumped the accompanying board fence — reminding me of that first night I schooled her through the triple in-and-out with Pop. Then I was down low, the tails of my grandfather Alfred's hunting coat flapping behind me. We raced to the little crowd at the finish. I pulled her up, and everybody swarmed around us, patting the filly on the neck, slapping me on my legs, congratulating us. Wassie was there, with his broad face beaming. He grabbed the reins and looked up at me. "God damn, boy, you looked just like your old man over that last fence!" I bit my lip. I patted and patted my filly.

After a little awards ceremony I was cooling the Voss filly out, walking her around the trailer. Mom and Wassie were leaning up against the side of our trailer, relaxing. Sheila Jackson, fit and athletic, walked over and spoke to them for a few minutes. Grinning, she approached me and the filly, congratulated me, and gave the filly a pat between the eyes. "Does she go as well out hunting on a calm day, when they're not doing much, as she did today?" Mrs. Jackson asked in her exuberant way.

I suddenly realized what was going on. "Yes, she's goes very well out hunting," I replied, my tone flatter than intended.

"That's a good girl. That's a good girl," Mrs. Jackson said, as she walked around my filly, giving her a close look.

"You've done a nice job with her, Patrick," she said. She gave her a pat on the neck and walked away.

Mr. and Mrs. Voss hadn't attended the Old Fashioned — but Wassie had given them the results. They had the exact same idea as Pop did, which was to enter the filly in the Elkridge-Harford Point to Point — a more formal race — held right on their thousand-acre Atlanta Hall Farm. This would be my first real race.

A few days before the race Pop and I walked the course together. It consisted of three miles over twenty fences: post-and-rails and board fences, all from three to three-and-a-half feet high. It was a "trappy" course that didn't allow riders to build much speed as they galloped around the Voss' house, main barn, indoor track, and cow barn. It even had an in-and-out between the indoor track and the cow barn, where riders jumped a big board fence, landed, took two strides, and then jumped a good-sized post-and-rail. The in-and-out would slow down the bigger and faster horses but would suit my filly just fine.

We had a serious walk around the course. It was the first weekend in April. The dull brown of the winter grass had been replaced with a rich green, and the ground no longer had any frozen spots; it had a nice give to it. Pop pointed out how to angle certain turns, where to ease up going up a hill and give her a breather, where to "let her roll" going down a hill, and where to make my move. He advised that I let her go easy the first mile. This was her first race, she was small and light-boned, and she had to carry a full 165 pounds. I only weighed 145, and thus I'd have to carry a lead pad, along with my saddle. Late in the race this 165 pounds might affect her more than the weight would the other bigger, stronger, and more experienced horses.

Jack Graybeal was the starter. Ten of us circled around and around, and just when it was most advantageous for me, Jack dropped his arm holding the red flag and yelled, "Tally ho, boys!"

We took off around the course in a tight pack. The first three fences took my breath away as we galloped into them full blast without much control. Then, rounding the indoor track, the riders took a hold of their horses for the next couple of miles. My filly jumped well — hitting just two of the fences with her front legs. With three-eighths of a mile to go, she felt strong. We jumped the third to last. Two horses were head and head five lengths in front of us. I asked her to run. She sped up for a few strides, and I was just getting comfortable with how we were reeling in the two in front when she suddenly stopped her forward drive. She didn't feel right. I eased her over the last two fences and hand-rode her to the finish.

Pop, Emmett, and Tiger were waiting. "Good job, Bud," Pop said, taking hold of one of the reins as I prepared to hop off. "Nice race, girl, nice race, yes — good girl," he said to the jigging filly, patting her. She was breathing hard and her neck was in a full lather, steam rising up all around her.

"Nice race-riding, jock, nice race-riding," Emmett chanted. "You can't pick 'em up and carry 'em."

"Let me take her, Boss. I got her," said Emmett, taking the reins from Pop.

"Okay, let's keep her walking, Emmett. I don't want her to tie up," said Pop, referring to the phenomenon of horses — fillies especially — sometimes cramping up after they've overly exerted themselves and haven't yet cooled out. "She's got a big heart. Hold on a second, Emmett."

He bent over and gently ran his hand down one shin, between the knee and the ankle, and she flinched away from his hand. When he did the same to the other shin, she flinched again. "Bucked both shins," he said, pulling himself back up. Emmett immediately started walking her. Tiger reached up and patted me on the back. "Well done, young man. Don't worry; she'll be fine in a couple of weeks."

Steaming horses were milling all around us. I was huffing and puffing a bit myself. Horses were jigging and blowing, and their eyes were expanded. Grooms were hanging onto them as the riders got off and tried to maneuver through the spectators to the scales. Pop and Emmett walked off, and I was trying to understand what had happened to my filly. I was confused over what to do. I knew that horses usually bucked their shins as two-year-olds and then never did it again. Then Pop and Tiger were beside me, and Pop said to Tiger, "Ed, could you go back to the barn and help Emmett? I'll be right there." Tiger headed for the barn.

"Let me give you a hand with that tack, Cowboy," Pop said.

I handed Pop my lead pad and saddle, about fifteen pounds altogether. He swung it over his right arm and we walked to the scales. At first I felt bad about her bucking her shins, thinking it was because we'd hit the top rail of one fence pretty hard and I should've made her jump it better. "There's nothing you could do," Pop explained. She'd never run in a race before, and the pressure of running in the race, carrying the extra weight, combined with whacking a couple of fences with her front legs, had caused her to buck. "She would've galloped," he said, meaning won easily, "if she hadn't bucked. She'll be all right in just a week or two. Don't worry, Bud."

* * *

I took the tack back from Pop and waited while two riders in front of me weighed in. It wasn't Carlyle Cameron checking the scales at this little race meet. It was Mr. Maher whom I'd hunted alongside on the Voss filly many an afternoon throughout the winter. We'd often jumped fences together — head and head — for the fun of it, and after a big run, late in the day, just when I was getting tired, Mr. Maher would open up the sandwich case attached to his saddle, hand me half of a ham sandwich, and then his flask of port and whiskey.

"Good job, Potstick," Mr. Maher said, grinning excitedly as I stepped onto the scales. He kept his eyes directly on mine, "Your filly went well. All our jumping head and head must have helped."

"Definitely," I laughed. "It definitely helped." I weighed in and headed back to the pick-up to leave my tack off. I felt short, stubby, as if I were covering very little distance with each of my human strides. Wassie Ball and Sheila Jackson stepped out of the crowd together. Beaming, Mrs. Jackson shook my hand. "Looked like she jumped well," she said.

"Thank you. Yes, she really went well," I said, realizing that again, my remark to Mrs. Jackson, had come out sounding flat. I marched on, past the wagon on which the winning jockey, owner, and trainer were standing, preparing to receive their trophy. I ducked going past a couple of photographers lining up their shots of the winning team.

Then I saw Mr. Fisher — Janon Fisher Jr. — the owner and trainer of the legendary timber horse Mountain Dew, whom I had watched fly over five-foot fences and win timber race after timber race, including the toughest timber race of them all, the Maryland Hunt Cup, since I was ten years old. Mr. Fisher — in his sixties — was dressed in a green tweed jacket (everyone else was in an overcoat or parka), a thickly woven yellow plaid vest, a tie, and corduroys. He wore no hat. He looked sharp, trim, fit. His hair was gray and short-cropped. He was talking to Pop, and Pop was nodding his head affirmatively. I headed for the pick-up when Mr. Fisher walked up to me, shook my hand, and congratulated me on riding a good race.

He said he'd also seen me ride in the Old Fashioned. "I like the way you ride into a fence," he said. He explained that his son Janon (Janon Fisher III, one of Pop's best friends) would be riding Mountain Dew, who was getting older, in the Grand National and then the Maryland Hunt Cup. Janon didn't want to ride anything else. Would I like to ride two of his horses the next weekend at the Manor Races? "Talk it over with your dad and call me back tomorrow."

Pop drove the pick-up, pulling the trailer home, and I sat beside him. He quietly told me that he had spoken to Wassie after the races and Mrs. Jackson was definitely buying my filly. I didn't say anything. He looked over at me. "Bud, you couldn't find her a better home." He explained that Mrs. Jackson wanted to pick her up right away.

We drove along quietly. "You know, Bud," he said, "it'd probably be better for the filly to rest up at our place for a week or so, and then go over to the Jackson's. What do you think?"

"Yes, I think that's a good idea."

"I'll give Wassie a call tonight."

He reached over and put his hand right above my knee, as he used to do when I was a kid, and gave it a hell of a squeeze. My leg leapt up, and I felt like I was going to jump out of the truck. We both laughed.

When we got home, we brushed any remaining sweat off the filly, tossed a light blanket on her, and gave her a hot mash. Pop put bandages on her front legs. Her shins would heal fast over the coming week, and one day while I was at school, Mrs. Jackson would load her onto a van and take her away.

While Pop and I worked on the filly, we discussed Mr. Fisher's proposition. Sunday morning I called Mr. Fisher back to tell him I'd accept the two rides. They would be my first rides in formal races sanctioned by the National Steeplechase and Hunt Association.

# 12

## Moonlore

A week later the first horse of Mr. Fisher's — a dark bay gelding — went poorly. I could not get him to stand off and jump. He propped — slowed — going into each of the four-foot fences and then put in an extra stride and "got in too close" to the fence, which slowed him down and caused him to smack his front legs against the top rail. The second horse, Moonlore, was a good-sized chestnut filly. She had a long neck, a long back, and beautiful lines running from her chest to her tucked in stomach to her high rump. She jumped like a deer and finished strong.

Mr. Fisher asked whether I'd like to ride her the next week in the Benjamin H. Murray Memorial, a race for novice timber horses held forty-five minutes before the Grand National — in which Mountain Dew would be running. The Grand National was the last prep race for the Maryland Hunt Cup, held the following Saturday.

I accepted. I was a junior at Gilman School and on the junior varsity lacrosse team, which had gotten me in good shape. On Monday after lacrosse practice, I walked the Murray Memorial timber course of big, solid, straight-up-and-down fences with Mr. Fisher. While walking, Mr. Fisher asked if I could exercise Moonlore — get to know her better — in the early afternoons approaching the race. I was a little worried about missing lacrosse practice, but the next day when I explained the situation to Mr. Menzies, my coach and my former sixth-grade teacher, he told me the whole team was rooting for me and I'd better go exercise that filly.

I was having fun and had no idea of what I was getting into. I had gone from the quiet contentment of training and riding my own horse, the Voss filly — feeling as if she were actually mine — to suddenly riding in a race that was paired with the prestigious Grand National. It was meaningful to me that the race was named in honor of B.H. "Laddie" Murray, whom I remembered well as one of my parents' best friends.

The day of the race I was "on my own." Pop had Count Walt entered in the timber race at Middleburg. Pop's great friend Tommy Walsh was riding "Walter," and Pop had the horse in perfect shape. Plus, he was running a couple of hurdle horses — so he had to go down the road to Middleburg while Mom and I made the short drive to Butler, Maryland.

I wasn't nervous and neither was Moonlore. She was led into the paddock and calmly circled the inside perimeter of the red snow fence while other horses kicked and jigged and reared. Mr. Fisher and I tacked her up, and next thing I knew we were at the start. Tom Voss was alongside me on his stallion, Suspendido, who was acting up, and Tom was busy trying to keep him under control. Charlie Fenwick, a recent Gilman graduate, was there on another horse, as was his brother Bruce, just a year ahead of me at school. It was like we were going out for a hunt.

The starter yelled, "Let 'em roll," and Moonlore and I galloped around a few lengths behind the leaders, jumping well. We crossed the driveway, two horses in front of us, the riders pushing them hard — Tom on Suspendido and Charlie on Arno. Mr. Fisher had told me to wait until we reached this point and then to ask her to run.

I clucked to her, and we had all kinds of speed held in the reserve tank. We passed Tom and Charlie over the third-from-last fence, flew over the last two by ourselves, out in front, and galloped down the stretch the winner. It seemed as easy as could be. It felt as if I had been doing this for years and would for years to come. I pulled her up, jogged back to the stewards' stand, a rickety platform made of metal poles, waved my stick, and got permission to dismount. I felt calm, peaceful. I wasn't blowing at all.

I weighed in, and soon I was up on the wagon accepting the trophy with Mr. Fisher, his daughter Kitty Jenkins, who was the owner, and the Murray family.

Early that evening Pop and Tiger returned home from Middleburg. They hurried in the front door and down toward the den, where Sue Sue and I sat waiting. With Tiger standing behind him, Pop hesitated on the step that led down into the den, holding his briefcase under one arm, looking at us expectantly. Sue Sue blurted out that I had won. Pop glanced into my eyes and then looked down, paying more attention than usual to the step as he descended. When he looked back up and walked toward me — the dogs now careening into the den, rubbing up against him and smacking their tails against his legs — he was grinning and his eyes were tearing up.

For a second neither of us knew what to do. He was standing there. I was standing there. Sue Sue headed back into the kitchen. I could tell he felt the exact way — maybe the flip side of the coin — I felt. He wished he could have been there. He wished I could've had my first win in a sanctioned race on a horse he trained. I felt slightly let down he hadn't been there. The whole thing seemed unreal. Suddenly, I had gone off and won this race without Pop, and, simultaneously, Pop had gone off to Middleburg and won the big timber race. We had both gained something. We had both lost something. We didn't hug, or shake hands, or anything.

Then Tiger stepped past my father, grabbed my hand, gave me his steely shake, and said, in an unusually serious tone, "Well done, young man, well done," and Mom came in, delighted Pop was home early, and heard the good news about Count Walt, whom she had ridden all winter. Tiger kidded Pop about Mom being the one who had done all the work on Count Walt while Pop got the credit. Pop put his briefcase down by his favorite deeply cushioned armchair. Fending off the dogs, he headed for the kitchen. "Ed, let's have a drink," he said, pulling off his tweed jacket and hanging it on the back of the chair. I fixed two Old Grand Dads and water, easy on the latter, "remember the drought." Tiger went into the living room, where we could hear him joking with Sue Sue and Sallie. I noticed Tiger was wearing the 1920s-styled riding jacket and antique, but well-polished, boots old Mr. Voss had given him. The coat had been too large and the boots too small. Last summer, I'd driven up to see Tiger one afternoon, and there he'd been, in the bathtub in the middle of a hot day, sipping on a jar of iced-down cider and wearing the jacket and boots. I roused him up to go for a ride. He hung his jacket out in the sun to shrink and wore the boots the rest of the day until they had stretched and fit him perfectly.

Sue Sue and Sallie helped Mom set the kitchen table, and Pop, Tiger, and I pulled on light jackets, preparing to go out to the barn and check on the horses. But first Tiger insisted Sue Sue go, too. The four of us worked together, throwing down some bales of hay and straw, Tiger alongside Sue Sue, unnecessarily ready to help her if she needed it — Sue Sue had Mom's uncanny wiry endurance. She never gave ground in any sort of strength contest. Whether arm wrestling or Indian wrestling, she could often whip me through sheer willpower. She never admitted feeling any pain. Like both her grandmothers, when she went to the dentist, she refused any Novocain — and instead practiced her Christian Science "mind over matter" as the dentist cranked up his drill. I'd once seen a terrible pony we were training run off with her. The pony had charged right into an electric fence, fallen, gotten tangled up in the wire and rolled all over Sue Sue, the electric shocks continuing to shoot through both the pony and my sister. Sue Sue extricated herself from the pony's thrashing legs and the coils of wire. She led the pony away from the wire, adjusted her tack, climbed back on, and continued with the ride. She didn't shed a tear; she didn't complain. She just bore down with full concentration on her riding, waiting for that pony to give the slightest hint of trying to run off with her again.

Soon we were all back in the kitchen having a big dinner. After giving a congratulatory toast to Pop and me, Tiger proclaimed that now I would probably have to ride in the Maryland Hunt Cup. Pop took notice and looked — forehead furrowed, right eyebrow raised, left eye squinting — across the table at Tiger after he'd made the remark.

The next morning, Sunday, Mr. Fisher called and said he was thinking about running Moonlore the following Saturday in the Maryland Hunt Cup. She would be running as an entry with the great Mountain Dew, who had won the Grand National half a dozen times and the Hunt Cup three times. Would I ride her? He thought that Mountain Dew was not 100 percent this year. Mountain Dew was getting a little older and had a leg problem, but Moonlore had a shot at doing well. In fact, if she could get over the big fences, he thought she had a better chance than Mountain Dew.

The Maryland Hunt Cup is the longest, toughest timber race in the world over the biggest post-and-rail fences in the world. Four miles — the other races in which I had ridden had all been three miles. Five-foot fences — the other races had fences ranging from three to four feet in height. Straight up and down — the fences at the Elkridge-Harford races leaned slightly away from you. The Maryland Hunt Cup had twenty-two fences and at least six were more than five feet high. All but four were made of big, thick telephone-pole-like posts and rails. They did not break.

The next thing I knew I was walking the course with Mr. Fisher. He knew everything about the Hunt Cup. He had bred Mountain Dew on his farm, only miles away from the Hunt Cup course his daughter Kitty Jenkins foxhunted the horse all winter, and his son Janon rode him in the spring races. This was the quintessence of a Maryland tradition.

## Chapter 12

We stood at the first fence, a normal-sized fence under four feet, and we looked down to the second, and then to where you crossed the road, and then at the third fence, huge, solid, more than five feet, on the other side of the road. Mr. Fisher took out a chunk of tobacco, stuck it in his mouth, and asked if I'd like "a chew."

"Sure," I said, like it was something I did all the time.

Then I was walking along with Mr. Fisher, toward the second fence, climbing over it, and crossing the road with this big wad of tobacco growing, swelling, in my mouth. We reached the third fence. Its nickname was the Union Memorial, after Union Memorial Hospital in Baltimore where many riders had awakened after galloping into it. It was almost as tall as I. Each panel consisted of five rails; each rail was thicker than my thigh. The posts were so thick they looked as though they had been made to hold back the elephants of Hannibal's army, about which I'd been reading in my Gilman Latin class, where for one solid week my classmates steered our teacher away from all things Latin and toward anything to do with the Maryland Hunt Cup. By this time the tobacco was causing an explosion of saliva in my mouth. Mr. Fisher didn't spit out any tobacco juice; his cheek wasn't even puffed out. Thinking it wouldn't be polite to give a big spit right in front of him, I held the juice in my mouth.

Mr. Fisher asked what I thought of the third fence. "I don't think I've ever jumped a fence this big," I said through the tobacco juice.

"Don't worry," he said, "neither has your horse."

I swallowed a gulp of the juice, and we continued around the course. I had to walk the remaining three and a half miles with the tobacco juice swishing around in my stomach. We looked at the sixth fence, which was big, and the thirteenth, huge, and the sixteenth, even bigger, more than five feet, because you jumped it going up a hill.

Monday through Friday my classmates at Gilman asked me about the race. I went ahead and practiced with the lacrosse team most days. Coach Menzies allowed me to miss two practices so I could drive to the

Fishers' and exercise Moonlore.

On Saturday morning, the day of the race, Pop gently woke me. "Go back to sleep for a while," he said, "I'm going into Pimlico and then I'll meet you over at the Voss barn."

Soon I was driving the three miles over to "the Voss barn." We had eight horses stabled in the barn belonging to Jen Voss, Tom's mother. Tiger was there. In his sixties he would still come over in the mornings — though not too early — and gallop a few horses with us. According to Pop, Tiger's riding, along with his handiwork around the farm — he'd build a fence, patch a porch, screw edges onto an old pair of wooden skis, split logs for firewood — paid off the drinks and meals he consumed at our place. Mom laughed at such a notion. Tiger had bronzed, weather-beaten skin, and a body hard and resilient as coiled steel. He had taught me everything I knew about canoeing, camping, using a chain saw, and drinking hard cider. That spring I often drove up to Tiger's, tapped into his keg of cider, hopped on one of his horses, and followed him over the course of wild-looking fences he'd set up in the woods. This was just about the most pure, hell-raising, alcohol-intensified fun I'd ever had riding. Sometimes I laughed so hard that it felt as if the top of my skull would pop off out of the sheer exhilaration and celebration of the moment.

All week Tiger had teased me unmercifully about the Hunt Cup. He had brought rolls and rolls of toilet paper to the barn and kept joking that after I crunched at one of the gigantic fences he would use the toilet paper to mummify me. He pushed it a little past the point of being funny.

"Far and wide all the damsels, all the young beauties on 'The Manor,'" he sang out the word manor in a snobby, country-club way, poking fun at the blue-blood heritage of My Lady's Manor, where we all lived. "All the lily-white virgins will lie crying on their four-poster beds, distressed, devastated, destroyed, ruined for life, after the funeral procession of young Sir Patrick. He will be knighted posthumously, and each and every one of them will vow never to kiss anyone else again." Tiger had gotten a deal at the Manor Tavern on a case of cheap champagne, and we'd been sipping champagne on Sunday mornings all of April, after we got the last set of horses out. This was not a Sunday morning, and we hadn't gotten all the horses out, but Tiger popped open a bottle, toasted to my demise, and offered me a taste — which I declined.

Tiger had earned his nickname from attending Princeton — the Tigers — as well as from his relentless ferocity when in any form of competition. He had written his thesis on Robert Smith Surtees, a sort of fun-loving Dickens or, better yet, an Anglicized, aristocratic version of Twain. Surtees wrote witty satires of the English foxhunting lifestyle and never had his name listed in a book. The title page would say: HAWBRUCK GRANGE (in large type) or, *The Sporting Adventures of Thomas Scott*, Esq., (in slightly smaller type), by the author of "Sponge's Sporting Tour," "Ask Mama," etc., etc. (in the smallest of type). Tiger had an entire edition of his books, each containing hilarious pen-and-ink drawings of hunting scenes, lining the wall of his ramshackle woodstove-heated den. Tiger's thesis on Surtees had not been accepted, and Tiger never received his degree. Surtees, who wrote in the mid-nineteenth century, had funny, alliterative nicknames for his characters, and Tiger liked to deal them out himself. Mine, which was not repeated much, was "Sir Fuck A Lot." My friend Tom Voss, who always had to fight his weight, earned the sobriquet "Sir Loin." Tom and I shared the same godfather, Garry Winants, who could go on a rage and out-cuss Huck Finn's father, and Tiger had knighted him "Sir Cuss A Lot." Best of all was the name Tiger had given his mischievous calico cat: "Miss Conduct." Everyone who came by the barn that morning took a few drinks out of the series of champagne bottles, teased me about being an "amateur" and riding in the Hunt Cup, and asked if that was what I had to do to get laid. (Only amateur jockeys were allowed to ride in the Hunt Cup, which then had no purse.) The air buzzed around me. The dew on the grass shimmered. The sun was bright. Everyone talked and talked about the Hunt Cup, about my chances, asked how I felt.

Soon it was late afternoon, a sunny day, the grass a brilliant green, and I was in the paddock of the Maryland Hunt Cup, with thousands of hard-drinking, pot-smoking — this was 1968 — spectators swarming around outside the perimeter of the red snow fence that formed the paddock. And there was Moonlore — what had happened to her? No longer was she the quiet, sensible filly of the week before. She was wild. She was rearing and plunging. She was difficult to tack up. When I got up on her, I could barely hold her on the ground. Later, I learned that she had gone "into season," meaning her body was preparing for breeding. When a filly goes into season, she prances around with her tail up and acts a little crazy.

We were at the start with the other horses and we took off. She was a handful. We flew the first, flew the second. We were humming right along, going into the third. Moonlore was pulling hard. She was acting frantic. I couldn't get her to keep her head down and to pay attention. We were in front and flying. I saw Janon on Mountain Dew to my left heading into the fence. He was off my hocks — half a length behind me. This was usually not a good place to be. Sometimes the horse half a length back will take off to jump at the same time as the horse half a length in front. Mountain Dew was my stablemate. He was my entry. I took back just a little on Moonlore so she wouldn't stand off as far as usual to jump the fence.

The image of Janon and Mountain Dew over to my left is the last thing I remember about the race.

There is a stunning photograph in a book on horses showing Moonlore flying through the air, crashing through the top rail of the fence. She is on an angle, her legs projecting off to the side. I am hanging on with a worried expression on my face, and it is obvious that when she comes down from this height she will land on me.

I was in a moving vehicle. It was throwing me in one direction, then the other. It was an ambulance. Someone was telling me to stay still.

## Chapter 12

We were roaring along. I tried to get up. I was pushed back down and told to sit still. There was a terrible screaming noise. What was it? Someone must've gotten hurt.

I was dreaming I was riding the race again. We had had a fall. I was chasing Moonlore. I would catch her and get back on. I ran across the field. I had the reins. I hopped; I jumped, trying to get back on. She danced and jigged away from me. Would someone, anyone, please give me a leg up? I looked around to see if a spectator would give me a leg up.

I was back in the ambulance. "Let me out of here." I was gently pushed back down. And then I was out.

I awoke on a hard — very hard — cot. I was on white sheets. It was cold. I was shivering. A woman in white was standing over me. Who was she? Where the hell was I?

"What are you?" she asked, peering at me. "Are you in some kind of a band?"

Was I in a band? No, I didn't think so. What would I play? What was she talking about? She stared at me. My neck hurt. My back hurt. I lifted my head slightly to look at my body … "Don't do that! Don't raise your head." She gripped my skull tightly with both hands and eased my head down, but I had seen the grass-stained and dirt-smeared boots and britches and silks and wondered if she'd once seen Mick Jagger in a similar outfit. My head spun. She spun. I felt like Dorothy in *The Wizard of Oz* awakening from the tornado but instead of cute little Munchkins, there was the Wicked Witch in white leaning over me. "Look at this," she said, and she flicked her hand across the white sheet, which was wrapped hard and fast over the cold, steel-like surface of the cot. "You're getting grass all over my clean sheets … How'd you do this to yourself? … You'll need X-rays …" And that was it. I drifted off, back to the green turf of the Hunt Cup. My feet were in my father's riding boots, and I was jogging through the thick green turf — I could feel it through the thin soles of the boots — to Moonlore, standing there. But as I got closer, she jigged away. "Catch her!" I yelled. "Let me get back on. I have to get back on and finish the race."

Then I was in my bed at home. The bed was soft. The mattress was not made of stainless steel. The length of the bed was up tight against the wall, with a window down by my feet. Tippy was curled by my chest. But it was light outside. What was I doing in bed when it was still light out? What was this discomfort? I moved slightly. What the hell was around my neck? I couldn't move my head. My neck was stiff and felt like it was in a cast. I was wearing some sort of neck brace, and I turned toward the wall to get away from the pain and smacked right into some damn big, hard splintery thing in the bed, and there it was, the thick, black rail that had caused all this. It lay beside me, running alongside the wall from my pillow down to my toes. Having been painted black with creosote, a wood preservative, it smelled like hot tar newly laid on a road. My Uncle Mikey — six-time winning rider of the Hunt Cup — and Tom Voss had gone out after the race, gotten the broken rail, brought it back, and put it in my bed.

Paddy Neilson won the Hunt Cup on Haffaday that year. In the most considerate of gestures, he stopped by the farm on Sunday to check on me and to encourage me in my career as an amateur timber rider. I was sitting in the living room with Paddy, Mom, and Pop. Paddy was telling me he'd heard Moonlore hadn't broken anything and was in pretty good shape, considering the seriousness of the fall, when the phone rang. Pop got up, went into the den, and picked it up.

"He's all right," I could hear. "He's going to be fine. No, I didn't tell him that … You go ahead …" Then Pop called out, "Paddy. Telephone, Paddy."

I got up stiffly, the brace tight around my neck. It was thick and spongy, and pushed my chin up into an uncomfortable angle, just like the one Pop had had to wear, and it made it so I couldn't turn my head; I had to swivel my shoulders and head as one unit. I went into the den. Pop was grinning. He handed me the receiver — I could hear someone talking fast, non-stop into the other end. I put the receiver to my ear, "Little-Paddy?" It was Evan Jackson; he said "Little-Paddy" as if it were one word.

"Yes."

"Little-Paddy, is this you?"

"Yes — hi, Evan …"

"Don't 'Hi, Evan' me, Little-Paddy. Now you listen. You've done your little aristocratic thing now. You won one and lost one. You almost broke your neck … How much did you get paid, Little-Paddy?"

"Well …"

"How much did you get paid for the one you won?"

"Well, I …"

"That's right. Not a cent. Now if any of those old blue-blooded Maryland people with their locked jaws ask you to ride one of their horses you just tell them you got better things to do …

"You've done your thing. All those cute little virgin prep-school girls saw you go to the post in the Hunt Cup. You can get laid in Maryland now. Okay? You understand?"

"Yes, Evan, but …"

"Look, I know your Uncle Mikey won that race half a dozen times — but what good did that ever do him? No one in New York has ever even heard of the Monkton Tin Cup or whatever it's called. No one at Belmont Park even knows what a timber race is — or an amateur rider for that matter …

"Little-Paddy, you do your homework tonight and get up in the morning and go to that school your mother and father are paying all that money for and forget all about the Tin Cup and all those Elkridge-Harford, Green Spring country clubbers down there who could care less if you broke your neck on one of their horses as long as they can be seen in the paddock before the race and have their pictures in the society pages …"

Pop was a little more succinct that Evan. He knew the lambasting I must've gotten from Evan. After Paddy and the others had left, he told me I'd paid my dues as a young Maryland gentleman, won one amateur race, lost one amateur race, hadn't been paid a cent, and had survived to remember it. That was it for the Maryland timber races and for riding for free. I could keep my amateur license so that I could ride in some races where professionals were not permitted, but I would be paid a fee to ride and I would receive a percentage of any purse.

Monday at school, I heard all kinds of stories from classmates who had been standing near the third fence and thought that I had gone to meet my Maker. Apparently, a young girl had run out after the fall, taken off my helmet, and rested my head in her lap until the ambulance came. She had cried and cried when they'd asked her to move so they could slide me onto a cot and roll me into the ambulance. Did I know who she was? No, I had no idea.

# 13

## Time To Get Going

**B**y the following spring of 1969, I was a senior at Gilman. I had won a timber race on Count Walt the fall before, riding against professionals as well as amateurs, and had been written up in some racing publications. Pop's stable was growing, and we were putting in some long days. At the track and at the farm, I rode with professionals. My focus shifted from riding in amateur Maryland races to riding in races with purses.

It was 5:15 a.m., and I lay in bed, living through a dream: I was crouched low, whip cocked, keeping a good hold of the horse's head as we rounded the last turn at Saratoga. Tote'm Home felt strong beneath me but he ran better from behind, and as Pop always told me, "Wait to make your move. Wait. And when you can't wait any longer, wait." As we straightened out and approached the last hurdle, I was coming up on the outside of Joe Aitcheson. He didn't know I was there. When he did, it was too late. He couldn't get in gear to keep up with us. Our momentum carried us forward over the hurdle half a length in front of the other horse. I was about to growl, crack Tote'm Home once hard across his rump, and dig in with the spurs when it seemed something was wrong with my thigh. Was it cramping from the reducing, I wondered? Then I was jolted out of the dream by the firm grip of Pop's right hand.

"Come on, Bud, time to get going," he whispered.

I lay in the bed, my shoulder up against the Hunt Cup rail, which neither I nor anyone else had ever gotten around to moving.

I lay there, thinking about the dream, wondering about it, reliving it. I let it drift away and adjusted my mind to the reality of the upcoming day. I was seventeen. Over two years had passed since Pop's fall; he had recovered most of the use of his body, but lately he'd had to fight to keep the weight on. The upward curve of healing after the paralysis had leveled off; he couldn't seem to gain any more weight or strength. He'd also had two blackouts. After years of overcoming broken arms, collarbones, ribs, and then paralysis, he was now trying to overcome, in the same persistent way — by ignoring and pressing on — a more insidious ailment, one the doctors were at a loss to diagnose. They'd told him the usual: Don't work so hard and stop all drinking. The neurologists added that he should never get on a horse again. They said he could be crippled for life if he had another fall.

Pop was training a good stable of horses: seven flat horses at Pimlico, eight jumpers over at Jen Voss' barn, and another ten on our farm, including "Frankie," whom Evan Jackson had sent us and whom a syndicate headed by Frank Sinatra owned. And just recently, Pop had hired an assistant trainer — Salvadore "Sal" Tumenelli, who specialized in working with the flat horses.

"Up and at 'em, Buddy," Pop said, rubbing my head. "Coffee's on. Cow prod's out of order." He walked out of the room, fully dressed for work.

One morning earlier in the winter I had been awakened in a far different manner. I'd gotten my second car, a little black Ford Falcon with a big V-8, and had started taking out girls and staying out late on weekend nights. (I had totaled my first car, my grandmother's old Corvair; I had also totaled the Falcon, but I had it patched up and kept driving it;

soon, I had totaled yet another car, Pop's, for which I felt terrible guilt and about which Pop never said a word.) Pop had a hard time getting me up on Sunday mornings to go to the track. He'd walk by my room, loudly whisper, "Paddy, Paddy, time to get up," and I'd say, "Okay, be right there," roll over, try to remember what I'd done the night before, and go back to sleep. So one morning Pop walked by and said, "Paddy, Paddy, time to get up." I'd opened my eyes, the room had twirled, my stomach felt like it was bubbling up a beer and scotch-fueled fizz that was gurgling into my brain, and I'd said, "Be right there." A few moments later it suddenly felt like a horse was biting me in the rear, taking a painful chunk out of me, and surges of electricity were pulsating through the horse's teeth, into my rump. I jumped out of bed to see an audience gathered in my bedroom. There stood Pop and Sue Sue, with Tiger, who had spent the night in the "Grand Canyon" right beside me — the traitor! They were laughing. Pop was holding a cow prod made for moving two-ton bulls. It looked like an extended flashlight, two and a half feet long, but instead of a bulb at the end there were two electric prods. For the rest of my life, whenever I heard Pop saying, "Paddy, Paddy, time to get up," I might not have always hopped out of bed, but I at least sat up, put two feet on the floor, and prepared to rise.

\* \* \*

Quietly — so as not to disturb the sleeping Tippy — I climbed out of bed knowing that by now Pop was probably out working in the barn. It was still dark outside.

Entering the kitchen, I heard the straight-eight of the pickup roar, and I looked out the kitchen window toward the barn where I saw thirty or forty tall thin ribbons of light seemingly hovering in midair. I pictured the powerful light bulb in the hayloft casting its rays through the finger-wide gaps in the vertically spaced sideboards of the barn. Suddenly, the glowing ribbons were gone. It was black outside. Then headlight beams lit up the shed next to the barn, causing two ponies to raise their sleepy heads and blink their eyes. Pop must've just thrown on a load of hay, and from the way the lights jounced as the truck rolled out of the barn, down the grass bank, and onto the driveway, I could tell it was a large one. I thought about the written ultimatum the doctors had issued after Pop blacked out twice over the winter and admitted he was feeling weak. "Mr. Smithwick should neither physically exert himself nor imbibe any alcoholic beverages until he is fully recuperated from his current illness."

Pop drove the twenty-five miles to Pimlico Racetrack, just inside the Baltimore city limits, while I dozed off, leaning against the door of the truck with a musty horse blanket wrapped around my legs, my parka fully zipped, and a wool cap pulled down over my eyes. Pop liked to drive to work, thinking about what the horses would do that day, then relax on the way back, letting me drive. On chilly mornings like this one, instead of turning the heater on and being warm and sleepy, Pop cracked his window open — the theory being that the fresh air would wake him up and acclimate his body to the cold before he had to get out and work in it.

Again, he awakened me from my dreams with his strong right-handed grip on my thigh. "We're almost there, Bud." I remained leaning against the door. A big, lighted sign floated by overhead, and I knew we were about to pull off the Jones Falls Expressway onto Northern Parkway. Take a right, head west, and go up the hill to Pimlico, home of the famous Preakness, the second leg of the Triple Crown. Take a left, head east, and you would go up the hill to my other institute of learning, Gilman School, with its puritanically strict devotion to the development of every boy's mind, body, and spirit, as well as to the educational theme that after graduation every Gilman alumnus should serve his community and work to make the world a better place. Gilman pushed you just as hard physically as it did intellectually and even spiritually.

On school mornings I'd fire up the engine of my old Ford Falcon, walk around to the trunk, pop it open, and get out my sledgehammer.

## Chapter 13

After its latest accident, the car went down the road sideways, like a basset hound, but with the wheels all rolling in parallel paths and with the rear end jacked up like a hot rod owned by one of those bootlegging rednecks Emmett so disliked. The more I drove the car, the farther the rear fender on the driver's side would jut inward until the fender was grinding against the tire, giving off a terrible rubber-burning smell and causing the whole side of the car to shudder. So, each morning I'd whack the hell out of the fender with the sledgehammer, knocking it out and away from the wheel. I'd leave the farm at 5:15, race into Pimlico. At Pimlico I'd get on a few of Pop's tougher horses, my first one at 5:45 in the dark. In the winter Pimlico — Old Hilltop — is a cold place to gallop a horse. Once I was off the last horse, the men in the barn all kidding me about going off to school, I'd hop back in the Falcon. Some mornings, in the dead of winter, Pop's assistant, Sal Tumenelli, would talk me into stopping by the Uptown Bar and Grill, offering to buy me a healthy breakfast of eggs, bacon, and juice. There, at the bar, Sal would self-righteously order "Professor Smithwick" a hard-boiled egg, a slice of beef jerky, and a shot of blackberry brandy before I drove down Northern Parkway, across the Jones Falls Expressway, and back up to Gilman. Between shifting gears, I'd be unlacing my riding boots, left hand on the steering wheel, right on the laces, head part way under the dashboard. I'd rumble onto the campus, sweater half pulled over my head, blocking my vision for a hold-your-breath moment, feet tangled in boots between brakes and clutch, trying to make it on time to hear Headmaster Redmond C.S. Finney in morning chapel.

* * *

Pop was leaning against the door of the pickup, holding the top of the steering wheel with his right hand, a cigarette between his fingers, his left hand by his side, the window cracked open letting in the chilly air, peacefully driving down the empty Jones Falls Expressway — it was Sunday morning — on the way to Pimlico. The brim of the fedora was

Rider-trainer combination of brothers A.P. "Paddy" and D.M. "Mikey" Smithwick (top); for Pop, making weight posed a constant challenge; Pop and Colorado Prince

Pop and Uncle Mikey with their parents (above); my mother, Suzie Smithwick, me, and sisters Sue Sue and baby Sallie (left); Pop and Mom with my godfathers, Morris Dixon and Garry Winants

Pop and I relaxing at home with our dog Chips; our farm at My Lady's Manor

Pop on the great
Neji (top) and on
Bon Nouvel (left);
he shows off his
famous style over
a water jump at
Saratoga (middle)

Crag, Pop, and I (above) before the Rochelle Tin Cup; Pop and I before the Maryland Hunt Cup (right); First Lady Jackie Kennedy (below) awards Pop a trophy after a race at Middleburg

Our groom Tanza (above) holds Curator, Dave Mitchell up; Crag, Pop, and I win the Tin Cup; Wassie Ball presents trophy (left); Moonlore and I on our way to winning (bottom)

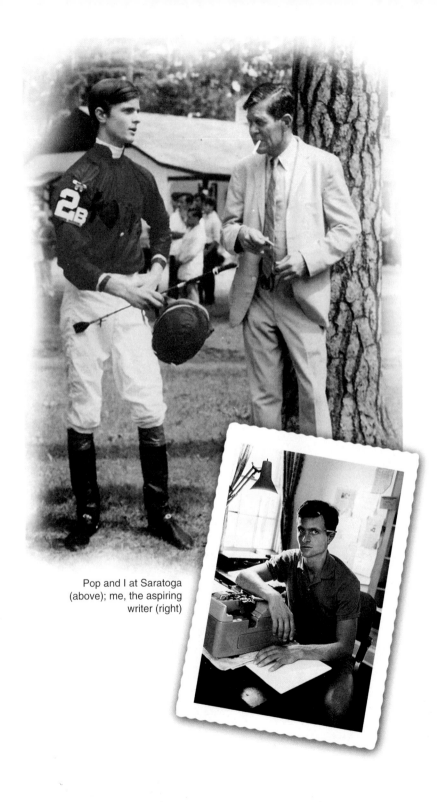

Pop and I at Saratoga
(above); me, the aspiring
writer (right)

I accept the honors for Pop at the Hall of Fame ceremony (above); Ansley and I (left); with Uncle Mikey (below)

pulled down low over his eyes, and he looked like he was concentrating on something. His face was fuller, more bronzed and weather-beaten now than back during his heyday when he was the country's leading steeplechase rider and the women were after him and the clothes companies had him modeling their English-cut jackets. Standing there beside the tall, slender, cosmopolitan-looking female models, Pop always had a mischievous grin on his face, as if he were about to pinch the sophisticated peacock on the ass, or had just done so.

We stopped at the red light at the end of the exit ramp leading onto Northern Parkway. I asked why. We usually just went on through it this time of the morning. Pop pointed to a police car with its lights off parked on the shoulder just down the road.

The light changed, and we roared along in first gear. Pop pushed in the clutch and popped the three-on-the-tree into third, barely touching the gearshift. He had it floored as we gathered momentum to get the lumbering load up the approaching hill. "That's not good for the engine," I said.

"Neither is driving it eighty miles-per-hour down the Manor Road," he said, referring to a warning a Baltimore County policeman had given me on a recent evening. After he'd written up the warning, the policeman had proceeded, unbeknownst to me, to follow me as I raced ten miles on country roads to my Grandmother Whitman's house, where we were having a family dinner. He pulled into the driveway in his patrol car, siren blaring, lights flashing, right behind me, causing my relatives — my two teetotaler Christian Science grandmothers, Granny and Um; my hard-drinking great uncles, Uncle Joe and Uncle Charlie; and my Aunt Edie, to come piling out, surround his car, and voice their opinions on what an upstanding student and citizen I was — after all, I attended the Gilman School and was on the honor roll there! — and how the officer must be mistaken about my speeding. Mom and Pop came out, too; luckily for me the officer had recently won a bet or two on a couple of horses Pop trained and might have been promised a good tip in the future.

Pop coughed. He placed his left hand on the bottom of the steering wheel, took his right off the top, and inserted the stub of his cigarette between the fingers of his left. Then he reached across to roll down the window, a smirk on his face. Before he touched the handle, I said, "Use that left hand." He wound the window six inches down with his right hand, picked the cigarette out of his left and waiting for me to react, gestured as if he were about to toss it out the window, which would not only be littering, but which could also cause the whole load of hay to catch on fire.

"You've got to start using that left hand more," I nagged, reaching across, grabbing the stub out of his hand, and putting it out in the ashtray. "You know that's what the doctors said." They had given him all sorts of pulleys and ropes and hand squeezers. The contraptions hung unused from the door to the cold pantry until Mom put them in a trunk.

"Sometimes, Bud, I don't think those doctors know what the hell they're talking about." I thought about that for a stoplight and another jump from first to third gear. If there was one thing I had learned from working with Pop, it was that when it comes time to make a big decision, go ahead and listen to the advice of veterinarians, blacksmiths, doctors, trainers, riders, friends, relatives — but in the last analysis, trust yourself.

"Light me another cigarette, will you please?"

I grabbed the soft, compact red pack of Pall Malls off the dashboard, pulled one out, stuck it in my mouth, tasted the dry tempting earthiness of a few flakes of tobacco on my lips, lit it with a match, gave it a pull until the end was red and burning, and handed it to him. He coughed and took a drag. I wanted to give him hell for smoking the damn thing but I didn't.

"You know something, Bud," he said, keeping his eyes on the road, "you may have to start learning how to use your left hand and your left leg."

"What do you mean?"

He looked to both sides of the road for cops and took a sharp and illegal left, through a gap in the concrete medium strip, into the two eastbound lanes of Northern Parkway. This was his early morning short cut. We headed west on the eastbound lanes, a couple of cars rounding the corner up ahead, their headlights and ours pointing straight into one another for a brief hold-your-breath moment. Then Pop took another left and we were across Northern Parkway and rumbling up a pothole-infested one-way street the wrong way.

"I'm going to give Brendan one more chance on that new horse today. If he runs out again, you'll start riding him."

I sat up. "I thought if Brendan was going to ride him this summer, he'd keep schooling him." I was speaking of an Englishman who'd been a jumping rider as a youth over in the old country but had developed weight problems after he'd had his dose of success and started drinking heavily as an antidote to the reducing. He'd gotten in some barroom brawls, then turned this aptitude of communicating through his fists into a career as a boxer. But again, the weight was a problem. His trainer had demanded he move down to a lower weight class. He told the trainer and the whole world of boxing "to bugger off" and moved to the States to start riding again.

Brendan had a temper. He had a broad forehead, hair combed straight back, a broken, pushed-in nose, broad shoulders, and big fists. A head shorter than I, he weighed in at about 160 and swore he would get down to 130 by summer. I felt okay riding with him, but on the ground he was quick to taunt you with his fists, and I hated being alone with him. He tended to pick on me, being the boss' son. Pop was giving him a chance to straighten up, work off the weight, and make a comeback.

"No, I think that black bastard is going to be your kind of a horse."

I wondered about my left hand and left leg.

"What side does he always run out on?" Pop asked.

## Chapter 13

I decided to carry a stick in my left hand on every horse I galloped for the next few days. I'd practice hitting with my left hand and switching the stick from one hand to the other while breezing horses.

The "black bastard" Pop mentioned was Tote'm Home. Our one-and-only groom, Tanza, christened Tote'm Home "that black bastard" the moment the horse came leaping and rearing and kicking off the van from New York.

At age seven Tote'm Home was ruled off running on the flat at any racetrack in America because he "stood" in the gate. The bell would go off, the gates would fling open, the horses would charge out, and Tote'm Home would freeze, refusing to come out. He did this one too many times. His career as a flat horse was over, but he would be allowed to run in steeplechase races, where starting gates were not used, if we could teach him how to break from the starting tape. Racetrackers call a horse such as Tote'm Home a rogue, and owners and trainers knew that if you wanted to get a rogue straightened out, you sent him to Paddy Smithwick.

I'd been watching Brendan struggle with this horse for two months at the farm, and I thought Brendan was afraid of him. Tote'm Home had reared up and flipped over once or twice, almost crushing Brendan. While hunting the Voss filly, I'd learned how not to let her bluff succeed when she started to rear up. After all, she, or any other horse, doesn't really want to flip over any more than you do. As she starts to go up, you stand up in the stirrups, keep your weight far forward, take your whip and crack her between the ears while jabbing the spurs into her sides with your heels, and preparing, as she goes down, for her to twist and turn and buck and try to rear again. Do this two or three times, and the habit is broken. Of course, the main thing, which was far more subtle, was to keep her moving, walking, jigging, or trotting and never letting her stand flat-footed. If she were still and you squeezed with your legs and asked her to move forward, that was exactly when she would "freeze," and if you then tried to force her to move forward, she would rear.

Tote'm Home also had a habit of running out at fences, but what really got you nervous was that he sometimes froze in one spot, like he used to do in the gate, and started to shake all over. He bent his legs, so his head and chest were close to the ground, and refused to budge. When a horse does that, and you're sitting on him, you start to wonder. You don't know what he's going to do next.

Tote'm Home was long and lean at sixteen hands (each hand being four inches) and one inch at his withers, the high point where a horse's shoulders come together. His black forelock was always whipping from one side of his face to the other; his teeth were flashes of white beneath his raised upper lip.

Returning from his gallops, he jigged, danced, and bucked. While Emmett — and only Emmett — washed him and you held him with a long shank, the chain wrapped around his nose, he never stopped stamping his feet, swishing his tail, and baring his teeth at you. Take your mind off your business for one second, and he'd be glad to take a nice chunk out of your arm or face, especially if you were Brendan. (We were suspicious that Brendan had ducked in Tote'm Home's stall when no one was around and "worked him over." Tote'm Home hated Brendan.) Constant motion, aggressive — yes, but also fluid, graceful.

You didn't have to be Sherlock Holmes to see that Pop liked this horse, and if he were still riding he would've been on Tote'm Home from day one, and there would have been no running out at fences, no refusing, no rearing. In fact, there was a strange connection here, one that Pop and I never discussed. It was odd that this horse's name, Tote'm Home, as well as his behavior, was so close to the name, and the behavior, of the horse that had almost killed Pop, Totem II.

We coasted through the entrance to Pimlico Racetrack, said good morning to the guard, and because we had a load of hay, instead of parking outside the gates and walking into the barn area, we just sailed on in. To tell the truth, the guard nodded to Pop and let us sail on in every morning, hay or no hay. It was early spring at Pimlico when after the sun rises all you need to wear is a turtleneck, a sweater, and a windbreaker — clumsy winter gloves have been happily cast aside — and the warmth of the sun puts all the riders in a good mood after months of fighting the cold and the frozen track. I couldn't wait to get on my first horse.

Out of the truck we headed for the tack room, Pop with his right arm around his briefcase. Pop walked on by the tack room, listing to port, in that fast, short-striding step of his, continuing around to the other side of the barn, and I wondered why.

I said good morning to Sal Tumenelli who was in a stall, taking off a horse's bandage. I stepped into the tack room and was warming my hands over the fluttering flames of the rusty gas heater when Pop entered, slapped the briefcase down on the old, gray-metal WWII army desk — the exact same type teachers had at Gilman — and said, "Give me a hand, will ya, Buddy?" We walked out to the truck and he asked me to hop up on top of the load — a good distance up, and it was still dark out. "We're going to unload now?" I asked. When we had a full load like this one, we usually unloaded at the end of the morning, after the horses had all been out and were being fed and the slapping down of fifty-pound bales of hay onto the asphalt wouldn't disturb them. Then, with the hangers-on thick around the tack room we might actually get a helping hand or two although usually all we got was a couple of old-timers, sipping cold bootleg beers, pointing out to me, the "bug boy," how I should throw those bales down a little quicker, pick them up a little faster, and work off some of that excess winter weight if I ever wanted to make a rider out of myself.

"Just get your rear end up there and throw down the top row," Pop said in the singsong, exasperated, kidding tone he used with me when I asked too many questions.

The moment the first bale bounced off the asphalt, Pop ran the fingers of his right hand under the two strands of baling twine, and leaning to the left, carried it past our feed and hay room to the other side of the barn where an old black trainer was stabled. There were not too many black trainers on the track; in fact, he was the only one I knew of on the Maryland–Delaware circuit. I threw down a dozen bales, climbed down, worked the fingers of both my hands under the two bands of baling twine without getting a stalk of hay stuck under my fingernails, lifted, and followed Pop, carrying another bale. The old trainer had fallen on hard times; only two of his six stalls were filled with horses, and he hadn't arrived at work yet. There wasn't much work to be done. Just the week before he'd had four horses, all doing well, for a new owner. Then one got claimed in a race. (If you put your horse in a claiming race, you're always taking a chance on someone claiming, or buying, him out of the race for the exact price listed in the program.) The owner threw a temper tantrum and took away the other three. One of the two remaining horses had a bad knee and hadn't galloped for a week. The old trainer was down to one horse in work, and that horse was owned by a non-paying customer, the trainer himself. We stacked the bales in the old trainer's feed room. When I returned for the last bale, Emmett was standing there grinning and shaking his head. "Didn't know we'd gone into the giving-away-hay business," he said.

"Emmett," Pop called out.

"Be right there," Emmett answered. He walked over to the back of the truck. He and Pop wrestled with a couple of bales and the two of them pulled out a fifty-pound bag of oats, each of them holding it by the corners. They walked toward the barn, lugging it, side-by-side, and Pop's left side began to slip. I saw Emmett's body tense. "I got it, Boss," he said. He flung it up onto his shoulders and marched into the barn and around to the old trainer's feed room. Pop's eyes caught mine for a second — they had a piercing worried-embarrassed look. He limped a step or two, bending over farther than usual, then straightened up and walked to our tack room where I knew he'd write out, on a legal pad, exactly what he wanted each horse to do that morning, the flat horses at the track as well as the jumpers we'd be riding out at the farm in the afternoon.

I glanced into a stall. The water bucket was full of clean water — not a stalk of hay or straw in it. The stall had been mucked out and the horse was standing in fresh, deeply bedded-down straw and nibbling around in his feed bucket for the last remains of his breakfast. Emmett must've gotten here at four to have mucked out, watered, and fed seven horses, a job that a pair of grooms not so conscientious as Emmett could drag out an entire morning.

Emmett walked back to his wall-box, pulled out a curry comb, stiff brush, soft brush, hoof pick, and rub rag, and ducked under the webbing into the first stall, closest to the tack room. I stepped into the tack room to get my tack together for the first horse.

No telling how old Emmett was — probably in his sixties though he said he was in his forties. He was almost my height, five eleven and a half, but built more powerfully. He'd learned to box when serving in the army and when he got out, fought as an amateur at the tracks. He'd even ridden some jumpers at the hunt meets. Emmett had a handsome, wily face and plenty of young girls to go along with it. His hair hadn't a fleck of gray but when he "broke bad," hit the bourbon and didn't shave for a few days, the whiskers were white as snow on his coffee-colored skin. When Pop had been in New York Hospital, Emmett was one of the first to visit him, and he told Pop that as soon as he got out of the hospital and started training full-time, he'd have the best foreman on the track. Many people promised many things to Pop when he was in that hospital. Emmett delivered.

# 14

## A Leg Up

The morning flew by for me — I was off one horse and back on another. Some freelance boys hadn't shown up, as usual on Sunday, so Pop let me pick up some gas money — three dollars a horse — by galloping half a dozen horses for other trainers in between our own horses.

All morning our tack room was a bus stop. Trainers, flat riders, ex-jumping riders, gamblers, owners, bookmakers, Pinkertons stopped to chat with Pop, who stopped working just long enough to step into the tack room and give whoever it was a shot of bourbon.

Jocks' agents were the most persistent visitors. They were usually retired jockeys who knew Pop well, who might even have spent some time in a "hot car" heading up the Jersey Turnpike with him and a thermos of screwdrivers. When a jockey retired, he could in a way keep living the life of a jockey by becoming the agent of a younger rider. An agent "took a rider's book" and was paid a fee, and a percentage of the winnings, by that rider. Every flat jockey had an agent, and a good agent could make a great deal of difference to a jockey's career. Pop tended to "name" older riders on his horses, riders he knew well from his days of being in the jocks' room with them — classy, knowledgeable riders who were also excellent horsemen, such as William Passmore, and fast-talking, risk-taking, hard-drinking, barrel-of-laughs, nervy types who knew how to get the job done, such as Nick Shuk, who always rode in white gloves.

After we finished getting the horses out, we met some friends at the Pimlico Hotel bar for a Bloody Mary. On summer weekdays we usually just stopped in for a quick one at the Uptown Bar and Grill, where you could buy some sort of "hot" item for an unbelievable price — cookware, telephones, watches, something that had been packed in a big box and had mysteriously disappeared when being loaded from ship to tractor-trailer down at Baltimore's docks. Pop was a sucker for this sort of thing. One morning he bought half a dozen hot watches, fake Rolexes. He gave me his trusty Timex, put on the "Rolex," and gave the rest to friends. Within days all the Rolexes fell apart, as if on cue, and I grudgingly returned the Timex. Another time he bought Mom a large tea set. We used it once, Mom making tea and cinnamon toast for the family on a snowy winter afternoon. Sipping out of the little cups, eating off the quaint plates, we praised Pop's purchase, and Pop acted a bit smug about the deal he had struck that morning at the Uptown Bar and Grill. After tea Mom put the set in the dishwasher and turned it on. Soon there was a terrible clattering noise. All the handles had come off the cups and most of the saucers had cracked.

This was a Sunday morning, and the Uptown Bar was supposed to be closed. The Pimlico Hotel bar — a bit higher-priced than the Uptown — was open because it was, theoretically, part of the restaurant, though I'd never seen one soul in the dining section. Pop laid a hundred dollar bill on the bar and bought a round for half a dozen of us younger horsemen. Pop had a draft Michelob. Beer didn't count as "an alcoholic beverage," Pop told Sal Tumenelli, seated beside him. "Besides," he added, "I need to put on some weight."

Sal nodded in agreement. On the barstool next to me was Ann, daughter of Johnnie and Kitty Merryman, great friends of our family.

Ann had been galloping horses on the weekends all winter. She and I were talking about going to college, and Sal was giving her a hard time about her intended major — anthropology.

I took a sip of my Bloody Mary and stared at the long row of liquor bottles neatly lining the bartender's counter before us, and then at the image of Pop, Sal, Ann, and me caught in the mirror behind the bottles. Would I some day be going to a far-off leafy campus adorned with ivy-covered buildings? And, if so, what would I be studying in those buildings? Or, would I be seated here, as on this day, having finished galloping for the morning and preparing to hop in a hot car, race to a hunt meet, and ride steeplechase races?

We drove back to the track, to our barn. Pop got out of the truck, walked down the freshly raked shed row, glancing into the stalls. All the webbings were neatly snapped; the halters had been cleaned and soaped and hung from nails outside each stall. Each horse had its head in the corner of the stall; each was eating out of its feed tub.

I slid over to the driver's seat; Emmett got in, then Pop. I drove the truck home while Pop dozed against the door and Emmett tried to nap. Every time I accelerated or put on the brakes Emmett twitched, awakened, asked me what the hell I was doing, and informed me we were not on the Indianapolis Speedway. He was a nervous shipper. Finally, we were out of the stop-and-go Sunday traffic, and Emmett was snoring. I shifted the truck, lightened of its heavy morning load, into overdrive and relaxed as we headed north on the Jones Falls Expressway and then east on the Baltimore Beltway.

There wouldn't be much of a chance to talk to Pop on this morning, but most of the conversations I had with him took place on the road. In bars there were usually too many people interrupting to maintain a conversation. I was tiring of sitting around in bars after work and before races, and I often tried, sheepishly, to coax him into leaving while the friends and hangers-on tried to get him to stay. At home it was too hectic with owners calling to ask about their horses, and

## Chapter 14

friends always stopping by and ponies getting loose or some other minor emergency occurring. But here we were on the road, where we'd had some interesting conversations over the years.

I pulled off the beltway onto Dulaney Valley Road, as Pop and I had done together hundreds of times, and cruised along, the trees thick on either side. Crossing Loch Raven Reservoir and preparing to turn left off Dulaney and onto the Jarrettsville Pike, I thought back on a discussion we'd had crossing this same long, narrow bridge, the last winter Pop had worked with Mikey. Pop had told me he was going to retire soon — but he wanted to ride his last race the day I rode my first.

As I downshifted to get up the first steep hill of the Pike, Emmett began a new type of snore with jagged intakes, almost as if he were about to sneeze, followed by long, sonorous exhalations. I took my hand off the steering wheel and gave his shoulder a shake until he stopped. Three miles later I slowed as we passed the half dozen businesses that made up Jacksonville: Carroll's Store, a little grocery store with wooden floors, run by Perry and Buck Carroll who had gone to school with Pop; the drugstore where you could get a sandwich and where Mom loved to order chocolate milkshakes, especially if she'd been raising a little hell the night before; the Starting Gate, a small bar and restaurant; and the Amoco station, run by George and with Shorty manning the pumps — you could place a bet with Shorty on any horse at any racetrack in the country while he filled your tank. Most importantly, just across the Jarrettsville Pike from George's was an unwieldy, sprawling wooden building, the Four Corners Corral, a bar and restaurant better known as Goldberg's.

I eyed the mud-splattered cars and pick-ups parked outside of Goldberg's. In the winters just about everybody in the horse business, especially the steeplechase part of it, who had been working at Pimlico or on farms in the Long Green Valley, on My Lady's Manor, and even over to the West in the Worthington and Western Run valleys, would convene for lunch at Goldberg's. We'd all be there: Fishers, Reeds, Gills,

Smalls, Vosses, Secors, Bosleys, Pearces, Merrymans, Bennetts, Rosenthal; blacksmiths, vets, riders, trainers, starting gate men, van drivers; and on off-foxhunting days, Dallas Leith, the huntsman, and Jack Graybeal and Bill Norris, the whips, all working horsemen and horsewomen sitting at Formica tables, having a late breakfast or an early lunch washed down with beer and brandy and coffee. At night Mom would load us up at home in the station wagon and we'd meet other families at Goldberg's. Once, late at night, after returning home from Goldberg's, I'd written about it for an English assignment as being a "modern-day example" of something Huck had said in *Adventures of Huckleberry Finn*: "What you want, above all things on a raft, is for everyone to be satisfied, and feel right and kind towards the other." Our parents would talk and carouse. Everybody knew everybody, and Abe Goldberg knew us all and kept a close eye out. Stories were told, people laughed, and Jamie Hruska played the piano, and it was the way life was meant to be — you knew the person you were eating and drinking beside, and you knew Abe Goldberg.

I watched my youthful step around Abe. In the summers, when I used to show ponies with Mom, we'd pull her station wagon and our blue-gray Rice trailer into George's gas station on the way home, say hi to George, and check with Shorty on the gambling industry. Across the Pike, Abe would be out back, where a boxer's speed bag was hung, and Abe — bald and graying with the wrought-iron belly of a woodstove — would be out there in a string T-shirt moving those fists (if not the feet) like Sugar Ray Robinson.

Goldberg's, the Manor Tavern, the Starting Gate, the Brass Rail, Scotty's Paddock, Sperry's — horsemen had spots like these outside tracks that held steeplechase, as well as flat races, up and down the East Coast. I learned you could cash a check, take out a loan, make a friend, make a phone call, find a lover, do just about anything in these establishments. There were three other major enclaves of steeplechasing: one in the Middleburg/Warrenton area of Virginia, another in the

## Chapter 14

Unionville/Radnor area of Pennsylvania, and a third in the Camden/Aiken area of South Carolina. There were also horsemen from Louisville and Lexington, Kentucky; from Nashville, Tennessee; from Tryon, North Carolina; and from Far Hills, New Jersey. We were a big family that was on the move, and trainers often referred to these family meeting spots as "the office." "Hey, Bud," my father would say, "I have to go to the office to make a few calls."

\* \* \*

Pop and Emmett woke up as we were bouncing down the long gravel driveway to the barn we were leasing from Jen Voss. Emmett lived in a room at the end, and Tom and I had spent plenty of time with him. He usually had a stash of bourbon or, sometimes, grain alcohol. Tom and I, under Emmett's tutelage, had experimented with drinking and driving, drinking and shooting pool, drinking and chasing girls, and drinking and burying in the manure pile the convertible of a handsome, athletic newcomer to My Lady's Manor (he'd been getting cocky and moving in on our girlfriends). Emmett had lived there for years, ever since he'd rubbed horses for Tom's father, Eddie. Tom and I were inextricably linked: We were cousins (sharing the same great-great-grandmother); Eddie and Pop had grown up together and been best friends; and we shared the same godfather, Garry Winants, a loyal childhood friend of our fathers. We also were both on the receiving end of Garry's searing commentary on the "high-flying, social-climbing, ass-kissing, nouveau-riche members of the fucking mink-and-manure set." Garry and Tiger Bennett were two of Pop's best friends and both confirmed bachelors stuck in their ways, but they rarely were with Pop at the same time. Tiger called Garry, "Mister Gloom and Doom," or, as I've said, "Sir Cuss A Lot," and Garry called Tiger, "the Aristocratic Gentleman Farmer" or "Your Friend Mister E.H. Fucking Bennett," or "His Highness Hoity-toity Himself."

I parked the truck and we hopped out. Brendan, Tanza, and Tom had six horses "knocked off" — curried, brushed off, rubbed, feet picked out, and ready to go. Tanza was also knocked off and ready to go. An Elmont, Long Island man, Tanza hated being away from "the action" at the track. As a way of fighting the boredom and country blues, he had lately been consuming large quantities of wine. To make matters worse, his wife, Bessie — all three hundred pounds of her (Tanza, at five-nine or so, weighed in at 130 at the most) — had just arrived from New York. Most men on the track straightened out when their better half arrived. Not Tanza.

Brendan, Tom, and I got the first set of three horses out quickly. We jogged them half a mile and gave them a good two-mile gallop across the open fields. Walking back, Tom and I remained quiet as Brendan, who thought he was the next Lester Piggott, criticized our style of galloping horses. For the second set we got on Road Trap, a horse I'd been schooling, Tote'm Home, and Kangaroo, a horse Tom had been schooling.

Easing Road Trap up from his usual gallop, I could tell Pop was planning for us to do something special. We had an audience: My mother's car was parked up by the first of the three new hurdles that ran alongside the driveway, beside Pop's pickup, and Tanza and Bessie's dilapidated Oldsmobile. The hurdles looked fresh and inviting. Tiger had made the "boxes" — the three-foot-high wooden frames into which he, Pop, Tom, and Emmett had stuffed the brush (Tanza jokingly claimed his union contract did not allow him to use his delicate hands for construction work), bringing each hurdle up to a height of four feet, with the top six inches being brush the horse must skim through. Layers of brush lay in front of each hurdle, making the "roll." Tiger had made the hurdles wide enough for two horses to jump head and head, and he'd built a set of wings for each — high, white-painted panels fanning out on both sides to help funnel the horse into the jump.

As I trotted closer, I saw Tom's mother, Jen, in the front seat of her station wagon with Mom. Bessie and Tanza were in the front seat of the

Olds, sipping on something. Pop and Emmett were walking around in front of the first hurdle tamping down the divots — hoof-sized swatches of turf torn out when a couple of horses had schooled over the hurdles the day before.

Pop gave us our orders. I was to give Tom and Brendan a lead over the three hurdles alongside the driveway and pull up. We were not to continue over the hurdle at the top of the hill — which was fine by me. None of us liked it. After you jumped the third hurdle, you had to turn to the left near where the driveway intersected Monkton Road and start up the hill, with the road and speeding cars twenty yards off to the right. Standing at the peak of the hill, the fourth hurdle was a spooky-looking thing. Galloping into it, neither the horse nor the rider could see the ground on the other side. You felt like you were about to take a leap into outer space.

I dropped my irons down a couple of holes, checked the girth, circled, and cantered into the first hurdle. I was sitting there half asleep, and Road Trap put in a short one — an extra half-stride — and popped awkwardly over it. Upon landing I woke up, gigged Road Trap with the spurs, and we headed for the next hurdle at a faster pace. I listened for Kangaroo brushing through the hurdle behind me, heard the *swish*, *swish*. I listened for the second swish, swish of Tote'm Home but didn't hear anything. I hesitated for a split second. Road Trap had shifted into high gear. I was already preparing to jump the next hurdle, and I thought, the hell with turning back, and galloped into and over it.

Coasting, easing up, Tom and I circled back to the first hurdle where Brendan was beating Tote'm with his stick, cussing loudly, unable to get Tote'm to go within eight lengths of the hurdle. Brendan had his stirrups jacked up too high to have any control of the horse and too high to use his spurs.

Tote'm reared straight up and Brendan panicked, kicked his feet out of the irons and slid off. He landed on his feet, still holding the reins, and started slashing Tote'm across the face with the stick. Pop's face was flushed and his eyes were contracted. He would never hit a horse from the ground like that; he would never whip a horse across his face.

He called Brendan over to him and began to lengthen the leathers on Brendan's saddle. I wondered why, and no doubt Brendan, and everyone else, was wondering the same thing. Then Pop seemed to change his mind about something, called me over, and told me to take my saddle off Road Trap. As I did, Pop pulled the saddle off Tote'm Home. Pop snatched Tote'm's reins from Brendan and told him to get on Road Trap. I threw my saddle on Tote'm, feeling the waves of animosity from Brendan — about ten years older than I — and thinking of the methods I would use to master Tote'm when Pop said, "Here, Bud," and handed me the reins.

As Tote'm jigged and danced in place, Pop loosened the left leather buckle with his right hand and with his left elbow pressed against his hip, and left hand on the stirrup, jerked down with his upper body and pushed the buckle pin into the lower hole with his good hand.

He had pulled the stirrup down far lower than I would have wanted it, and suddenly I realized what was going on. It wasn't until he asked for my spurs and stick and I was taking a spur off while he was putting one on that everyone else realized what he was planning: He had adjusted those leathers for himself, and he had switched saddles because the leathers on Brendan's didn't go long enough. This would be the first time he'd jumped a hurdle, or so I thought, since he'd ridden Totem II at Monmouth Park and had the fall from which he was still recuperating.

Mom started yelling, "Paddy, no; Paddy, please don't; it's not worth the chance ..."

I would have loved more than anything else in the world to hop on that horse myself, but Pop was angry. I knew better than to try to reason with him. Besides, the situation was awkward — it would have been hard on Brendan if I succeeded.

I lengthened the right stirrup. Emmett asked, "You sure you ought to do this, Boss? Don't you think Little Paddy might … ?"

"You got him, Emmett?"

"I got him." Emmett was standing directly in front of Tote'm Home with a hand on each rein, gently jiggling the bit and talking soothingly to the horse. Pop put the stick in his mouth, something I'd never seen him do, grabbed the pommel of the saddle, and cocked his left leg up. I gripped it under his ankle and hesitated for a split second as the realization whacked me in the head that here I was giving my father a leg up on a horse who had almost the exact same name as the horse that had ended his riding career, and I was doing this after all the doctors had said he should never sit on the back of another horse. That split second of hesitation was all Tote'm needed. He lunged forward, knocking Emmett down. I released my hold on Pop's leg. Tote'm reared straight up, pawing at the air. Pop still had his left hand on the left rein and was keeping his balance by hanging onto the stirrup leather with his right.

"Get back! Get back, Paddy!" he yelled at me as he took his right hand off the leather. He put it on the rein beside his other hand and pulled with all his falling weight, forcing Tote'm — coming down now — to twist in the air away from Emmett and toward himself. With his feet almost beneath Tote'm, Pop could do nothing but hold his left arm out to break his fall. I made a grab for Pop's arm while simultaneously a long-fingered black hand hooked under his armpit, and we catapulted Pop clear of Tote'm's down-crashing shoulder.

Mom was crying. Pop, Tanza, and I were in a heap. Tote'm was up in a split second and backing up fast. Pop was jerked away from us, his left hand still clamped around the rein. I jumped up off the ground. Tanza lay there, looking like he'd had the wind knocked out of him. Mom was screaming, "Paddy, let loose, Paddy, let loose!" as Pop was dragged across the ground. Emmett grabbed the taut rein. Pop released his hold, and Emmett was pulled back ten yards before he could stop Tote'm. I leaned over, put my hand under Tanza's armpit, and helped him up.

Pop limped over to Tote'm, now in a lathered-up frenzy. Blood was trickling off Pop's left hand. He turned his back toward the cars and looked down at his hand. There was a gash in the fleshy part of his palm where the toe caulk of Totem's shoe must have cut him. Pop pulled his red bandana out of his hip pocket, spread it across his palm, and looked me in the eye. How many times had we gone through this ritual of hiding injuries from Mom, from trainers, from track doctors, from owners. I wrapped the bandana tightly around his hand and tied a square knot over his knuckles.

This time as I lifted Pop up, Tanza was holding Tote'm. It was hard getting him up there. He got on stiffly, not bending at the waist, and he felt heavy, as thin as he was.

The second Pop was on, Tote'm tried to shy away, but Emmett was standing on the other side and Tanza was in front. Up Tote'm went, breaking Tanza's hold on the reins. Pop grabbed the stick out of his mouth and cracked Tote'm between the ears. Tote'm came down, ears pinned back, head shaking. Pop thrust his feet into the irons. Tote'm lowered his head and began wildly, crazily, furiously backing up when Pop let out a bone-tingling growl, dug in with his spurs, and cracked Tote'm hard on the rump.

Mom was still crying. Tanza was helping Brendan get up on Road Trap. Bessie was leaning on the Oldsmobile chanting, "Oh, Lord, help us, oh, good Lord, please help us ..." Tom was circling around on Kangaroo, trying to settle him down.

Emmett grabbed a halter out of the pickup, snapped a shank on it, and he and Tanza walked closer to the first hurdle. I followed them. As usual, after being up on a horse for most of the morning, I felt short, powerless, awkward down on the ground — having to take all those little steps in the thick grass to get anywhere, my line of vision coming from so low down, the ground so close I felt like I was suffocating. I'd have given anything to be on that horse.

## Chapter 14

Pop circled Tote'm clockwise in a large loop a few times, far off, away from us. Then he slowly galloped around toward the first hurdle, riding long, with a shorter hold on the reins than he was renowned for using back when he was the Babe Ruth of steeplechase riders. As he approached the wings, you could hear a growl and then see his whole left arm swing stiffly from the shoulders, out and back, and hear the stick smacking Tote'm hard on the shoulders.

Tote'm tried to jam on the brakes but was too late. He hopped over the hurdle, landing on all fours, immediately ducking to the left and trying to drop his head between his front legs like a bronco. Pop was sitting back. He didn't change his expression or his seat a bit; he just snatched Tote'm's head up and kept his eyes and balance focused on the next hurdle.

Close to the second hurdle, Tote'm tried to bolt to the left. Pop caught him with the right rein. Tote'm slowed and then suddenly picked up speed. No stick had been raised; Pop must've given him a good squeeze with the spurs. Tote'm dived over the hurdle, dangerously low, smacking the wooden box in front and behind and ripping out the brush. When Tote'm landed, a front leg buckled and his nose skimmed along the ground. Leaning back, Pop let the reins slide through his fingers and then, gripping the reins, pulled Tote'm's nose up off the ground and maintained the same steady confident expression.

Jen was repeating, "He's all right now. He's all right now." I knew Mom wouldn't be watching. I pictured her sitting with her face in her hands saying, "I just can't watch. Tell me what happens," as I had seen her do so many times when Pop was whipping and driving into the last fence at Saratoga Springs, Belmont Park, Aqueduct.

Tanza was hollering, "Whoa, Boss; Whoa, Boss," and Pop was squeezing with his legs and heading into the third hurdle faster than that horse had ever dreamed of going into a fence. A few strides away you could just barely notice the horse flinching, thinking of ducking out. Pop had the whip cocked now, held like a conductor's baton. He simply waved the stick along the left side of Tote'm's neck. Tote'm met the hurdle just right, jumping a little high but landing fine.

Emmett hollered, "Goddamn — just like the old days, Tanza!" I cheered to myself, and Emmett slapped me so hard on the back that I had to catch my footing in the deep grass as I was jolted forward. We all felt giddy with relief. I laughed aloud, let out a sigh, wheeled around, and stepped back toward Emmett and Tanza, preparing to watch Pop ease Tote'm up and gallop around to us. But something was wrong; I glanced at Tanza's face expecting to see him grinning but instead saw a furrowed forehead, thick eyebrows uncharacteristically pinched, deep brown bloodshot eyes squinting in concentration. Suddenly, eerily, all laughter and crying and hollering had stopped; there was dead silence except for hooves rhythmically, powerfully pounding the sun-baked afternoon ground.

As I turned to see what had happened, Tanza whispered, "Oh no, Boss; oh no," and I saw Pop and Tote'm at an open gallop heading up the hill toward the fourth hurdle.

Pop looked as he had ten years earlier on Neji or King Commander or my favorite, Crag. He had his hands down low and had lengthened his hold on the reins and had Tote'm pulling against him. "That black bastard" was moving in long, beautiful, sweeping strides up the hill.

Nearing the wings Pop drove him forward by squeezing with his legs, making him lengthen his stride, and confidently asked for a big one. Tote'm stood off and brushed through the hurdle better than any other horse on the place had yet done, Pop looking as he did in those old winning pictures covering the walls at home: whip cocked, hands low, feet a little out in front, rear end a few inches off the saddle, ready to land with all his weight in the stirrups. I would have bet he also had that slight mischievous grin on his face, the same one he had in the photos with the models, the same one he had in the photographs at home, crossing under the wire ten, twenty, forty lengths ahead of the opposition.

## Chapter 14

Emmett and Tanza laughed and shook their heads in disbelief. Mom was crying again, Jen trying to calm her, and Bessie was chanting, "Oh, Lord, thank you, Lord. Thank you, good Lord ..." Pop cantered Tote'm Home back to us. He was loosely balanced in the saddle, his legs rubbing back and forth out in front of him like a cowboy's.

Emmett and Tanza stood on either side of the horse, each grabbing a rein. Pop's face and shirt were drenched in sweat. The bandana had come off his hand. The left thigh of his corduroys was smeared red. He kicked his feet out of the irons and Tote'm's sides quivered. I glanced down and winced when I noticed the palm-length gash in Tote'm's left side where the spur had sliced through the skin, and looked up just in time to see Pop's hand over his head. He was holding his old race-riding stick, whalebone covered in leather, and then the stick was spinning and twirling through the air toward me. I snatched it out of the air as I'd seen Pop's valet, Dick Dwyer, do hundreds of times. It was slippery, with sweat I supposed. I almost dropped it. I looked down at my hand gripping the handle and saw the blood squeezing up between my fingers.

When I looked back up, Pop was standing on the ground, bent over with his hands on his knees, coughing hard. As I began to go to him, he stood up, his left side sagging, and walked toward me with a slight limp, his eyes still contracted into a piercing glare. He stopped and straightened all the way up, the piercing focus subsiding. He grinned, looking into my eyes, and said, "Come on, Bud. I'll give you a leg up."

# 15

## Death in the Morning

Pop pulled his car up to the curb in front of Scotty's Paddock on Union Avenue in Saratoga Springs. We'd just finished with the horses for the morning. Racing fans and gamblers were already walking in the entrance to the track across from Scotty's. Pop held the door to Scotty's open for me. I stepped into the smoky hubbub of the long, narrow barroom, polished bar on the right running down the length of the room, small tables set up on the left, with Pop right behind me. The place was jammed with steeplechase trainers, jockeys, and exercise riders.

We always stopped by Scotty's after work in the morning — except when we had more time and went to Sperry's with Evan Jackson. Pop had told me he had first come up to Saratoga when he was eighteen, back when it was a wide-open town with big-time gambling and plenty of gangsters and prostitutes, and he'd bought a drink or two at Scotty's. It wasn't until he got back to his hotel room and checked his money clip that he realized the bartender had inadvertently given him a fifty dollar bill instead of a five for change. Fifty bucks was a lot of money back then. The next morning after work he returned to the bar, handed over the fifty dollars to the "bartender" — who ended up being Scotty himself, and ever since, we Smithwicks have been treated like royalty at Scotty's Paddock.

We nodded to Scotty, working behind the bar. We sidestepped past a dozen eating, drinking, and smoking members of the hunt and jump set, each of them saying hi to Pop or asking him a question, and sat down at a little table in the back that could hold four. Pop ordered a beer and I ordered a vodka and grapefruit juice. It'd been a hectic morning at work, and I was looking forward to discussing my upcoming race with Pop. The next day, August 7, 1969, was National Steeplechase and Hunt Day, and I'd be riding Tote'm Home in the Cottesmore, a "maiden hurdle" for horses that had never won a major race over hurdles. It had been a long hard road from the day Pop schooled him at the Vosses. I had been the only one on his back every morning since that day. And I had ridden him in my first, and his first, hurdle race at Delaware Park. Neither the horse nor I could believe how fast and wild the race had been, with horses all jumping so tightly bunched together, but we finished fine, in the middle of the pack and gaining. Most importantly, the stewards had been watching him carefully at the start; I had kept him on his toes, and when the starter dropped his hand and snapped the tape, Tote'm and I were instantly at a gallop.

A waitress set our drinks on our table. A shapely redhead about ten or twelve years my senior, in tight-fitting jeans and a light-blue, low-cut, V-neck cashmere sweater, walked in and started looking for a table. Pop stood up and waved her over to us. She walked through the gauntlet of tables, turning the heads of all the men. I stood as she approached. "Hi, Paddy," she said to Pop, kind of bouncing off her toes, everything in the V-neck jiggling around. She turned to me and caught me staring at the V-neck. She looked me in the eyes, gave me a big knowing grin, and then looked back at Pop.

"Who you got with you today, Paddy?"

Pop introduced us. She put her hand out and we shook. She was in no hurry to let my hand loose.

Pop pulled out the chair next to his. "Come on and have a seat with us, Sam," he said.

"Thank you, Paddy," she said. He did a half bow. She sat down and he pushed the chair in. She was seated directly across from me.

Pop ordered Sam a Bloody Mary and asked where she was staying this year. She explained that she was living just a few blocks down Union Avenue in a boarding house on the corner run by a landlady who'd drive anyone crazy. It wasn't much of a room, but it was close to the track. She thought Pop was kidding when he told her that we had just taken a room in the same boarding house. I backed him up — yes, we were in the same house with the same crazy landlady. We had a good laugh and traded stories about her.

Sam and Pop had sandwiches, and I had a poached egg on a slice of whole wheat toast. I was doing 140 the next day, which meant I had to weigh 135. I'd been reducing throughout the entire summer and had lost twenty to twenty-five pounds from my original 160 since graduating from Gilman in the spring.

At first Sam was flirting around with Pop, and I wasn't paying much attention to the conversation — I had heard all this before — and then, the next thing I knew, after her second Bloody Mary and my second vodka and grapefruit juice, she was rubbing her foot between my legs and looking me in the eyes all funny, and when we stood up to leave, she hooked her elbow around my arm, winked at Pop, and said, "I'll give him a ride." We drove back in her car, went up to her bedroom, and she got down to business pretty fast. Afterward, we talked for a few moments — she'd gone to college for a couple of years, had gotten bored with reading books, and had decided to focus her energy on sex. But the men on the campus weren't too exciting, so she got into riding, including some steeplechase races, and had found some good lovers along the way. She explained she was now working as an assistant trainer for a major outfit and that she occasionally had sex with the exercise rider for this outfit — he was a singing, talking, bantering, tough-as-nails "galloping boy" in his thirties who got on twenty-five a day and rode every horse exactly the same, with his stirrups jacked up high and with a big stick. I'd seen, and heard, him in the mornings. She talked about her adventures in this field, gave me a subtle pointer or two for the next go-round, and then fell asleep. This was all an eye opener to me, and a bit of a flashback to Kelly at Belmont Park. It differed greatly from my experiences with girlfriends at home. I tried my best to fall asleep but had so many thoughts whizzing around in my mind that it was impossible. I pulled on my pants and tiptoed back down to Pop's and my room. Pop was lying there, snoring, having a good nap as the honking and brake-squealing of the race-going traffic picked up. I pulled on wool socks, thermal underwear tops and bottoms, and a rubber sweat suit, tying the elastic bands tight around my waist, wrists, and ankles. Then, I put on old corduroys, a turtleneck, a wool sweater, a rain jacket, a wool cap, and tennis shoes.

Walking down the hall, I passed a door that was ajar. Through the opening, I saw Joe Aitcheson in jockey shorts and T-shirt, sitting on the edge of his bed. He had a barbell in his left hand, his elbow on his knee, and he was curling the weight. The veins were popping out of his arm and his bicep bulged, the striations of muscle clearly defined. Sam had hinted she might have gone a few rounds with him — and had had very successful experiences. I felt as if I were now competing with this man of iron on two fronts — in the bed as well as out on the hurdle course.

Head down, I walked out the front door into the August heat. From behind copies of the *Morning Telegraph*, a couple of old men in creaking porch rockers peered out at me over their bifocals. I stepped into my black Ford Falcon with its V-8 and fierce heater, cranked the engine, wound up the windows, flipped the heater on full blast, and took off. I drove around Saratoga for half an hour and finally pulled into the parking lot of the town playground and playing fields. I jogged slowly toward the quarter-mile cinder track. The sun was bright and I was sweating nicely.

Children were swarming over the grounds, screaming and laughing and hopping in and out of the cool spray of the fountain. I spied a tan teenaged girl. In athletic shorts and a loose white softball jersey that made you curious about the newly developed curves you could only imagine, she sat on the edge of the fountain, her bare feet in the water. About my age, she had to be the babysitter of one or two of the children splashing in the fountain. I watched as two little boys in shorts ran laughing and splashing over to her. Reminding me of my girlfriend at home, she leaned back and down, reaching for something on the grass, and her long blonde ponytail swished across her sharp shoulder blades, touching the grass. The babysitter sat back up and handed each little boy a glistening can of Coke. The saliva shot from the glands in my mouth. I looked away and jogged on past the busy swings, slides, and tennis courts.

I ran six laps at a steady pace, then a seventh, the sweat popping off my face in large pellets, the salt stinging my eyes. On the eighth lap, heading into the last turn, my lungs began to burn. I tried to keep up the fast swish-swishing of the steaming clothes, but a slight side ache was turning into a hot coal in my gut.

The track, the kids, and the playground went into a spin. My legs started to go out of control, heels hitting me in the rear. I pictured jumping the last fence and riding for the wire, holding myself together, sprinting for the wire, and slam I was under it. Then I was crouched over, massaging the ache in my side, blood pounding through my head, heart slamming against my ribs. I walked to a goal post, leaned against it, and focused on a single blade of grass. Then I did sit-ups, push-ups, wind sprints, and the duck walk for thigh-burners.

That night Pop took Sam and me out to dinner. Siro's. I had the usual, steak and salad. The steak came with another plate holding a big, beautiful baked potato, with the thick, crisp skin that I loved, and a shot glass-sized cup of the thickest-looking sour cream you've ever seen. I cut an end off the potato, forked it onto my plate with the steak. I knifed into the sour cream, dabbed it onto the potato, and, imitating something Pop did, covered it with black pepper. I had forgotten about Pop, Sam, the upcoming race, even the steak. I hadn't had a potato, even a potato chip, in two months. Pop and Sam were conversing. I easily cut through the skin of the potato with a sharp steak knife, stuck a fork in the morsel, and heard, "Paddy." I looked up. He glanced at the potato and then up into my eyes, without letting Sam know. But I knew, and I momentarily had this terrible sinking, guilt-ridden feeling. I forked the potato off my plate onto the little plate it came on, pushed it and the sour cream away, and had a long sip of my scotch.

After dinner we went to the bar. Sam introduced me to the concept of the after-dinner drink, and in particular to the stinger — brandy and white crème de menthe. Pop had a bourbon. Sam and I were sipping on our stingers. It was getting late, and we were the only people at the bar when this big-breasted woman of about fifty, in an extremely tight, low-cut dress, and with a towering country singer-type hairdo, walked haughtily past us on the way to the ladies' room. We chuckled a little at her demeanor, went back to our conversation, and Sam went back to rubbing the inside of my leg. Then, the woman came out of the ladies' room. There were only four others in the bar, three men sitting at a table, and the old-timer bartender. The woman, head held high, strode regally through the bar, between us and the table of men, and as she passed we all observed that trailing from her dress was a fifteen-foot stream of toilet paper. Not one of us made a sound until she was safely out of the bar, and then we howled with laughter and the bartender gave everyone a drink on the house.

I had one more stinger to settle myself for the night's activities, and then we went back to the boarding house.

* * *

The alarm rang. It didn't sound right. Eyes still closed, I reached across the double bed expecting to feel Pop's shoulder but instead felt the soft skin of a bare shoulder. I slid my hand down and felt the roundness of a breast and for a few seconds had no idea in the world where I was or whom I was with. I watched as she sat up on the edge of the bed, facing away from me, with no clothes on, and pushed in the alarm. All woman. A full woman. How had this happened? What the hell had I gotten myself into? She turned, leaned toward me, red hair falling over her swaying breasts, said, "Good morning, lover," gave me a big kiss, and was off to the bathroom down the hallway. The cars and trucks were already whooshing by on Union Avenue, just outside the window. I glanced at the clock, 5:15. I listened as she turned the water on in the bathroom. My thoughts drifted. There was something going on today … Then it hit: At 2:30 this afternoon I'd be riding Tote'm Home into the first fence of a hurdle race at Saratoga Racecourse. One and seven-eighths of a mile. Ten hurdles. In just over three minutes of running and jumping, the race would be over and the winner declared.

I sat up on the edge of the bed, listening to the water in the bathroom and the cars accelerating away from the light on the corner. I felt drained, gaunt, and still I wondered what my exact weight was. The only clothes I had were my dress clothes from going out to dinner the night before. I pulled on pants and shirt, put the other stuff in a bundle, and tiptoed out into the dark, narrow hallway, past the bathroom door, past the doors of other tenants, down the steps to Pop's and my room. Pop was already gone. I felt a little guilty at first, and then as my eyes fell across the old set of scales, which I had painstakingly calibrated and carefully placed on a flat spot in a corner of the bathroom, I felt my spirits lift because I was confident I was light. I dropped the bundle of last night's clothes and prepared to take a leak, remembering the pounds I'd pulled the day before combined with all the evening activity.

I stood over the toilet and let the urine pleasingly flow — feeling I was getting lighter and lighter, the pounds visibly streaming out of me. I'd been eating just one or two poached eggs in the morning, steak and salad at night, with no salt, all summer, and it was paying off. Anything I drank — which was mainly coffee, juices, vodka after work in the mornings, and scotch in the evenings — went straight through me.

Skin tight against my ribs, cheeks taut, arms and legs honed to the muscle and bone, I stepped onto the scales. The needle wavered back and forth, and steadied on 139. I had to make 140 — which meant I still had four pounds to lose since the saddle, girths, pads, britches, boots, and the fly-weight "cheating silks" used for weighing-in added up to five pounds. I'd lose two pounds at a normal morning of work anyway. And I could pull on a rubber suit, beneath my galloping clothes, for the last few horses I'd gallop.

Later, in the jocks' room, if I weren't light enough, I could get in the hot box — but I wanted to dodge that option. It made me too weak, not to mention a bit sour. The week before, getting ready to ride Arnold W., I'd passed out in it. Luckily, Mark, the big German masseur, was there to carry me out and stick a cotton ball soaked with smelling salts under my nose. I had to make 130 that day. "You're too big for this," Mark had said in his deep voice, lightly massaging me awake. "You got heavy bones like your father. This reducing is not good for you."

I left the apartment feeling good. I was fit and light, and Tote'm Home was fit and well-schooled. All I had to do was get through the morning and early afternoon. It wouldn't be until 2:30 when Pop would be giving me a leg up on Tote'm — until I had the rubber-sheathed reins in my hands, my honed calves pressing against the leather flaps of Pop's old two-pound saddle, my toes in the same aluminum stirrups he had used for years — that I could relax.

Tote'm Home would be a longshot today. That was fine with me. Pop and I had spent countless hours with him, me in the tack with spurs and whip, and Pop on the ground behind him with a buggy whip. We'd taught him to jump, taught him not to rear, not to flip over, not to wheel, not to run out, not to refuse. We'd taught him to go straight.

We'd taught him to respect us. And most of all, we taught him to go when I touched his sides with the spurs and hollered a low hoarse growl. We had to obliterate from his mind the thought of ever again standing at the start.

Heading for our barn, I drove in the entrance to Horse Haven off East Avenue, just a hundred yards from Scotty's Paddock, through the row of trees along the oiled dirt road, took a right, and wound through a maze of barns, manure piles, tractors, walking rings, parked cars, and coffee-sipping horsemen.

Two lithe bays covered with blue-and-white checkered wool blankets were walking around the dirt ring in front of our barn. The trainer in the barn across from ours often sent these two out early, even in the dark, when he "breezed" them. To further cover up his training tactics, he'd have his hot-walkers cool the horses out on our walking ring, instead of his own. He thought he was going to win a big bet on them and didn't want anyone to know how fast they had worked. In particular, he didn't want Old Blue, the clocker who timed the horses when they worked or breezed three-eighths, one-half, or five-eighths of a mile, to catch his horses doing a fast work, and then put the time in black type in the following day's *Morning Telegraph*. If the gamblers saw it, they'd put their money on the horse, bringing the odds down, ruining the trainer's chance to win a bet on his own, personally manipulated longshot. I saw the trainer standing outside his tack room talking to his rider — a galloping girl who had just probably breezed one of the horses. She was wearing black cowboy boots, tight black chaps over blue jeans, a tight red turtleneck, and had a black cover on her helmet with a red pom-pom on top. She looked familiar. She had long blonde hair in a braided ponytail coming out the back of the helmet and was taking a drag from a cigarette as she listened in a non-interested, sulky way to the trainer pulling a filibuster, and I realized that she was Megan McFarlane, my old Saratoga girlfriend — now a hot-shot galloping girl — and still smoking like a chimney. I thought of her smoky breath and of the big breakfasts and the wonderful massages she and her sister used to give Mike White and me after work, and I drove on past her, around our barn, and parked in the back. I walked around a manure pile and up to our shed row.

Steam spurted from the rapidly expanding and contracting nostrils of the two horses walking around our ring and seeped up from under their dampened wool blankets. Between two oaks in the center of the ring, a misty vapor floated lazily out of the rusty-red barrel holding water for washing down the horses. The blue-red flames from a gas burner hissed and beat against the bottom of the barrel and licked up around the sides. When I was a kid, one of my early morning jobs had been to scavenge around and gather up old newspapers and splintery pieces of wood to be used for fuel under those barrels.

There was a background of low, soothing murmurs and rustling in straw, horses snorting and water sloshing, metal clanking against metal. The sharp antiseptic pungency of disinfectant flowed out of our dark blue/light blue — the colors of the Smithwick silks — painted buckets arranged in a line beside the barrel.

"Come on, jock!" hollered Emmett. "Give me a hand." He stood outside a stall holding the twisted corners of an overloaded mucksack — two burlap bags laced together with baling twine and filled with manure. I strode over to him.

Jack, a sharp-witted, sharp-tongued Native American, leaned out over the webbing of Tote'm Home's stall, a rub rag in his hand. "You'd better get your big ass in gear if you want to make 135 today," he hissed at me. Pop had just hired Jack when we arrived at Saratoga and had given him Tote'm Home as one of his four "to rub."

"Mind your own damn business, you lazy Injun, and stop playing around with that horse. You're making him nervous," retorted Emmett.

"This jock is my business. I'm gonna put my paycheck on him this afternoon and if he's not light enough this morning ..." I knew what was coming. I'd heard it a hundred times: "... I'll wrap him up in blankets and bury him in the manure pile ..." — that's the way Jack used to lose weight in his riding days, back before the advent of saunas and airtight cars with heaters; he claimed he'd run a few miles in a sweating outfit, then bury himself up to his neck in the manure pile and drink a pint of Jack Daniels. Jack had a chip on his shoulder and was always criticizing everybody in the outfit, except Pop. He was about five-eight or so, shorter than Emmett or me, and in his sixties. He had thick, powerful forearms, and besides having been able, as he put it, to outride anyone in the country from the quarter pole to the wire — he had actually showed us a few impressive photographs of himself winning races in the 1940s — he had fought in the ring, "had a killer jab," and most likely could have taken the title away from Sugar Ray Robinson or Jake LaMotta, but the Mafia got involved and screwed him over. "That's a lot of shit. Don't believe a word he says," Emmett would tell me. "That Injun couldn't fight his way out of a wet paper bag."

I grabbed the bottom of Emmett's mucksack, dug my fingers into the wet and dirt-embedded burlap, took a deep breath, inhaling the thick ammonia-like fumes, and yanked the heavy sack upward as Emmett rhythmically swung the load onto his shoulders. He took one off-balance step, regained his balance, and grinned back at me. "I got it, jock."

About this time a big, old, rumbling, low-to-the-ground Oldsmobile pulled up in front of the barn. Its seats were crammed with slouched-over figures. A door opened, someone gave a push, and out stumbled Tanza — thin, his cap on sideways, his eyebrows and moustache thick and bushy. Focusing on the idling car, I could see Bessie, his sumo-wife, at the steering wheel. Things had been quite peaceful, and Tanza had been working hard until she rolled into town a couple of days ago. We all knew she was supposed to go back to Long Island in the afternoon and that we just had to get through one more day with Tanza being a zombie. He staggered up to a stall and hung himself over the webbing. Pop walked over to him. "Tanza, why don't you come back in the afternoon at feed time?"

Hanging onto the webbing, Tanza looked at Pop, "Ah, Boss-sh," he slurred. "Ah'm all-ri. Jush nee a cup-a'coffee."

"Tanza, see you at feed time."

Emmett went to Tanza and said something to him. The two of them walked back to the car, Tanza's path not too straight. Tanza fell back into the car and off it rumbled, Emmett shaking his head, "It's that damn wife of his and that damn rot-gut wine."

Emmett walked to Pop, who was sitting on a footlocker outside the tack room. Pall Mall dangling from his mouth, Pop was neatly writing on a legal pad a list of all the horses and how far and fast each would gallop this morning.

"He'll be straight this afternoon, Boss."

"Okay, Emmett."

"I know where he's staying, and he'll be straight."

"Good — we could use him here while we're running the horse."

I stepped across the neatly raked black dirt of the shed row past Pop, on the way to the tack room. I was feeling a little awkward, unsure of what to say.

"Got you a black coffee, Bud. It's on the trunk," Pop said.

"Thanks," I said, stepping into the narrow tack room, feeling relieved. I pulled off the plastic top and inhaled the raunchiness of track-kitchen coffee. It mixed with the relaxed scent of well-soaped leather girths and saddles and bridles that I had cleaned outside in the late morning sun the day before. And with the dewy country smell of fresh wet clover that had just been dropped off.

Pop and I had discovered a few mornings earlier why Emmett, Jack, and Tanza, who usually could not agree on anything, were all suddenly united in their concern that our horses have fresh clover every morning. Pop had picked up a pitchfork and sauntered toward the mound of clover, lying wet and deep green on a burlap bag in the center of our walking ring. Tanza, coming out of a stall a lot faster than usual, had piped up and said, "Oh no, Boss. I'll take care of that. You just leave it right there. I'll move it when you're out on this set."

"Okay," Pop had said, walking away from the clover and winking at me. Tanza went back inside the stall. Pop told me to go up and lean on the webbing of Tanza's stall and be sure he couldn't look out. I did as told.

We'd gone out on a set of horses, and when we returned, a gloom had descended on our three men. We cooled off the horses and got another set out. I still didn't know what was going on until Pop, standing in the tack room, handed me three still-cold, long-necked Budweisers and told me to put them back under the clover. It seemed that the clover man had set up a little sideline business. We went out on our next set, returning to find Emmett, Tanza, and Jack seemingly contented but eyeing us suspiciously.

* * *

I liked to get on an easy horse first each morning to get the blood flowing, and a horse the men had dubbed "Rolling Rock" had been the one all summer. He was a big, good-natured gelding and a great jumper — all you had to do was take a good hold and squeeze with your legs, and he placed himself perfectly at every hurdle, adjusting the length of his stride on approaching a hurdle so that he took off to jump it from just the right spot. He was a joy to school. Some long-striding horses are difficult to set. You end up in a spot where you either have to ask them to stand way off, the fastest way to get over the hurdle but also risky, or you let them put in an extra stride, which is safer but slower and can cause you to lose a length or two on other horses in a race.

We knew Rolling Rock didn't have the speed to break his maiden at Saratoga, but Pop wanted to run him once or twice to let him get some experience and then win some races with him at the hunt meets in the fall. It would be particularly good to have him run well at the Rolling Rock Hunt meeting in Ligonier, outside Pittsburgh — because he was owned by one of the Mellons from Pittsburgh, and then perhaps Mr.

## Chapter 15

Mellon would send us a few more horses to train. The men had heard that the horse might have gone out hunting a few times with the Rolling Rock Hunt Club, and because when we first got him he was "big and fat as a hunter," they'd been disdainful of his prospects as a racehorse and had so nicknamed him. However, there was a play on words here; they'd also been thinking of the beer called Rolling Rock, which was brewed near Ligonier. At first, I hadn't really liked this stable name. Every time someone said it, I pictured a little green bottle of ice cold Rolling Rock beer, but soon the name Rolling Rock was not the beer and not the club; it was this very nice, calm, well-mannered chestnut horse.

With Pop on our "pony," Crag — who still had the fiery temperament of a racehorse — and me on Rolling Rock, we headed out to the training track. For the hell of it, I jacked my irons up short like a flat rider's, shorter than I would on any other horse in the barn because Rolling Rock was so quiet and trustworthy. I felt good, toes in the irons, legs thin and bent sharply, fingers loosely gripping the reins, stick in my left hand, on a big, strong, easy-going horse. We had plenty of rough ones back at the barn waiting for me. Wadsworth, a big strong chestnut, would pull your arms out. He liked to move, full tilt, with his long neck stretched way out and his head close to the ground, leaving you sitting up there with nothing but a lot of air in front of you. I had schooled him one morning at Delaware Park in June as an exhibition for a grandstand full of visitors. He'd taken off with me and had run down over the hurdles as fast as a horse can possibly go, on the flat or over jumps, so fast, his stride so long and powerful that I hardly noticed going over the hurdles. Also waiting for me in the barn was Arnold W., a skinny three-year-old who when you were trying to give him an easy gallop would pull and then as soon as you took a hold of the reins, throw his head to one side, then the other, then flip it right back in your face. There was nothing worse than being hit in the face by a horse's poll — the hard bone between their ears — it would almost knock you out, and you'd be seeing stars for half a dozen strides. Then he'd plunge and dive, never giving you a moment's rest. And there was Tote'm Home, black, sleek, and clever: Pop had taught me never to let him get away with even the slightest trick, his favorite being to wheel — to stop suddenly and spin in the opposite direction.

We walked along quietly, laughing at Crag, who spooked and misbehaved more than Rolling Rock. It was just a few years earlier that I'd been foxhunting him in the winters and riding him in horse shows over the summers. Seeing Pop on a jigging, snorting horse, Tommy Walsh, who had recently retired as a jumping rider and turned trainer, yelled out, "Hey, Paddy — you making a comeback? Who's riding that horse this afternoon — you or Little Paddy?"

We made our way onto Oklahoma, the training track. All business now, I clicked into full concentration. I nodded to Old Blue, the clocker in his little green stand, clucked to Rolling Rock, who broke into a canter. I didn't have to inform Blue that I was breezing. He could tell. Pop wouldn't be riding over to the rail and pulling out his stopwatch if I weren't going to breeze. I tapped Rolling Rock on the shoulder, squeezed with my legs, trying to get him to pull against me. We shifted into a gallop, and I shortened my hold on the reins, focusing on the track directly ahead of me, the horse between my legs. Going around the turn, I blocked out everything else — the dozens of horses walking along the outside rail, the horses all around me pulling up from galloping, the trainers leaning on the rail with their coffees, stopwatches, and cigarettes. I knew Red's coffee truck was pulling up outside a barn and all the men — black, Panamanian, Cuban, Puerto Rican, English, Irish, French, Australian, Canadian — were rushing out and ordering coffee, doughnuts, and hotdogs, and yet I kept it outside the range of my direct vision and concentration. I was ready at any second for one of those horses on the outside rail to bolt into my path, ready for the horse in front of me to stumble and the rider with his irons up too high to go flying off. I kept my rear end low to the saddle, and we galloped around the turn, onto the straightaway on the backside.

Nearing the five-eighths pole, with its black stripes, I pushed with my legs, making Rolling Rock pull harder. I grabbed the stick out of my left hand with my right, growled, and — getting in a little practice on my whip handling — cracked him on the rump. We dropped in on the rail and passed the pole just as we hit top speed.

I couldn't believe how good he felt, how fast he was going. I was down low, keeping a good grip on the reins, out a couple of feet from the deep going on the rail. The white posts holding up the shiny aluminum rail flashed by. I felt lithe, agile; I felt like I was a part of Rolling Rock. If he could keep up this speed — hell, he might win a race here at Saratoga.

Around the turn, through a cloud of mist, I relaxed on him for a few seconds as Pop had taught me to do before asking a horse to make his stretch drive. I felt him swell his chest and then release it. I reached up, took a shorter hold, and started pushing to the rhythm of his long stride. We were almost under the wire — I was preparing to stand up and catch the breeze on my chest knowing everything would be sharp and shimmering and more alive than at any other time — when suddenly his head lurched down.

Instinctively, I let the reins slide through my fingers, leaned back, pulled his head up. He continued to gallop frantically, wildly, one shoulder jerking down with each stride, feeling as if he might flip. I pulled him, lurching and bobbing, to the outside rail, and jumped off. He reared, pawing at the air, struck me on the shoulder, ripping my jacket.

Then he fell on his side. His foot was flopping below the ankle. I watched him bring himself to his knees, force his body to an upright position, and then try to stand on the fractured leg, the ankle bone jabbing into the dirt.

Pop yelled he was going to find a vet. Then Emmett was there. He jumped over the rail: "Go on, jock — I'll take him now."

"No," I said. "No."

Emmett unsnapped the girth, grabbed the saddle to pull it off. Rolling Rock reared, his foot flapping obscenely. Emmett pulled the saddle off just before the horse came down on his side. I was looking into Rolling Rock's frantic eyes, trying to keep the reins from being snatched out of my hand when Emmett flung himself across Rolling Rock's head, grabbed an ear and pinned the horse to the ground. "Whoa, boy. Whoa, boy, that's a good boy," Emmett chanted, stroking Rolling Rock's face.

"You all right, jock? You all right?" Emmett asked.

"Yeah, I'm okay."

"Your shoulder all right?"

I hadn't even thought of it. I cringed and glanced at my right shoulder — hoping it was all right, that there was no problem with it that could prevent me from riding in the race that afternoon. I was wearing my favorite lightweight blue jacket, and the shoulder of it was torn, revealing the ripped checkered lining beneath. I hadn't been in pain, but now the shoulder began to throb.

The vet's truck pulled up to the rail. Pop must've gotten him. "Where's Pop?" I asked Emmett.

He looked up at me. "You know better than to ask that." We both knew Pop didn't want to be there to watch what he knew the vet would have to do.

The vet ducked under the rail, held Rolling Rock's leg, examined it. He ran back to his truck and returned with a huge needle. He stuck it into Rolling Rock's shoulder, the horse thrashing, trying to get up. Emmett hung on. I stood there, uselessly holding the reins, looking into Rolling Rock's terrified eyes, the same gentle eyes that had greeted me first all summer when I ducked under the webbing into his stall to give him a rub on the white star between those eyes and tack him up. I thought of a game we'd played: Every morning, after patting him, I'd turn away from him to get my saddle; he'd nip my bandana out of my rear pocket and then turn around in the stall, facing away from me, the bandana drooped from his mouth, and as I walked toward his head to get the bandana, he would keep turning, until I'd finally make a grab for it, and he'd release it.

Rolling Rock gave a last struggle, his body big and powerful and beautiful, and then, unbelievably fast and all at once, his entire body — his head, his neck, his legs, his tail — collapsed. The big brown eyes stared out vacantly, non-blinking, still, and he was just a huge, heavy, non-breathing, very awkward-looking, impossible-to-move body lying in the dirt, and I was standing there in the deep dirt of the track feeling short as horses and riders approached, slowed, swerved out away from us, and jogged by, the riders not saying a word.

"You go on now, jock," Emmett said to me. "You go on back to the barn. Someone'll give you a ride back."

A little crowd had gathered by the outside rail. I dreaded asking anyone for a ride. I heard, "Pa-trick. Pa-trick," in that way Sam said my name, stressing the first syllable and letting the second trail off. I got in her car.

Back at the barn the mood was somber. No one said a word as I walked down the aisle in front of the stalls. The others had been through it before. They knew it was part of racing. In the tack room, Pop asked me to pull off my jacket and turtleneck. There was a two-inch gash. Pop felt my collarbone and shoulder bones to make sure nothing was broken. He cleaned out the cut with some antiseptic. Letting it dry, he cut four strips of athletic tape, placed them over a square of gauze, and then applied the gauze and tape to my shoulder. "It might be a little stiff by this afternoon," he said. "Get in the hot box for a few minutes to loosen it up; then take a good hot shower and it should be all right."

We kept going. Owners stopped by throughout the morning. We acted as if nothing had happened.

# 16

## Victory in the Afternoon

I galloped my second horse of the morning, Wadsworth, without much enthusiasm, but the mist was clearing, the chill was gone, and the sun was coming out. While galloping Arnold W. at a rather fast clip, I saw Sam, standing in the clocker's stand with half a dozen trainers. We had eye contact; she discreetly nodded and shot me a heart-warming grin.

I tacked up Tote'm Home — Jack had him glistening as if he were going into the show ring at Madison Square Garden. Pop wanted me to jog the troublesome gelding around the Horse Haven pony track and then hack him around just to relax him before the race. Jack was leading Tote'm around the walking ring, giving me all kinds of directions on how to ride the race that afternoon when Betty Bosley Byrd, a childhood sweetheart of Pop's for whom we trained three horses, pulled up in her Rolls-Royce. Jack halted Tote'm, stood directly in front of him, and with one hand on each rein, jiggled the bit in his mouth, and spoke to him in a low, continuous voice, "Whoa, big boy, save it for this afternoon. Whoa — this is our pay day today. You're going to tote home all the money, and old Jack is going to have some fun with his honey ..."

Pop gave me a leg up, and Jack started walking Tote'm Home again. "Paddy," Betty drawled at Pop from her Rolls. "Paddy."

"Yes, Sister."

"Paddy, please get in."

"I can't right now, Sister. We still have a couple of horses to get out."

"Come on, Paddy. I want to show you a horse I'm thinking of buying. Only thing is, he has a problem that may hinder his future as a stallion …"

Pop laughed at Betty's joke and got in the Rolls. Off they went.

\* \* \*

Just a few weeks earlier Pop and I had driven over to Betty's farm in Unionville, Pennsylvania. We were staying at the Skyways Motel, outside of Delaware Park, forty-five minutes from Unionville. Pop and Betty had been very close since childhood. Following is Pop's entry in his diary for Tuesday, June 18, 1935:

*This was one of the nicest*
*days in my life.*
*Betty Bosley came to spend*
*the night at our house.*
*We rode Spotty.*
*Once we all three got on*
*together and she bucked*
*us off but we caught*
*her and put her in*
*the stable.*
*We went wading in*
*the spring-house and*
*we all got wet.*
*On the last ride we*
*saw some gypsies*
*in the woods.*
*We galloped away.*

Three weeks later, on Wednesday, July 10, 1935, Pop began his diary entry:

*To-day I felt lonely*
*without Betty but we went*
*for a ride with Miss*
*Waggonner* [sic].
*Spotty went well*
*I watched some men*
*Making a driveway.*
*Spotty gallopped* [sic] *home*
*And every once in a*
*While I gave her a piece*
*Of sugar.*
*I rode my bicycle and*
*went so fast on the*
*had [hard] road that I bounced*
*up in the air and fell*
*down.*
*I cut my knee which hurt …*

Upon our arrival at Betty's farm, Betty fixed Pop a drink and then asked him to come down to the barn to take a look at the breeding apparatus of her stallion. Seemed he had some kind of wart. I walked down with Pop and a half dozen adults, laughing and carrying their drinks. Pop ducked under the webbing, stepped through the deep straw in the stall, rubbed the colt's face, talked to him. He ran his hand down from the colt's head, down the line of the neck, across his back along the spine. He gently rubbed the horse over his kidneys, whistling to him and talking to him in a whisper. The horse's cock began to drop, to come out of its sheath, not bone-hard, just tumescent. Pop reached under, gripped it, and pulled it toward him and us. It was the thickness of the most muscular part of my arm and the length of my arm from wrist to shoulder, and it had a mushroom-shaped head on its gradually stiffening end — where there was a big black wart. Pop examined the wart, let go of the cock. It swung back and forth. Pop soothingly patted the colt along his flanks and stepped through the deep straw, ducked under the webbing, and was out with us. He pronounced the wart not only safe but also an advantage for this young stallion in his line of work.

Laughing and drinking, we all adjourned to two long tables set up for dinner on the back lawn. Candles, china, white tablecloths, glittering silver, champagne, toasts … I drank a glass of champagne. Then, I heard something. I heard galloping hooves; they were nearing. Instinctively, I thought: a loose horse? Then, out of the darkness our hostess appeared in a white dress, bareback on a big Thoroughbred, galloping toward the four-foot-six-inch post-and-rail fence to a paddock just twenty feet from our table. You could hear everyone inhale deeply and hold their breath. The horse stood off, jumped the fence perfectly. Sighs of relief. Guests reached for their drinks. Chatter. Laughter. Horse and rider turned, and galloped back in, over the same fence. Applause.

Our adrenaline was pumping and we assumed Betty was walking the horse back to the stable when we heard the hooves again, coming up from behind us. I put down my champagne glass, and before I could turn around to look, a horse — 1,300 pounds — was flying over the table with Betty in white flowing fabric aboard and hooves whooshing through the champagne glasses, sprinkling them across the table — leaving puffs of smoke from the snuffed out candles and Betty's deep-throated Bosley laughter hanging languidly over the tables as she galloped away from us.

We left late that night, headed back to the Skyways Motel, Pop driving on the country roads. Then we were on a highway, which was raised up high and turning sharply to the left, the two lanes steeply banked. Pop pulled over, our car just barely fitting on the narrow shoulder between the guard rail on the right and the traffic speeding by on our left. He said he couldn't drive another second. He had to take a short rest. He leaned heavily toward me. I argued. We couldn't stop here. It was dangerous. He said he couldn't stay awake; he needed a little rest. The champagne had my head spinning. Pop lowered himself across the front seat and fell asleep, his head in my lap. The cars streaked by. I didn't know where we were. I didn't know the way back to Delaware, back to the motel. The cars flashed by inches from our left side. I grabbed my jacket, folded it. I pulled Pop's heavy head up, placed the jacket under it, and slid myself out. I climbed over and around Pop, got behind the wheel, pushed his legs over, and when there was a gap in the traffic, I stomped on the accelerator. The tires squealed on the hot asphalt as I tried to get us back into the stream of oncoming cars without being hit. I drove down the highway until I found an exit ramp, pulled off onto a country road, and dozed off. Soon Pop was rubbing my head, rubbing my hair, "Okay, Bud, Okay, Bud, why don't you climb in the back. I'm all right now." I climbed over the front seat, into the back. I heard the click of his lighter and smelled the butane, then the burning tobacco. I slept all the way back to the motel.

**\* \* \***

I galloped three more horses in my sweating clothes. When I reached the jocks' room, I was light enough to skip the hot box.

The cut on my shoulder had stopped bleeding and a bruise was forming. I spent a few minutes in the hot box, as Pop had recommended, then the steam bath, and took a cold shower. Dick put some gauze and athletic tape over the cut. I pulled on Pop's old britches and boots, and a T-shirt, and sat outside on a bench in the dappled shade. While the flat riders weighed out, I studied the past performances of every horse in my race: One was a bad jumper — I didn't want to get stuck behind him; another, I remembered from the spring hunt meets, jumped to the right; and there was a gray horse I didn't want to be near at the start because he kicked. Knowing who the early speed horses were, I rehearsed the way I'd like to ride the race. Tote'm Home was definitely an all-out, one-drive, come-from-behind horse. I wanted to make my move going around the last turn and catch the front horses at the last hurdle — because I didn't exactly ride a finish like Angel Cordero. I envisioned Tote'm Home and me landing in front over the last hurdle and pulling away to the wire.

Finally, I was standing under a tree in the paddock beside Tote'm Home — black, long neck lathered in a soapy sweat, teeth snapping at Jack and Emmett, shoulder muscles twitching, front legs stamping, rear legs kicking. I kept an eye out, making sure none of the spectators got too close. Jack talked soothingly to him while jiggling on the leather shank. Pop and Dick Dwyer — Pop's former valet, now my valet — saddled him. Pop checked the blinkers — two leather cups adjusted to the outside of Tote'm's eyes so that he could not see anything on either side and would focus on what was straight ahead. Pop adjusted the figure-eight, pulling the two thin leather straps down, under the bit, and buckling them behind Tote'm's chin. This was to help steer him; without the figure-eight, he tended to open his mouth wide and the bit slid through his mouth without having any effect. I buckled my chin strap.

Jack led Tote'm around the walking ring in the paddock in a line with the other horses. The clerk of the paddock called out, "Riders up!"

Both of us standing by the horse's shoulder, Pop said, "You know what to do, Bud." He reached down and grabbed my left leg just above the ankle. I sprung up into the saddle. Walking along beside me, Pop set my left foot in the stirrup. I slipped my right foot in the other stirrup and tied a knot in the long jumping-rider reins while Jack led Tote'm Home, jigging and dancing, around the paddock, behind the other horses.

Heading for the gate out of the paddock, leading us through the gauntlet of pot-bellied, T-shirted gamblers holding their programs with one hand, their beers with the other, Jack looked up at me, "All tied on, jock?"

"Yeah, I'm okay. Thank you, Jack."

"See you in the winner's circle," he sang out, unsnapping the buckle of the shank. Tote'm Home took a leap forward. I was ready for it and patted him on the shoulder, "Whoa, old man, take it easy, whoa …"

As we passed under the clubhouse archway, the bugler gave his call. One by one we filed onto the track. At that moment, with the bugler playing and Tote'm dancing onto the freshly harrowed track and with the distance between us and the mobs of people increasing, the tension left me and was replaced with an inner calm.

Tote'm's neck was arched, and he was shaking his head. "Hey, Smithwick," a railbird yelled out at me, "I hope you gave that four-legged chicken a heart transplant!" Another yelled out, "Hey, bugboy — Smithwick! Can you make that horse jump any better than he comes out of the gate!" Still another, "Why if it isn't big bad Tote'm Home who I lost all my money on at Aqueduct. Thought you'd been toted off to the glue factory. Ain't nobody but an idiot going to bet on you today …"

Then I saw this red-faced man running down the rail, waving his newspaper at me. "Mish-ter A.P. Smithwick, Junior, Mish-ter A.P. Smithwick, Junior." He caught up with me, and the other gamblers stared at him as he jogged along, slurring his words. He was in an old tattered tweed jacket and corduroys and had a greasy cap pulled down tight on his head. He looked up at me wildly, "Tell me Mish-ter A P. Longshot Smithwick. Is he ready? Does your old man have him ready?" It was Danny, Danny the gambling addict I hadn't seen for years.

"Yeah — my old man has him ready," I said.

Railbirds were yelling comments at the other riders — "I got my money on you, Joe. Hey, Joe, keep him out of trouble today, will you." I kept my ass low to the saddle and a tight grip on the reins, prepared for Tote'm to spook or wheel at any moment.

We jogged down the track, through a gap in the rail, across the turf course, across the hurdle course, and into the infield. We all cantered slowly, peacefully, in and out of the trees, and then over to the starter. I stuck the middle finger of my right hand through the rubber band that was wrapped around the handle of the stick — a trick Pop had taught me.

"All right, jumping riders; let's go, jumping riders!" the starter yelled, calling out the order of post position. A circle of horses formed around him, jigging and dancing while the riders sat calmly in their saddles, watching the starter.

We circled twice and then started to pull out in a line, by order of our numbers, across the hurdle course. Tote'm Home was feeling a little too quiet beneath me, a little sulky. I seesawed on the reins, pulling the bit back and forth through his mouth, pretending, for the starter's sake, that I was trying to settle him while I was actually giving him a light poke with the spur on the side the starter couldn't see. I couldn't let him stand flat-footed for even a split second — he might stand at the start, refuse to go, which, after all our work, would ruin his entire career; he'd be ruled off running in steeplechase races as well as flat races.

Then we were all even in a line, the elastic tape taut before us. I squeezed my legs; the starter dropped his flag, yelled "Let 'em go!" and the tape snapped.

Instantly, in an incredible burst of speed, we went from standing and jigging into a full gallop, the pack all gathered together, charging the first hurdle. I was closed in, too tight. I pulled Tote'm back a length or two so he could see. The jockeys in front, Ronnie Armstrong and Heinz Schwab, disappeared over the first fence. Surrounded by horses and going too fast, we were swept into the hurdle.

The turf was hard, and the hooves made a loud drumming noise. I got on the inside, saving ground. The lead horses were ten lengths in front, but I knew they couldn't keep up the pace. We galloped around once, all maintaining our positions, jumping four hurdles on the backside, three in front of the stands.

The second time around the clubhouse turn and headed into the backstretch, I heard the jocks behind me start to ride — sticks cracking on rumps. Pop's words, "Wait to make your move, Bud," resounded in my mind. I forced myself to wait. After jumping the first hurdle down the backstretch, I pulled to the outside, wanting a clear path.

I couldn't wait any longer. I asked Tote'm to run.

Ahead of me Ronnie Armstrong's horse took off to jump the hurdle. Ronnie's right arm shot up and he leaned back. Brush flew up into the air. Ronnie's horse was going down. I rode hard into the hurdle, wanting Tote'm to concentrate on it and not on the falling horse. We got in just right, and he jumped it well, whooshing through the top layer of brush. In the air I looked down and saw Armstrong's horse sprawling to the left of me, Armstrong rolling to get away, and another horse, Chapel Street, going down with his jockey, Heinz Schwab, in the confusion.

There were still three in front. I gave Tote'm a breather for a few strides, waiting, as Pop had taught me, until I felt the horse's chest swell on the intake of a deep breath and then contract as he exhaled. With a sense of release, I took my right hand off the rein for a split second, opened my palm, and spun the stick around so I was holding it like a baton. I got my rhythm, letting him take one stride, then another, and then, simultaneously, I gave a low growl, raked him with the spurs, and reached back and cracked him with the stick. Upon making contact with him, I felt a bolt of pain shoot through my shoulder. I felt Tote'm respond, dig in. I felt him trying with all his heart. We passed two on the turn. I was pushing hard; my thighs were on fire and my lungs were bursting. Now there was only one left, Marocco, with the classic rider Joe Aitcheson in the saddle.

We were gaining on him, reeling him in. Joe was going easily — sitting still, hugging the hedge — not knowing we were coming. We sneaked up on his outside. Then we were head and head, and Joe looked over at me, startled. He pushed, trying to keep up, and I heard him whipping as we galloped past him.

Three or four strides away from the last hurdle right in front of the grandstand, I had the choice of pushing Tote'm to lengthen each stride, and asking for a big one, or letting him get in close. I didn't want to risk falling, so I let him take an extra stride; we got in a bit close, had to slow for a split second, and he whooshed through the top layer of brush, popping me slightly forward. Then we were headed for the wire.

The crowd was roaring, and I couldn't hear if there was anyone near me or coming up from behind. "Never look back," Pop had told me. "Throws a horse off balance. You should sense where the other horses are." I cracked Tote'm one more time with the whip and kept my eyes focused straight ahead. Lungs sucking in fire, thighs burning, begging me to rise up, stand up, release the pressure, I stayed in my tuck, I pushed and pushed, the wire approaching, nearing, no one around us ... and we were under the wire.

Instantly, everything went from speeded up and burning and pushing and fast as hell to slow motion. I stood up straight in the irons, catching the air on my chest, leaning back on the reins, releasing the tension in my neck. Tote'm Home put his head down lower than usual, stretching out his long neck, inhaling the oxygen he needed, and leaned against me. I eased him up going around the clubhouse turn, in no hurry, while the other riders, all older, many of whom had ridden with my father, galloped up alongside me and congratulated me: "Well done, Smithwick," "Nice job, Little Paddy," "Way to ride," "Your old man couldn't have done it any better."

One of the groundsmen opened a gap in the rail to the track. We filed out onto the track, the dirt at first feeling foreign, deep. We galloped back around the clubhouse turn, easy, floating, so easy, letting Tote'm catch his breath, letting the others go ahead of us, savoring it, thinking back on the winter's work, on Pop schooling him that one day at the Vosses', on all that had gone into this win, on how Pop always stood by this horse when others said to get rid of him. Nearing the winner's circle, I slowed to a jog and then pulled up. I looked up at the stewards in their box in the clubhouse, waved my whip at them. One nodded and pointed to me, giving me permission to dismount, and I tossed the stick, spinning, twirling, through the air toward Dick Dwyer. And Pop, beaming, standing there beside Emmett and Jack, both beaming — a laugh ran through my chest as I thought of Jack winning his big bet, his whole week's pay on this horse, a longshot! — Pop stepped forward in front of Dick, snatched the stick, his old whip made of whalebone covered with leather, out of the air as he strode toward me, looking — happily, proudly — up into my eyes.

# PART IV

# BREAKING AWAY

# 17

## Going Home Again

We sat at the bar in Esposito's. It was Pop and I, the three Esposito brothers — John, Ralph, and Junior — and a few others. Pop and I didn't usually go there in the evening, but there we were, and it was getting late, and I was trying to make a decision.

I had enrolled at Washington and Lee University in Lexington, Virginia, and classes were about to begin. It was early September. We had shipped the horses from Saratoga to Belmont Park, and I had ridden a race that day. Pop needed help at the barn. He needed someone to gallop the horses. And there would be horses running in steeplechase races during the fall meet at Belmont Park. I wanted to skip college and stay at Belmont with Pop and ride races. I sat there drinking double scotches, and John, Ralph, Junior, and Pop — not one of whom had ever attended college — talked me into going.

The next morning I packed my bag and met my old Saratoga buddy, Willie Dixon, at Esposito's. We had one for the road, hopped in the car — the turncoat had traded in the Packard for a grandmotherly 1960s sedan — and started the long drive to Virginia. Willie was returning for his second year at a small college in southeastern Virginia and was nice enough to make a detour and drop me off at Washington and Lee.

## Chapter 17

Neither of us had ever seen Washington and Lee. We philosophized all the way down.

Driving into Lexington, we saw some rigid, militaristic-looking buildings, thought they were Washington and Lee, and almost turned around and went back up the road. Lost, we headed up an alley, where we spotted an old friend, Matt LaMotte, who was standing out on a porch, in bow tie and jacket, sipping a gin and tonic. It turned out he was attending a welcoming cocktail party for freshmen. Matt explained we had been looking at Virginia Military Institute, a place I later came to know and respect. He directed us to my dormitory.

I spent a year and a half at Washington and Lee. The first fall I lived in the dorm, attended classes, ran every day, ate almost nothing, and intermittently flew up to Belmont Park to ride a race for Pop. I was riding Arnold W., who always got in light, sometimes at 130. There I was at college; the Vietnam War was going on, my classmates were staying up until 1:30 or 2 a.m. drinking beer, smoking pot, arguing about politics and the war, eating pizzas, and I was reducing. There was no racetrack near the university, and I couldn't stay in good shape. I couldn't keep my timing for jumping the fences, my feel for the horse, or my fitness for riding a finish. It took forever to get to Belmont from Lexington: I had to drive the hour down to Roanoke, catch a puddle-jumper, take it to a major airport, and then wait for a plane to Kennedy Airport. By the time I got to the last few fences of the race on Arnold W., I was wrung out. The steeplechase season ended in November, and my body immediately shot back up to its normal weight of 160 and past that to 165.

In January I started looking in earnest for a farm where I could gallop some horses so I could get fit for the spring races and make some money. Pop had a good little timber horse we called Big Eyes, and I was supposed to ride him that spring. While I was in the classroom at Washington and Lee, Pop was working with Big Eyes every morning. One Saturday I drove over to Charlottesville to meet a renowned horsewoman who I'd been told could set me up with some horses to gallop. It was too long of a commute, but I was so desperate that I drove over to see what might be available.

At sixty-five or so, she was fit and tough. The moment I arrived we took off "beagling." On foot we followed a pack of beagles that were on the scent of a rabbit for miles and miles around the countryside. At every estate we passed through, the well-dressed owners would greet us in front of their house with a tray filled with glasses of sherry. We returned to my hostess' house for dinner. She and I and her older but equally hard-drinking sister had dinner and drank and laughed and told racetrack stories late into the night before I drove the two hours back to Lexington.

I roared into the parking lot of the Beta House. I was joining the Beta Theta Pi Fraternity ("Never Date-a-Beta"), the wildest house on the campus, because my good friend Matt LaMotte said that was the thing to do. I didn't understand the fraternity business; it made no sense to me at all. Here Mom and Pop thought I had gone off to college to learn from books and professors, and my first two weeks on the campus all I did in the evenings was walk from one fraternity house to the next to drink beer and answer silly questions about fast-driving, hard-drinking, car-wrecking nights I'd lived through, nights I'd thought I'd come to college to get away from.

"Is it true you once …?" the fraternity brothers asked. I had thought that on coming to this university more than two hundred miles from home I would leave behind this notoriety. It had developed in the normal way — from people witnessing and laughing and gossiping about my escapades, most of which were good-natured and harmless. Nevertheless, some of these larks, especially when inflamed by alcohol, were driven by something deep inside me that I did not even try to understand — this desire to do the wildest thing, to take the biggest chance, to do what no one else would on a given night: drive the car at sixty miles per hour off the road and between two gas station pumps and back onto the road; turn off the headlights late at night on approaching an intersection with a stop sign at top speed, yell out, "Columbus took a chance," and barrel on through; climb up a two-story ladder, scuttle across a slippery slate roof, then shimmy up a rain spout into a girl's room; dive into a friend's swimming pool through a hole in the ice in February, swim the length of the pool under a three-inch layer of ice, then pop out through a hole in the ice at the end.

On arriving at Washington and Lee, I thought I would be leaving behind whatever it was that spurred me to tilt the bottle up, forget all worries, and burn through the night. I thought I would ease up on the drinking. Yet, here I was living in some kind of anachronism: I had entered a world out of another century, out of the post-Civil War era, a world where one was judged by how fast he could drive, how much he could drink, how many escapades he could squeeze into one night, how well he could fight, how many nights he had spent in jail.

To top it off, once I signed up for this fraternity, matters worsened. We began having "hell nights." I'd be sound asleep at 2 a.m. up in the dorm when an older fraternity brother would sneak in my room and roughly awaken me. Along with the other "pathetic, slimy, snotty-nosed, disrespectful, neophytic, pencil-dicked pledges," I would rush down to the Beta House. There, an older fraternity brother, a true ass-hole, would torture us for about three hours, putting us through all sorts of athletic endurance drills, wearing us down until we were a trembling, crying, vomiting mass of "pledge shit." We had to do everything together. If one of us screwed up, then we all had to make it up.

*  *  *

Returning from my day of beagling and night of drinking with sixty-year-old women, I pulled my Falcon into the back parking lot of the Beta House, noisily skidding to a stop on the gravel. I strode in through the back door. It was late, and I was showing off. It was Saturday night, or early Sunday morning, and half a dozen fraternity brothers were sitting around the living room, drinking, smoking, and playing poker. When they saw me, instead of walking up and slapping me on the back and asking where I'd been, they all quieted down and my "big brother," Joe Bosley, a wonderful and brilliant junior from Shreveport who was pre-med and had an impossible 4.0 average, told me there was an emergency; I should call home right away.

There was only one phone in the building, a pay phone, on the right where you walked in the back door. Joe gave me some change. I dropped the coins into the slots, called collect, and squeezed into the nook.

"Hello." It was Mom. She sounded groggy.

"Mom, what's going on?"

"You need to come home," she said, her voice muffled. "Your sister Sallie ..." she stopped talking for a few seconds. I pictured her holding her hand over the receiver. I heard her take a breath. "Patrick, Sallie was in an accident and you need to come home." She was whispering. She was trying not to awaken Pop.

"What happened, Mom? Could you tell me what happened?"

"She was burned. She has burns all over her body ..."

Joe walked up to my room in the dorm with me. I was going to leave immediately. I wanted to leave that second. He talked to me, calmed me down, reasoned with me, talked me into getting some sleep first.

I collapsed in bed, slept a few hours, then raced home early the next morning, hitting eighty, ninety, one hundred miles per hour as I chanted prayers the entire way. I drove directly to the Greater Baltimore Medical Center. At first the doctors were not sure Sallie would survive. She was ten years old and flames had exploded on her as she was doing a routine household chore. The doctors were not sure her body could withstand the trauma.

I got up early every morning and rode Pop's horses at the track, then helped around the farm. I went to the hospital to see Sallie in the afternoons. Mom spent almost all her time at the hospital. My grandmother Whitman lived at the hospital for three weeks, twenty-four hours a day. My grandmother Smithwick visited the hospital frequently but her main focus was on around-the-clock prayer, positive thinking, and total immersion in the practice of Christian Science healing, accomplished in her house on the Hydes farm and while walking through her favorite fields.

Mom was shattered. Pop was weakened. Sallie kept hanging on.

I was over at Tom Voss' one afternoon having a good time with my girlfriend, Phini, who was a senior at the nearby Oldfields School. There was an eclipse that day. Phini and I had been celebrating the eclipse out in a field at the farm by drinking Bloody Marys, and I had been drinking to forget about my sister's pain and future. After a while we drove over to the Vosses to see Tom and some of the gang. My friends had gone off somewhere, but Tom's older brother Ned, who reminded me a little of Elvis Presley and was about as cool as you could be, was there with his group of friends. Ned raced motorcycles. A few of us were standing around as Ned and some of his friends roared their motorcycles down the long drive, pulled them up in front of us, and then took off again. Then Ned climbed off his bike with great style and went into the house to get something, leaving his shiny, brand new, high-powered dirt bike parked in the driveway..

I threw my leg over the bike, put my hands on the handle bar grips, and tried to get a feel for it. One of Ned's friends came over and told me I should probably get off the bike. I said I would, but asked if first, he would show me how to get it started. "All right," he said.

The engine hummed between my legs and I eased the motorcycle out onto the gravel driveway and then I yanked my wrist down and gunned it, and ... it took off, even reared up. I went flying out the quarter-mile driveway. Faster, faster. The wind ripped at my hair, pulled at my eye sockets. It felt magical, powerful. Faster than breezing a horse. The driveway was ending and the road was coming up —

Monkton Road, a major road. I had no idea where the brakes were. I didn't know how to stop this thing. It roared louder and louder. I flew onto Monkton Road, swerved to the left, shot down the road twenty yards, and swerved to the right into another driveway, the Secors' entrance.

I realized that to slow down, I had, out of instinct, pulled back on the handlebars, as if they were the reins of a horse, and it hadn't worked. I still had no idea where the brakes were. I eased my grip on the handlebars, and the intensity of the roar lessened. Just then I hit a speed bump in the driveway, which flung the motorcycle up into the air and shot me back. The engine roared — trying to hang onto this machine, my grip had tightened in the air on the throttle and twisted it back. On landing, I jetted forward. There was no way I could make the upcoming turn where the driveway curved to the right. I steered the machine off the driveway, onto the lawn. Forty yards before me was a four-foot stone wall. I was headed right for it. I was flying, bumping along on the grass. All I could do before I hit was lean to my right. I slammed into the ground, my right leg taking the pressure. The motorcycle kept going, hit the wall, flipped over it, and landed on the other side in the middle of a cocktail party. I was knocked out. I awoke encompassed by a circle of gawking bystanders. One adult lectured me, "You could've been killed. What were you thinking? Do you realize you just missed hitting a car on Monkton Road by a few feet ..." A friend of Ned's kept badgering me, "Look what you've done! You've ruined Ned's motorcycle! You've ruined his new bike. He was supposed to race it next week."

Tiger Bennett drove me to the hospital. Phini sat in the back of the car with my head on her lap as I moaned and groaned. My body felt shattered, but no one place felt worse than any other. I was sure I was just badly banged up, maybe a broken collarbone or some cracked ribs. I wasn't bleeding. I was an expert at going to the Greater Baltimore Medical Center emergency room.

# Chapter 17

Just a few years earlier Bobby Burke, the renowned show ring rider and a great friend of Pop's, had driven Tom, Tiger, and me there in the middle of the night after we had totaled Bobby's wife's car, a high-powered Pontiac convertible. Tiger had been driving us home from a party at the Merrymans, "schooling," that is, jumping, all the bumps on a very bumpy country road. We'd come down off of one jump, missed the sharp upcoming turn, gone through a telephone pole, through the side-rail of a little bridge, and landed, engine smoking, in a stream. Tiger and Tom had been knocked out. Steam and smoke poured from the engine. I was worried it would explode. I pushed and pushed on the doors, but they were jammed shut. Tiger and Tom lay up against the doors, on either side of me. I pounded on the window, trying to break it. Suddenly, a long, sharp knife blade punctured and sliced an opening in the canvas roof, just inches above my scalp. It was two men who had been on their way deer hunting. They drove us back to Mom and Pop's, where a party was going on. Blood spouted from a gash in Tom's forehead. A flap of Tiger's ear had been ripped off and dangled, leaking blood from his earlobe. No one paid much attention to us, and Bobby took us to the hospital.

On driving in, through the dark, Bobby's favorite expression, when he saw the headlights of a car approaching us, was, "Let's split those two motorcycles." Bobby looked worse and crazier than any of us. First of all, he was wearing my nineteenth-century jodhpurs with leather-lined calves and a big flair from the knee to the hips, and the jodhpurs had dried blood all over them. Secondly, he had a terrible black eye and cuts all over his face. They'd all just left Goldberg's and had adjourned to our house after Bobby, who'd been having too much fun, had been taken outside by Abe Goldberg, the owner. Bobby said, "Okay, you big fat bastard. You get the first three punches. I get the last three." By the time Abe finished with his three punches, it was time for everyone, including Bobby, to head back to Prospect Farm. When Tom,

Tiger, Bobby, and I arrived at the hospital, the emergency crew was waiting for us — Mom had called ahead — and they immediately went to Bobby. He had to fight them off and steer them to Tom and Tiger.

* * *

At the emergency room after wrecking Ned's dirt bike, I was put on a hard cot, given some drugs, and pushed in and out of X-ray machines. I drifted in and out of sleep, and then I awoke to Pop's hand squeezing my shoulder. I looked up into his face. It was stern. He was looking down at me. "You won't be able to ride Big Eyes now."

"What do you mean?" I asked.

"You won't be able to ride Big Eyes this spring."

"Yes, I will. Sure I will."

"Look what you did to your leg, Bud."

I had been lying there, still. At this, I tried to bend my legs. The left one bent. The right would not bend; my knee hit something hard. Pain knifed through the kneecap. I felt my thigh with my hand. Hard, hard — the doctor had put a full-length cast on the leg. Then the doctor was there. And Pop was gone.

"Why do I need this? When can I take it off?"

The doctor looked down on me. "You were very lucky, son. You are very lucky it wasn't worse," he said, tapping the cast, "Furthermore, you could have been killed."

"When do I get this thing taken off?"

"And no helmet. Why were you not wearing a helmet?"

"I don't know. I don't usually ride motorcycles. I just hopped on one and didn't know how to control it."

He stared down at me.

I tried to move my leg, and the pain shot through the kneecap again. "How long do I have to have this cast on?"

"Eight weeks. You have a break at the knee cap, and for this to heal you must not use the leg, bend it, or put weight on it for eight weeks."

Eight weeks, I thought. I could probably cut it to five. I'd be fine. I could still ride Big Eyes.

"You'll be on crutches. The only way this break will heal correctly is if you keep this cast on. And then, when you take the cast off, your leg will have lost all its muscle tone. It'll take another four or five weeks to get the strength back in your leg."

A stream of black, inky guilt enveloped me. I had let Pop down. I had let my sister down. I had let the family down. I wouldn't be able to help with the horses this spring. I wouldn't be able to ride Big Eyes. Sallie was in this same hospital, just a few floors up. Her injury was life threatening. It would affect her all her life. And here I had done this stupid thing.

"Son," said the doctor.

"Yes, sir." That's how we had always answered our teachers at Gilman, and I was comfortable with it.

"You look to me like you've been drinking."

I didn't say anything.

"Were you drinking?"

"Yes, I was."

"I'd advise you to watch the drinking."

"Yes, sir."

"You've been given a great deal, and you should be able to give back to society. You don't want to cut your life short."

I was quiet. I was no longer drifting in and out of sleep. I was awake in a nightmare. When I arrived home, I lay in my bed with Tippy, with the Hunt Cup rail, and with Phini. The heavy hospital painkillers wore off, and I awoke with sharp pain shooting through my kneecap every time I moved my leg. The next morning Phini helped me get the Hunt Cup rail out of the bed and toss it.

My sister Sallie was in the hospital for a long time. She underwent terrible pain. She began to heal. She went through operations. More pain. She pulled through. One doctor said he'd never seen such a recovery — it had to be the Christian Science, my grandmothers' praying and caring and practicing of Christian Science.

I returned to Washington and Lee and finished the spring semester. It was the first time in my teenage years I had been away from horses, away from the racetrack, away from reducing and trying to stay fit and getting up at five to ride before classes. I had an interesting semester participating in the intellectual life of Washington and Lee, which I had discovered outside the façade of the fraternities, and I even came to enjoy and appreciate my fraternity — along with some of the escapades that were Beta House inspired. I joined in the anti-war movement, went to rallies, marched (with crutches and cast) on Washington, D.C. I had amazingly dedicated professors who were devoted to treating every member of the class as an individual. My cast came off, and that summer I went back to work for Pop. I lived at home, helped Mom in the afternoons with the farm, and saw more of my sister Sallie, who had regained her strength and health.

I spent one more semester at Washington and Lee. I had always thought grades were a very silly by-product of education, and during my freshman year I had felt freed from their tyranny. In the fall of my sophomore year, I cranked it up again, played the grade game, received good marks, and painstakingly filled out a thick handful of forms and questionnaires so that I could be an exchange student at Johns Hopkins University in Baltimore for the spring semester, allowing me to be at home with my family, help Pop with the horses, and make money through riding to pay my tuition.

I went home for Christmas. I completed my interviews at Hopkins; all the paperwork had gone through. I took a deep breath, and suddenly Tom Voss announced he was going to Ireland for two weeks to visit some of the great racing stables, meet with some bloodstock agents and trainers, and go foxhunting. A friend of his family had set this up as part of his education as a horseman, but Tom didn't really want to go alone. Overnight, Mom, Pop, and Tiger decided I would go with Tom, and we would visit my many cousins.

## Chapter 17

* * *

It was late morning. Tom and I were in Ireland at my cousin Dan Moore's having one of the best times of our lives. Dan had kept us out until two in the morning, bringing us to every pub in County Meath, introducing us to his friends, and insisting we allow him to treat us to just one more. On arriving back at the Moores', I'd read a message written on an envelope and left on my bed: "Important — call Hank Slauson at Beta House." Hank was a wild man with curly red hair who'd become a great friend of mine at Washington and Lee. We'd gone on all kinds of midnight adventures, most of them landing us in the local jail of a Virginia town, where Hank would sing and carry on and misbehave and taunt the guards, even take his shoe and slap the sole noisily *thwapp-thwapp-thwapp-thwapp-thwapp-thwapp* down the wall of bars, while happily belting out a ribald ballad, causing me to think we'd never be released. It was a bit late to be making calls from the Moores' phone. I put the message on the bedside table, planning to call in the morning.

Late the next morning Tom and I were sipping scalding hot tea, preparing to go back out in the chilly rain and get on our third set of racehorses. I was talking to an international operator, giving out a complex formula of numbers, and calling and calling the Beta House. "No one is answering," the operator told me in her beautiful Irish accent. "Let it ring; let it ring," I told her. Finally, someone answered. Yes, he would wake Hank. Just then, Dan's son Arthur opened the door to the kitchen, looked at me on the phone in disbelief, said, "Come on, come on now, jockeys — the horses are tacked and the lads are waiting!" and shut the door.

Hank picked up the phone in the Beta House. I pictured him standing there in the telephone nook by the back door in his boxers. "Jesus, Paddy," he said, "couldn't you have called at a better time?"

"Sorry, what time is it there?"

"I don't know. Five-thirty? Fuck it. Paddy, we've got a little problem."

The semester had begun at Washington and Lee, Hank explained. The Hopkins semester did not begin for another two weeks. The Washington and Lee admissions people had received word from Hopkins that I could not attend as an exchange student — there was a problem with the paperwork — and the only way I could attend Hopkins was as a transfer student. "You're in limbo, Paddy. Right now, you're not enrolled here or at Hopkins. You're practically a fucking dropout. What the hell do you want to do?"

I took a sip of hot tea and told Hank, "I'll transfer to Hopkins." I hung up, stepped outside, and got a leg up onto a big beautiful Irish steeplechaser. Hank hung up, caught two more hours sleep. Then he got dressed, hiked up the hill to the Washington and Lee admissions office, talked to his friends there, called Hopkins, worked through the red tape, and got me a spot in the sophomore class at Johns Hopkins University at the end of January. He made it happen.

# 18

## "Hey, Mister Tambourine Man, Play a Song for Me ..."

By my junior year at Hopkins I had saved up some money and decided to quit the racetrack: to quit riding races and quit galloping horses in the morning. I was engaged to a young woman I'd been going out with, on and off, for a few years. We had been living together for a year, and I was now going to do the mature thing. I had had enough hanging around the drinking and cussing and joking and smoking and sexual high jinks of racetrackers. I had won a couple of scholarships at Hopkins that were going to help pay my tuition, and I had decided to concentrate on my studies without the distraction of horses. Pop had a string of good horses and he was doing fine; he supported me in my decision.

One February night I was studying in an office I had set up when the phone rang in the living room. Carol answered it, and I could tell from the way she was joking and laughing that she was talking to Pop. Then I heard, "Yes, he's here. I don't know. I don't know. You ask him." And I had a feeling about what was to come.

Pop had a new horse at the track, he told me, a little chestnut called Tambourine Man. The owner had sent him this one horse, a rogue, and the deal was if Pop could get Tambourine Man going right, could turn him into a jumper and win a race or two, then the owner would send him plenty more horses. Could I come down to Pimlico and get on him in the morning?

"In the morning?" I asked. "Tomorrow morning?"

"Yes — tomorrow morning would be good."

"Just one morning?"

"Well, maybe a few. How about a week? Just to get him going right?"

"What's he doing wrong?"

"None of these riders can get him on the track. I wouldn't ask you, Bud, if I didn't need you."

"All right ... I'll see you in the morning."

"Thanks, Bud. We'll have him ready."

I hung up and felt a wave of defeat and frustration collapse over me. I hadn't been on a horse for two months. I wasn't fit for riding. I was fit for studying. My mind was honed for books and professors and philosophic questions. I was reading short works and poems in French by Baudelaire, Saint-Exupery, Gide, and Rimbaud. I was reading Hemingway's "The Snows of Kilimanjaro," "A Clean, Well-Lighted Place," and "Fifty Grand." I was taking a journalism course and writing for the *Johns Hopkins News-Letter*. I was in a creative writing class, my first, with a graduate student. I pictured myself a graduate student at Hopkins one day, or a foreign correspondent stationed in France. And, I was off the sauce — not completely, but I'd reined in the drinking and hadn't pulled any wild nights for a couple of months. I definitely had not been having any drinks in the mornings.

Carol and I had had our differences on my leaving the track. She had been negative about the track and then, over the summer, had gotten attached to it. I felt like an alcoholic who has worked to stop drinking, practically succeeded, and then felt forced by family loyalty to have one drink every morning (knowing the one would lead to three or four) for seven straight days.

I drove down to Pimlico the next morning, feeling like the old-timer who had retired, the Hemingway fighter who had hung up his gloves but had to come back to the ring one more time. I was Jack in "Fifty Grand." It was cold as hell. I parked outside the barns and walked into the backstretch, head down, shoulders hunched, hands jammed into my pockets. The wind whipped pieces of hay and straw and sheets of old *Daily Racing Forms* up and down the asphalt between the barns. A sheet of newspaper would take flight until it swatted into a barn, looking for a second like it was plastered there. Then another freezing gust would come along and the sheet would go tearing and flapping off. Not good riding weather, especially on a horse no one could get on the racetrack.

I walked to the barn where Pop had the dozen stalls. No one was getting horses out on the track yet. The top and bottom doors to the stalls were still closed. I could see a line of light at the bottom of the tack-room door. It was 6 a.m. I had an 8:30 class in architecture. I had only signed up for the class at such an early hour because I knew I wouldn't be galloping horses. I had recently won a scholarship from an eccentric philanthropist for my ideas on how to improve life in American cities through innovative architectural concepts. That's what I won it for, in theory. I knew perfectly well that I had been chosen over the narrowed-down field of a dozen finalists waiting outside this old high-roller's office for a completely different reason. The other applicants in the waiting room were dour. They pored over their architectural plans as we waited. They looked over charts and diagrams and lists of statistics. One after another they filed into the big room and exited a few minutes later. By the time I was allowed in, the poor old man was bored to tears. A slick assistant, dressed in a pinstriped suit, sat beside the gentleman and gathered the materials. In my letter to the philanthropist, I had mentioned how I was working my way through Hopkins, paying my own tuition, by riding racehorses. He immediately inquired about this, and soon I was regaling him with racetrack tales — while his assistant grew more and more fidgety and kept trying to interrupt and ask me for the details of my architectural plans. Soon, instead of my just spouting off, we were conversing and having a good time. Our conversation drifted away from horses, to architecture, and I explained that my main ideas came from my love of the countryside, my studies of Frederick Law Olmsted, who designed Central Park in New York, and my love of running and riding. My plans focused on incorporating vegetation on the tops of urban and suburban office buildings. I thought cities needed to aggressively buy up and take over spaces, whether one building or whole blocks, and create more parks and green space. I wanted to clean up old railroad beds and turn them into places for people to walk, run, bicycle, and even ride horses. This was all talk. I had no specific plans and had no idea of how to do an architectural drawing. The assistant finally ushered me out. The philanthropist awarded me the scholarship, which paid for the class in architecture, plus one in art history.

I opened the tack-room door. My Uncle Charlie, who was actually my great-uncle on my mother's side, and Janon Fisher, with whom I'd ridden in the Hunt Cup a few years earlier, were sitting on the tack trunk opposite the door. Pop, in his insulated coveralls, was sitting on the corner of the desk, cigarette in his mouth, and Emmett was on a flipped-over bucket, his face a little thinner than usual. The thickness of the warm air from the fired-up gas stove, mixed with the sweet scent of whiskey, hit me. There was no sign of assistant trainer Sal Tumenelli, and I didn't bother to ask where he was. No one on the racetrack had days off or took vacations, but I knew it was a Monday, and I knew that Sal often had a big night Sunday — first, playing in a high-stakes poker game, and then, if he'd played well, investing his winnings in a brothel down on Baltimore's notorious Block, where Sunday nights were discount nights. Thus, on Mondays, Sal was usually late to work, laughing and happy as could be when he did arrive.

The wind billowed into the room, stirring up whirlpools of dust, and I forced the door shut behind me. Janon, in a pair of thick corduroys and a puffy down vest, said, "Hey, A.P., where you been?" (Alfred is my first name; Patrick, my middle.) I could see the necklines of a waffled insulated undershirt and a heavy sweatshirt beneath his green flannel shirt. His old Irish cap was pulled down over his eyes, as if it were sunny in the tack room. He reached behind the trunk and came up with a fifth of Early Times. "Have a shot of courage, A.P." Janon was a great friend of Pop's and trained four or five horses on the backside of our barn. "No thanks," I said.

"Maybe you'd better if you're getting on this horse," Pop kidded.

"Help your nerve," said Janon.

"Al," Emmett drawled, making it sound like two syllables. "You better hadn't be having any of that." He coughed a few times. "I want you on the ball …" Emmett, and a few others around the barns, had started calling me "Al" for my first name. "On the ball, Al, you need to be on the ball to get on this horse," Emmett asserted, still seated — unusual for him — on the bucket. (When I'd been riding races, I was listed in the program as A.P. Smithwick Jr. My father had always been listed as A.P. Smithwick. There wasn't enough room to use the "Alfred" or the "Patrick" in the narrow column of the program where the riders' names were given. So some of my racetrack friends called me "A.P." It was a nod to my life as a jockey. Yet, it was also what many of Pop's friends called him. One morning at work, someone had inquired what the "A" stood for. Soon, jokingly, they were calling me "Alfred," and then it was shortened to "Al.")

I compromised. I took the bottle from Janon, held it by the neck, tipped it up, and took a good swig. It felt smooth and sweet and like something from long ago pulling me back. It warmed my throat going down and felt good when it lit up my belly. I doubted that any of my Hopkins classmates beside whom I'd be seated in two hours were at this same moment having a swig of whiskey in a dilapidated tack room preparing to go out into the cold and force a rogue around the track.

"My, oh my, what would your grandmother say," quipped Uncle

Charlie, his old-time, stylish fedora tipped back off his forehead. Uncle Charlie was the youngest of my grandmother's eleven siblings and, now in his sixties, lived with my Grandmother Whitman at the Knoll, the Victorian house in which they had been raised. I had lived there on and off during my Gilman years and during college. It was much closer to the track, to Gilman School, and to Johns Hopkins than the farm. It was quiet, and I could get plenty of work accomplished there. I'd always been extremely close to my grandmother, and Uncle Charlie and I had become the best of friends. Uncle Charlie was, in some ways, the opposite of my Christian Science teetotaling Granny. He loved to raise hell, had gone through a spouse and several lovers, and over the past couple of decades had fought a drinking problem. He had been a great amateur steeplechase rider and an excellent polo player. He was such an athlete that during the winters he put away his riding boots, pulled out his skates, and played professional ice hockey. Uncle Charlie had then become a top trainer of flat horses. He now had one horse in training, stabled with Pop's horses — a big, fat, well-bred colt with whom I was soon to become very familiar.

Emmett braced his hands on the rim of the bucket and pushed with his arms to get himself up onto his feet. He looked over at Pop, "I'll tack up the new horse."

"Wait, I'll help," I said.

"No," said Pop. "You stay here, Bud. Emmett, take your time. They're still harrowing the track."

Emmett coughed into his hand, opened the door, and the arctic air blasted in, stirring the dust back up into whirlpools. The door shut and the dust eased back down to the floor and the palpable warmth from the hissing flames of the gas stove wafted through the room. "He's the only one that can go in the stall with him," Pop said. "I don't know what he did, but that horse respects him."

I asked Pop what the horse had been doing wrong, but he wouldn't tell me much. This was the usual. He gave me his old pair of rowel spurs to pull on. I strapped them over the heels of my riding boots, the tiny, sharp points of the rowels spinning around and around. He got his old riding stick out of the tack box and punched a hole in the cracker — the leather flap at the end of the whip. He stuck a strand of wire through the hole in the cracker, bent it back double, and twisted the two end pieces together into a knot.

Pop looked me in the eye. "Now, that sonofabitch does anything wrong, I want you to crucify him. Okay?"

"Okay," I said.

He folded the wire back so that it lay across the whip and gripped the whip at its end, with his fingers around the whip and the wire. Holding the whip backward, he said, "Carry it like this when you're walking on and off the track or when you're not using it."

I had one more shot of bourbon. Then Emmett proudly led out the horse. It was the first time I'd seen him. He was a light-boned chestnut. He had a thick wooly coat that made him look a little shaggy, and all four feet were never on the ground at the same time. He wasn't big and his neck wasn't long — which would make him a little more difficult for me, at almost six feet, to ride. He held his head high, looking at every little thing being blown about by the wind. He spooked this way and that, at a bucket being blown over, at a door rattling and slamming shut, at a gust of wind hitting him in the hindquarters. His eyes looked like the eyes of a horse escaping from a blaze.

Emmett walked him around the shed row a couple of times. Then he stopped, and held Tambourine Man tightly by the head while Pop gave me a leg up. As soon as I landed in the saddle, I felt at ease, my legs feeling long and at home wrapped around Tambourine's chest as he jigged and pulled on Emmett, who was leading us around the shed row. Knowing I had nothing to worry about with Emmett holding the shank, I relaxed, lengthened my stirrup leathers, and tied a knot in the long reins.

Emmett looked up. "Al, you be careful."

"I will, Emmett," I said. Tambourine Man jumped away from a gust, into Emmett, who was ready. Like the old boxer that he was, he sidestepped out of the way.

"Looks to me like you're the one should be careful," I said, laughing.

"I'm all right, Al," he said, coughing.

"What the hell's all that coughing, Emmett?" I asked, standing up in my stirrups for a moment, focusing on getting the feel of the jigging animal beneath me.

"It's nothing, Al."

"You seen a doctor?"

"Yeah ... The boss went and made me an appointment at the Veteran's Hospital. I got to go in a couple of days."

He led me out past the tack room door onto the asphalt. There was no dirt or grass between the barns. Except for the pale, buzzing, vaporous yellow illumination from the floodlights, it was still dark. Pop, Janon, and Uncle Charlie, their hats pulled down tight, were standing there waiting for me.

A sheet of newspaper blew under Tambourine Man's legs. He leaped sideways toward Emmett. Emmett had a tight grip on the reins and was pulled off balance as Tambourine lunged forward. Emmett was under him, and I yelled, "Let go!" as I could hear dull thuds instead of the clanging, ringing sound of steel horseshoes hitting asphalt. Emmett's weight pulled against the reins. I put my finger through the yoke and stayed loose and ready. Suddenly, Emmett appeared in front of the horse. Tambourine's head shot back and up, and I snapped my head back and out of the way in time to keep the poll from smashing into my face. Tambourine began scrambling backward, slipping and sliding on the asphalt, and then stopped dead. Emmett started leading Tambourine out across the expanse of asphalt to the entrance gate of the track, Tambourine jigging and dancing.

"I got him, Emmett."

"You sure, Al? Maybe I ought to walk you to the gate."

"I'm all right. You can let him go now."

"Okay, he's all yours. Bring him back in one piece, jock."

I had a short hold of the reins and was squeezing hard with my legs, ready to turn my heels in and use the spurs. There was no one around to see my illegal whip. I was ready to use it instantly. Out of the corner of my eye, I saw Emmett, Janon, and Uncle Charlie at the door of the grandstand. I knew they'd walk in through the hallway and up a flight or two of stairs, and then out to where they could lean on a rail and watch from two stories up so they could see the whole track.

Tambourine Man walked fine through an unlit area to the big wire gate, which led out of the barn area. As soon as we went through the gate and he was able to see the track entrance lit up by an overhead floodlight about twenty-five yards away, he tried to wheel to the left.

I jabbed him with the left spur and he stopped spinning but started skidding sideways across the asphalt to the left, crisscrossing his legs like a dancer sidestepping across the stage. I couldn't hit him on the left side with the whip because I was holding it in my right hand, and needing both hands on the reins, I couldn't switch it to my other hand. A gust of wind hit him from behind and he leapt forward.

I felt good. I was riding long and tied on tight. I snatched the right rein to make him go toward the track. As soon as I had him facing it, he faked half-jogging-jigging forward a few steps. I leaned slightly forward, going with his momentum, and then he threw his head back, the poll between his ears smashing me in the forehead and nose, the front of my helmet catching most of the blow. It made a cracking sound when I was struck and hundreds of sparks filled my sight. I dropped my head a notch, focused my eyes on a section of mane. Electric amoebas swirled before my eyes. I took a deep breath and relaxed, waiting for the dizziness to subside. This was it. Him or me. All or nothing.

I squeezed into his sides hard with both spurs, but instead of going forward he reared up ... up ... up. I stood up in the stirrups and threw my arms around his neck — we were teetering, we were on the verge of going over backward. I looked down at the straw and paper being blown beneath Tambourine Man's feet and thought about how hard that asphalt was. "Careful, Paddy; careful, Paddy," I heard Pop call out from behind me. I had thought he'd gone into the grandstand. I had thought I was all alone.

The second Tambourine's front feet hit the asphalt I let out a blood-curdling growl. I whacked him with the stick on his rump as hard as I could swing it. I dug in with the spurs, and he started sidestepping to the left. Out of the corner of my eye, I saw Pop walking up behind me, swishing a long buggy whip, just in case I needed any help. I switched the stick from my right to my left hand, let out another growl and hit him on his left side, the wire making a dull whopping noise when it bit into his heavy coat. Simultaneously, I heard the zing of the buggy whip, gripped my legs tight, and then heard it *thwapp* around Tambourine's hind legs.

The combination of the two whips catapulted us onto the track at the head of the stretch an eighth of a mile from the wire. We had it all to ourselves. The buzzing track lights eerily lit some sections more than others. Squeezing with my legs and digging in with the spurs, I got him down the homestretch, under the wire, and around the clubhouse turn, as he spooked and propped and tried to stop the whole way. I was sweating under my parka. My legs felt like mush. My lungs were burning.

Around the turn we had to pass the chute for the starting gate. I got my rear end low in the saddle and braced for him to try to stop, and instead he just kept galloping along and started pulling on the reins. I thought this was a good sign. He started picking up speed, and then, on the straightaway, by the five-eighths pole, he tried to run off. I stood up in the stirrups and leaned back with all my strength, the wind freezing the exposed skin of my hands.

He was getting away from me. The wind was blowing straight at me, harder and harder the faster we went. My chest and waist were drenched in sweat, and my hands and face and forehead and feet were freezing. I hadn't worn thick winter boots — knowing they would be dangerous on a horse like this; they could get stuck in the stirrups and I could be dragged — and the wind sucked all the warmth out of my thin ankle-high lace-ups. The reins were cutting into my fingers, cutting off the circulation. I was on the verge of losing control, and Tambourine was seconds away from being a flat-out runaway, which could put us both in danger and could injure his legs, killing any hope for a racing career and any hope of Pop getting more horses from Tambourine's owner.

Our speed was increasing. We flew past the three-eighths pole. The final turn was coming. The turn was banked and sharp compared to most tracks. Just on the other side of the outside rail was a tall page-wire fence, topped off with a roll of razor-sharp concertina wire, and in ten more yards a steady stream of traffic rushing by on Northern Parkway, car lights on, heaters purring — the drivers safely heading to their warm office buildings.

I pulled on the left rein. He didn't respond. I was afraid he was going to crash into the outside rail and flip into the page-wire fence topped off with a roll of razor-sharp concertina wire. I pulled up my hands, bit the mid-section of the whip out of my right hand, held it in my mouth, the wire knot flopping just out of range of my face. I clamped my right hand in front of my left on the left rein, and with one last recall of energy leaned back, yanking Tambourine Man to the inside rail, bluffing him, as if I wanted him to go through that rail. We went right up to the aluminum rail. He must've thought I'd gone crazy, which is what I wanted. He had to fight me to keep us from smacking into the rail, and he slowed.

I put my right hand back on the right rein and around the turn we went, slower. I relaxed for a second, and the bastard tried to bolt out the entrance to the track. I yanked hard on the left rein, took the whip out of my mouth, let out a growl, and slashed him across his rear. And then, my legs having completely given out and my rear end bumping on the seat of the saddle, I let out another growl, raked up with the spurs and in the world's worst form, hit him once more and forced him to "open gallop" the rest of the way down to the wire.

Back at the barn, Emmett grabbed Tambourine Man by the bit and I slid off. My legs buckled when my feet hit the ground and, embarrassingly, I almost collapsed. As I was attempting to unbuckle the girth with my numb fingers, Tambourine Man flinched, and I saw a thin sliver of a cut my spurs had made along his rib cage. I ducked around and looked on his other side. There was another cut.

Drops of bright red blood dripped from the cuts. I looked down at my spurs. "Don't worry, Al," Emmett said. "He'll be all right. You got him now."

* * *

That one February gallop on Tambourine Man marked the commencement of a glorious spring. I started to drive down every morning before my classes to get on him. I could sense the split-second he was thinking of wheeling or ducking out, and I'd give him a squeeze with the legs, maybe a little gig with the spurs, keep constant communication with him through the reins, and keep him going straight and forward. Every morning we jogged down the stretch of the track, toward the wire, warming up, getting ready to gallop, and I'd be singing "Hey, Mister Tambourine Man, play a song for me. I'm not sleepy and there ain't no place I'm going to ..." And I was happy. I was riding and studying, and in love with Carol, and excited to be back working with Pop. I was delightfully fit, and I was getting lighter without even reducing, and I was making all kinds of money doing what I loved.

Then one morning I breezed Tambourine with another horse. Three-eighths of a mile. Pop, Uncle Charlie, Janon, Emmett, Sal Tumenelli, and a few others were all in the stands watching. I galloped head and head with the other horse down the backstretch, keeping Tambourine pulling against me. We broke off gradually, so that when we hit the three-eighths pole, right where the turn before the homestretch begins, we were running right along. I kept him alongside and slightly behind the other horse. He felt great. A nice smooth stride. But I knew him, and I had my rear end down low and was ready for anything. Coming out of the turn, I let the other horse draw ahead about two lengths, and then I released Tambourine Man. I had my stick with the coat hanger ready. I let loose a hoarse growl, walloped him one time with the stick, and dug in with the spurs. Tambourine shifted into another gear, and we flew past the other horse and under the wire. I never hit him again.

In early March, Pop entered Tambourine in a flat race at the Casanova Hunt Point to Point in Virginia. Carol and I drove down in my car. Pop drove the trailer, with Emmett in the back. The races were held out in a broad field. There were hurdle races, a timber race, and a flat race.

Soon, I was up on Tambourine and we were in the race, and I was going around the last turn head and head with my childhood friend Mike White just like in the old days on our ponies. He glanced at me and yelled, "Hey, my chain's broken!"

The going was deep and the divots, clumps of turf, were flying back, hitting us in the face. The horse leading the pack was about seven lengths ahead of us. What the hell is he talking about, I thought. "Come on!" I yelled over at Mike. "Let's roll!"

"You got a tow line?" he yelled to me, a grin on his freckly mud-covered face.

I felt an explosion of white light and laughter in my soul as I envisioned him on his mud-splattered green bike towing me on my red three-speed up the hill out of Yaddo at Saratoga. Leaving Mike, I let loose a growl — that was the signal — waved my stick alongside Tambourine's neck without using it and squeezed his sides one time with Pop's old dime spurs. We took off, gaining on the leaders, passing them. The wire was nearing, one horse to go. We blew past the horse and were all alone, in front, no horses around, and we were under the wire. I stood up in the irons, leaned back against the reins, and eased Tambourine to a canter, to a trot, to a walk. I gave him a pat on the neck, pulled the mud-splattered goggles from my eyes, spit out the grit caught in my teeth, and jogged back to the stewards' stand at the finish.

Pop was there, grinning. Emmett was there, wobbling a little, having to work to keep his balance, meaning he'd hit that pint of Early Times pretty hard after he'd unsnapped the shank in the paddock and had called out, as Tambourine Man and I jigged away from him, "See you in the winner's circle, Al!" Pop and Emmett were grinning and laughing and congratulating me and patting Tambourine Man as I slid off. I glanced at Tambourine's sides and hindquarters — not a cut or slash mark on him. His chestnut coat was bright, luminescent; he was hot and lathered and blowing, and he had run his heart out. I rubbed him between his eyes before heading for the scales, and he lowered his head and rubbed his nose hard against my side, pushing me back a step or two. I laughed as I rushed to the scales.

Two weeks later we did it again, at a point to point held on the Middleburg racecourse. I galloped along behind most of the pack, and with an eighth of a mile to go, we flew by them, in one sustained run. And two weeks after that he was entered in a flat race at the Potomac Hunt Meet in southern Maryland. It was pouring and the going was deep. When I went to make my move, horses were all over the place in front of us, but Tambourine Man laced through the pack, and just at the wire we pulled out in front. That night, on the drive back in the car with Mom and Pop, Pop told me I had ridden him "like Arcaro." I will always remember that compliment.

I started picking up other rides at the point to points. Trainers saw I was winning. The phone was ringing. Every Saturday morning after galloping at Pimlico I would meet Carol and Uncle Charlie at the Knoll, and we would hop into my car and speed off to a hunt meet in Virginia. One Saturday we went to the Middleburg hunt meet, and I won the amateur timber race on a roan called Sand River, owned and trained by Virginians. I really liked Sand River and looked forward to riding him in more races. In fact, I thought I might get the ride on him the following week in a timber race that was open to professional as well as amateur riders, but the trainer named a young up-and-coming professional on the horse. The poor horse, only an eight-year-old, finished second, then collapsed in his stall after the race and died.

Pop had a flat horse called Wild Amber. He was a black, flashy speed horse. Benny Feliciano, a stylish Maryland jockey, rode him on the flat over the late winter/early spring and won a few, on top all the way, at sprint distances. But in the horse's past couple of races, Benny couldn't rate him. Wild Amber took off and burned out early.

Pop said he could be rated. He could be held back. No one believed Pop. I started getting on Amber every morning before classes. He was a smooth mover, graceful, like riding a rolling wave. His strides blended together so that you felt like you were cruising down the track on a hovercraft, just waiting for the right moment to push down on the throttle and release the full force of the jets. He never dreamed of stopping or wheeling or bolting like Tambourine Man. He just wanted the rider to ease him down onto the rail, let him open his stride up farther and farther, and take off, saving nothing in reserve, the poles to the inside rail flashing by impossibly faster and faster. We schooled him out at the farm, and he jumped well. Trainers, grooms, riders criticized Pop: No way this horse could go the distance — a mile and three-quarters — of a jumping race. No way he could be rated. He'd fly the first mile and spit out the bit. Pop was crazy trying to turn this speed horse into a jumper. I never said anything, but I knew that Pop thought I could rate him.

We had Tambourine Man out at the farm, too, and he also schooled well over hurdles. I was galloping in the mornings before classes at Hopkins; I was galloping a few on Saturday mornings and driving to the races and staying up late, carousing after the races. Sunday mornings, if Carol and I weren't off in Kentucky or Tennessee for a Sunday race, I was up and getting on half a dozen horses at the track, then going out to the farm and breezing and schooling horses. We were on a roll. Carol and Uncle Charlie and Pop and Emmett and I.

Soon Tambourine Man's owner, Mr. McNaughton, started sending Pop more horses. We didn't have enough stalls at the track and at the Voss barn. We were overflowing with horses. We refurbished the barn on our own farm, dividing the shed into handsome, sturdy stalls. Some days, I first rode at Pimlico, then went to the Vosses', then to our own farm. Horse after horse. I could ride as naturally as I could walk. I was as comfortable on a horse as people are in an easy chair. One morning, one glorious Sunday, we breezed most of the horses at Pimlico and then we shipped all the horses from the two farms over to the Elkridge-Harford Hunt Club, and Tom, Tiger, and I breezed horse after horse in the huge field out in front of the club, pushing our horses up the long gradual half-mile hill, and then finishing three-eighths of a mile along the straight, flat spine of the ridge.

Mr. McNaughton started to visit us on the weekends. It was always questionable when and if he was going to pay the bills for his horses. He was a big man, heavy, in his seventies. He loved to drink and talk. On Sunday afternoons I'd make a pitcher of Bloody Marys, and we'd drink them while we waited for the leg of lamb with potatoes and onions and carrots that Mom was roasting. We'd eat at the kitchen table and then move into the living room. Mom and Pop would sneak off, leaving me with Mr. McNaughton, who would sip on a bourbon and ask me about his horses. I'd be in mid-explanation about how a horse was going. The sunlight would be pouring through the tall living room windows, and Mr. McNaughton would lean his head back, close his eyes, and in seconds be snoring. I'd get up, leave, and when I came back, he'd sit up, ask for another bourbon, and start talking right where he left off. Soon we'd be down at Goldberg's and he'd be leaning back in his chair with a circle of admirers around him, reciting passages from *King Lear* and *Henry V* and *Hamlet*.

## Chapter 18

Then he would leave, not pay his bills for a month, and Mom would get worried. She'd call, and he'd threaten to take his horses away. His rickety van might even pull into the driveway. Mom would be in the kitchen, looking out at the van, while talking to Mr. McNaughton on the phone. She'd change his mind. The following weekend he'd be at our house, drinking all Pop's bourbon, reciting Shakespeare, waiting for Mom to cook another lamb or roast beef dinner ... the king in *Huckleberry Finn*.

# 19

## Dream Cottage

Carol and I were were to be married in June of my junior year at Hopkins. All spring I was galloping in the mornings at Pimlico, taking classes at Hopkins in the late mornings and early afternoons, and driving out to Mom and Pop's to get on a couple of horses at dusk and even in the dark. I had limitless energy. I loved everything I was doing. I loved Carol. I loved working for Pop. I loved being at Pimlico in the early morning.

I loved Hopkins. I loved arriving in the bluster of a winter's morning. I would park, peel off a few layers of my winter galloping clothes, and go directly to the cafeteria. If I were in a rush, I'd just get a cup of coffee and take it, splashing, to my first period class on American literature, where I could sit back with a hundred other students and listen as a brilliant Hopkins professor pontificated on the novel I hadn't quite finished reading for that week. If I had more time and if the weather was particularly cold, I'd get a bowl of oatmeal to warm my insides. The same big, beautiful black woman was seated there at the cash register every morning, and she'd ask, "How ya doing, Pat?" or, if I had time and I were ordering oatmeal, "Good morning, Pat, you have a little more time today?" Or, "Pat, why don't you have some eggs and bacon?

You need to put on a pound or two."

One morning I was there early and no one else was in the line. I asked her, "How do you know my name?"

"What do you mean?" she asked.

"I was just wondering how you know my name?"

"Oh, Sugar. I don't know your name. I just call you Pat because you remind me of Pat Boone."

After class I'd prowl the halls of Gilman Hall, the central building of the campus. (It was named after Daniel Coit Gilman, the first president of Johns Hopkins University, after whom Gilman School was also named.) Gilman Hall was gray and dingy with notices and printouts and posters hanging from doors and walls. I'd step outside and there'd be a rally protesting the war in Vietnam and all kinds of boycotts to sign. Back inside I'd go to the coffee bar. Students — young men and women, looking interchangeable, with long dark hair in ponytails — ran the show. They were pale and skinny and dressed in crazy, raggedy, tie-dyed T-shirts, flannel shirts with the tails hanging out, and baggy, ripped-at-the-knee army pants. Bagels and doughnuts. Hot coffee. Students and professors huddled around tables. Students madly writing in journals while all the commotion swirled about them. Professors importantly grading papers. Ideas, concepts, philosophies palpably floated in the air. The nostril-flaring stench of pot emanated from wool coats and thick, shaggy hair. This was headlong intellectual engagement. This was an all-out, do-or-collapse, drink-black-coffee-all-night, get-the-paper-written lifestyle. There was a crush of thinking; there was a collision of art and writing — Jean-Paul Sartre in one student's hands, Jorge Luis Borges in another; John Barth's conventionally written *The Floating Opera* being recommended by one creative writing seminar student, Barth's fantastically narrated *Giles Goat-Boy* being touted by another. It was the spring of 1972, and the intellectual atmosphere at Hopkins was so deep, so thick, so lush — you could dive in and swim through it.

Women! Young women. Intellectual women. Hopkins had finally

caught on and was admitting the opposite sex. They were in my classes. As students, they were different: They engaged more with the professor; they were more in the moment during class; they did not have the "this is bullshit that I am only doing because it is required of me" attitude. They boosted the energy level. They wore baggy T-shirts with no bras, and when they raised their hands to answer a question, you'd see downy hair sprouting from their armpits, and there were their breasts, pale and limber and jiggling just an arm's length away right in broad phosphorescent light. When they spoke to you, they looked you right in the eye. This was not Gilman or Washington and Lee.

I was an international relations major. I wanted to travel around the world as my mother's brother, Colonel Ned Whitman, had. A decorated World War II fighter pilot, he had worked and lived in most of the Cold War hot spots while with the State Department, and, finally, as a CIA operative, though he never admitted this to us. He'd advised me on how to get into the Foreign Service, and I was preparing to take the notoriously difficult Foreign Service exam. Yet I was enjoying the English classes more and more. It occurred to me that one could major in this sort of thing, but I wasn't sure how one could make a living from it. For the hell of it I signed up for an introductory creative writing seminar. Most of the students were freshmen and sophomores taking the course to fulfill a writing requirement. I was the odd duck in the class, but there was a sensitive female graduate student teaching it, and she liked my stuff. I wrote short, emotional pieces. I wrote about Carol. I wrote about Pop. I wrote about Emmett and Tambourine Man and drinking.

One night at home Carol had gone out with some friends, and I read a short story by Ernest Hemingway called "My Old Man," narrated by a boy about his father, a struggling steeplechase jockey in France. I loved it. When I finished, I thought: What the hell does Hemingway know about having a steeplechase jockey for a father? I pulled out a legal pad and pen and wrote the first draft of a short story based on living

## Chapter 19

through Pop's fall and paralysis. The next day I read it to the class of usually jaded and disinterested critics. They were fascinated.

I went to the library in Gilman Hall and studied. Students lived there, mainly the male students and mainly at the end of the semester. They had their books piled around them on the huge oak tables, and their clothes were spread around them on the floor, and more than half of the time they had so exhausted their brains, so pushed their capabilities, that they lay with their heads down, their long oily hair sprawled across the table top, and slept. Right there in the library.

Because I did not live on the campus, I knew only a few students. Kip Elser, a fellow amateur steeplechase jockey, introduced me to all the guys in his fraternity. I'd bump into them during the afternoons. I was very impressed; they were the old pros on campus. I took an intense course in the novel by a notoriously provocative and iconoclastic professor, John Irwin. He amazed me with his insight into what these American writers were doing. I fully accepted everything Irwin said, and then we walked out of the class one afternoon, and one of Kip's friends, Jamie McGuire, declared, "Isn't that bullshit? You know perfectly well Faulkner wasn't thinking any of that when he sat down to write." I took another literature course from Richard Macksey. He was enveloped in mystique. The students loved him. He was big and brash and belted out his lectures. The atmosphere of anticipation in the room before he arrived resembled that before a rock concert. Stories swirled about the size and value of his private library.

I started getting more rides in the "Midwest circuit" — which was what we called the schedule of spring races held in Kentucky and Tennessee. Jumping rider Greg Morris, who had been raised in Kentucky, was studying at the Maryland Institute of Art and freelance riding at Pimlico along with Kip and me in the mornings. He got me a ride on a mare called Dream Cottage.

Carol and I flew to Lexington, Kentucky. We were on an adventure. We were doing this together. We were in love. Carol helped line up the flights, helped with cleaning my tack. We flew down, all expenses paid. We rented a car, all expenses paid. We went to a ball, all expenses paid. The balls always had filet mignon for the main course, and we usually sat at a table with Greg Morris, which meant I could have two filets — Greg was a vegetarian. We stayed in a nice motel, all expenses paid. This was the life; this was love — all expenses paid.

On the morning of the race, I didn't have to rush off and gallop any horses. I didn't have to arise at five, fix a mug of black coffee, drive to Pimlico, get on half a dozen horses, and then race to Hopkins. I got up after the sun had already risen. The light streamed through the windows. I wasn't used to this. For years when I arose, it was dark outside. Now, sunlight was everywhere — it splashed onto the white sheets of our bed. I didn't have to put on a sweat outfit, go out and run. I didn't have to drive in a hot car. I didn't have to go to the hot box. All the weights in the Midwest were 160 or above. I had the morning off. These were precious moments. We lolled around and joked around and even had a light breakfast.

Before we knew it, we had to rush. Soon I was in the "jocks' room," a tent, leaving off my tack. Then I was walking the course with Carol, and then I was standing in the paddock, prepared. I was in Pop's old britches and race-riding boots. I had Pop's race-riding stick in my hand. I was relaxed. On this one afternoon I was perhaps over-relaxed due to the romantic nature of the morning's activities. I was confident. I was riding in my favorite saddle — Pop's old timber saddle. Greg had told me Dream Cottage was a "nice old mare" and there was nothing to worry about. He mentioned that the owner/rider might have had a fall on her that spring.

A young woman approached me in the paddock. She was the daughter of the new owners, and she said she had a list of points that should help me. She handed me a long, yellow legal sheet with a list taking up the entire page. At the top of the page, listed as number one, in scratchy handwriting, it said, "Bad jumper." Number two was "Rank.

Do not go to the front." Number three, "Doesn't run for the stick." I handed the list back to her.

She explained that the mare was rank and would want to go to the front. The former rider kept her in the back because she tended to tire at the end of the race. He had been lifting weights so he could control her. She fought against him and pulled like hell, but that was just how you had to ride her. She added that the mare was a bad jumper and had crashed through a few fences in the last race.

I listened to this, but not in the way she intended. I started to think that the mare should get a good start, be up with the front-runners, if not on the lead. I'd try to "drop her head," that is, ride her with a long hold and relax my grip on the reins. She'd probably jump much better up in the front, on her own, galloping freely, in contrast to being back with the pack with her rider swinging on her.

It was hot and the ground was hard and dry, and I was not feeling as strong as I'd like — definitely overconfident about my recuperative powers from the romancing back at the motel. I laughed at myself, thinking about Pop's plight in this arena. When he and Mom had gotten married, my grandmother Whitman had told Mom that they should never make love the night before he rode a race. It would drain him too much. He told me this, laughing, one morning, on the way to the track. "We got married, went on the honeymoon, first to New Orleans, then to Mexico ... We came back to Maryland, and the love life tailed off. I couldn't figure out what was happening until your mother told me what her instructions had been. I had to explain to her that her mother's theory just wouldn't work with my riding races five and sometimes six days a week."

I didn't know many of the Kentuckians in the paddock. They chatted with one another, and then the horses came in, and there she was — this was the first time I'd seen her: high at the withers, strong shoulders, long-necked, long-back, tucked up nicely between her rib cage and her haunches, and a nicely rounded rump. She was a dark bay with dapples and she was jigging. She was beautiful. I couldn't wait to get on her. The groom brought her over to my spot.

I went to pick up my saddle and pads, and the daughter of the new owners, gently gripped my arm. By this time I was wondering why she, and not her parents, had come to watch. I stopped and looked her in the eye. She told me that the former owner/rider of Dream Cottage had been a great friend of her parents; he had been killed in a race on the mare just two weeks earlier. Now that was something no one, including Greg Morris, had told me! She explained that the mare had run through a wing, and a board had gone through the owner/rider's chest.

That did it. I definitely would not try to hold her back. She must've been fighting against him. And I would have to talk to my good friend Greg Morris; could this latest news have had anything to do with his deciding not to ride this mare?

Would I try hard to win it, the young woman asked me. Her family would really like it if I could win this race in honor of their great friend.

I would do my best, I told her.

We threw on the tack, and then I was up and on Dream Cottage. I let all the remarks wash away. We strode out of the paddock, her long brown neck out in front of me. She jigged; she pulled against the reins. She felt strong, powerful.

She finished second that day. We went right to the front, led most of the way around. She jumped great. I took no chances having her in tight with other horses or having her in close to the wings. In front she relaxed, and we just galloped around sailing over the big brush fences. She had some age on her, and she got leg weary. Kip Elser came up on my outside. We jumped the last fence head and head. I carried him out a little, but he was on a big rangy horse and was whipping and driving, and Kip could ride a finish and Dream Cottage was tired. She was trying hard. I didn't touch her with the whip — except to wave it alongside her neck. Kip went on by and we finished second.

## Chapter 19

I went home and reported back to Pop how it had gone. I'd be riding her in a big race in Tennessee in two weeks, and there were going to be some tough horses in the race, including one classy, well-bred horse ridden by George Strawbridge. George, a history professor who was heir to the Campbell Soup fortune, was building what would become one of the greatest stables in steeplechasing, and he didn't skimp when he bought his horses. I wasn't sure if I could go to the front, make the pace for the entire race, and then have enough left to go on and fight off the challengers and win.

"Remember how Dougie rode the Tom Roby last spring?" Pop asked.

I visualized Pop and me standing at Delaware Park, by the rail up in the clubhouse where he liked to watch. Dougie Small had gone to the front on his horse and had galloped along, running and jumping well. With about five-eighths of a mile to go, the pack of horses swarmed up behind Dougie as they headed across the track and down the hill. He let two or three horses go by. I was standing there beside Pop. "Watch this, Bud; watch Dougie." Going back up the hill, and crossing the track, the riders were whipping and driving. As they came to the last hurdle, they started to slow, and, meanwhile, Dougie was right behind them, sitting still. They jumped the last in a bunch, and Dougie got down low, laced through the three of them, and went on to win. "That's called giving your horse a breather," Pop had said, and then, although he didn't gamble often, he went to collect his bet.

"Keep that race in mind," Pop said. "Remember that you need to let her catch her breath before you ask her to run heading into the last fence."

The course at Iroquois, Tennessee, was beautiful. The fences consisted of live brush, big but with lots of give. The course was in the shape of an oval on the side of a hill, with the spectators all on top. Once around was a mile and a quarter. We started at the top. Leaving the tape, I let Dream Cottage go to the front, where I planned to relax her, and slow the pace of the race from the front end. But some wild Kentucky rider — Mason Lampton — came up alongside, challenging me. Dream Cottage grabbed a hold of the bit, acting like a three-year-old, and took off down the hill. We flew over three fences head and head before Mason dropped back. I galloped a mile or so, by myself, out in front, on the perfectly manicured bluish-green grass. Dream Cottage was jumping well.

With five-eighths of a mile to go, we headed up the hill, and I heard them coming up behind me, yelling and whipping. We were going up an incline. I didn't want to wear her out going up this hill. I was on the inside. They were making their move, going up this hill, and they had to swing out and lose ground, to get around me.

I let three or four of them go by. I saw from their smug expressions that they thought we had gone out on top too fast and that we were washed up. I eased Dream Cottage up the hill. She was a lady with some age on her, and I didn't want to have her feel in the least defeated. At the top we had a three-eighths of a mile straightaway to the wire. There was one more fence between us and the wire, the water jump — a low brush fence followed by a four-foot-wide pool of water. I passed one horse, passed two, and only George was ahead of us. I held Dream Cottage together riding into the water jump. We were gaining, gaining. I let her get in close to the brush so she could jump it and sail cleanly over the wide pool of water on the other side. She jumped it perfectly, passing George in the air, and I was down, riding her to the finish — not using the stick, the one and only point on that list to which I had adhered.

A couple of weeks later Pop gave me a leg up on Tambourine Man in his first sanctioned hurdle race, a race for maidens, at Fair Hill. I walked the course that afternoon before the race with the legendary Dooley Adams, a retired steeplechase jockey. Dooley was a little older than Pop. The end of his career overlapped with the early years of Pop's. He and Pop had been colleagues but never close friends. They were rivals. Dooley had had an advantage over Pop — he was smaller. He didn't have to fight to make the weights, and he picked up rides on horses that got in light that Pop couldn't think of riding. As Dooley and I walked around the last turn and looked up at the long uphill stretch to the finish, he drifted out to the middle of the course, instead of walking close to the inside rail, where you would think he'd want to be to save ground. He showed me how the grass was greener and thicker, and the turf deeper, for about a ten-foot swath coming out from the rail. In the middle of the course, where we were walking, there was a slightly raised four-foot-wide ridge of turf, where the ground was firmer, the grass cut shorter. The ridge led like a path straight through the middle of the three hurdles and to the wire. "This is where you want to ride your finish, Little Paddy," he told me in his South Carolinian drawl.

Then, while talking about one of the all-time great riders who was still riding, he pointed over to the rail and got in a little dig: "Even if the going was two-feet deep in muck on the rail and there were five horses in front of him throwing mud back into his face, that is where he would be, on the rail. You ask your father if I'm not right."

That afternoon Tambourine Man galloped along, jumping well, in the back of the pack. With half a mile to go, after saving ground going around the last turn, we drifted out onto Dooley's ridge. I let out a growl and gave Tambourine a squeeze with the spurs. On up the hill we went, picking off each horse one by one, jumping the last head and head with one horse that was over in the deep going by the rail, and then I was down, lower in the saddle, "hand-riding him," "scrubbing," attempting to hold my lanky body in a neat tuck, and we were under the wire first. And back to the winner's circle with Pop and Emmett and Mr. McNaughton.

\* \* \*

A month later I was in the car with Tiger and Pop on the way to get married at St. Thomas Church in the Green Spring Valley, just half a mile from the Knoll. I knew the rector at St. Thomas rather well but in an awkward way, given the circumstances. He had a daughter I'd gone out with for a semester or so, and I'd sometimes visited their house on Sunday afternoons when the whole clan of fun-loving sons and daughter and parents enjoyed Bloody Marys.

Pop was driving, I was in the middle, and Tiger was to my right. Pop had been to work at Delaware Park, but I'd been given the morning off. Tiger had been kidding me, acting offended that I had picked Pop over him to be the best man. To give himself a role, he had proclaimed his title to be "best man to the best man." Job duties included talking Pop into having a shot of whiskey on the way and then trying unsuccessfully to get him to sing along as Tiger impersonated Eliza Doolittle's father singing "Get Me to the Church on Time." I declined both the drink and the sing-a-long. I wanted to be clear-headed and to remember this day.

We had a big wedding with all our best friends in it and a party afterward under a huge tent at the clubhouse of the Green Spring Hounds. We danced into the morning hours and didn't learn until a year later that we'd been married on the night of the Watergate break-in.

We spent our honeymoon in Paris and in the south of France. In Paris, I was reading Hemingway's *A Moveable Feast*, living the life of "the lost generation." We stayed in a hotel on the Champs-Elysées. I practiced my French, and we thought we were getting a great deal until it was time to pay the bill. In French I asked the man at the desk to please repeat the amount of the bill. He stated it. I looked at Carol and then back at the man, asked him to please repeat that amount one more time. He did so, and finally, to my complete embarrassment, I realized the amount I thought they were charging for our entire four-night stay was the amount per day.

We took off to the south of France in a rented car. Emulating the French drivers and celebrating the lack of speed limits and radar traps, I drove as if we were at Le Mans. We flew through the chateau country, downshifting at every turn, and accelerating coming out. We had wine-and-cheese picnics in the afternoons, late-night discussions with French couples at little bed-and-breakfasts. We had romantic times in sway-backed beds that Louis XIV's servants must have thrown out. In Nice we lay on chaise lounges set on the pebbled beach and ordered Niçoise salads and bottles of cold white wine.

In Saint-Tropez thousands of beautiful, scantily clad people paraded up and down the promenade along the docks and stared at one another. Going topless on the beach, Carol got a terrible sunburn. I paid too much attention to the other topless women on the beaches while Carol wore my white cotton Oxford shirt to keep the sun off her fair skin. Seventy-five-percent-naked women, beautiful women, stunningly shaped women with long legs and perfectly bronzed breasts, walked nonchalantly across the beach and into the water. Carol, rightly so, got tired of me watching the goings-on.

I ran every day. In Paris I had a favorite run along the Seine to Notre Dame and another up the Champs-Elysées to the Arc de Triomphe. Every morning I ran off the effects of the wine from the night before. I did pushups and sit ups in our hotel room, vigilantly not allowing my weight to go up. Every night at dinner the waiters spoiled us — the honeymooners, the newlyweds — treating us to free bottles of wine. We skipped and danced, hand in hand, down the sidewalk of the Champs-Elysées to our hotel. We were extremely young looking, Carol in particular. The concierges at hotels pampered us, gave us the honeymoon suites, bottles of champagne. We laughed and laughed. We were so young-looking that sometimes they didn't believe we were a married couple — they thought we were brother and sister and jokingly asked where our parents were.

One night in Saint-Tropez, Carol and I returned from dinner. The concierge had a message for me to call home. It was late. It was hot in the claustrophobic phone booth in the hallway just across from the hotel desk. The front door to the little hotel was wide open to the street, and the hotel was on a corner. The high-pitched squeal of motorbikes and the low growl of sports cars downshifting through the gears echoed in the hallway. I had to close the glass door to the phone booth so I could hear. It was stifling. Carol had gone up to our room.

Mom was on the phone. She sounded frantic. I could barely hear her through the static and the mosquito-like buzzing of the motorbikes. She told me Pop wasn't well. He was working himself to death — I had to come home and help, she said. Tambourine Man had started wheeling again. They had tried several riders at the track. Tambourine had dumped two of them while going around the track, and just yesterday the latest rider couldn't even get him onto the racetrack. "Your father won't ask you, but you've got to come home. He's thinking of getting on him himself."

"Mom — our scheduled flight is in just five days. Isn't there something you can do? We have a reservation in this hotel for two days, and then we're supposed to go up into the mountains where it's cool ..."

"After all your father's done for you ... Just this one time ... Couldn't you just do it for him?"

Two days later, instead of waking up to the gentle flapping of curtains and the soft Mediterranean early morning light and breeze wafting into our spacious room through six-foot French windows, Carol lying beside me, both of us under one white sheet, I woke up in the pitch-black, cramped bedroom of our one-story house, the old air-conditioning unit noisily humming and rattling. I poured black coffee into a big mug, pulled on my leggings and riding boots, stepped out into what seemed like the middle of the night, and drove over to the farm to catch a ride up to Delaware Park in the pickup truck with Pop, a full load of hay in the back. I soon learned that Emmett wasn't at the track, which was part of the problem. The groom working on Tambourine Man was afraid of him. Emmett had gotten weaker. His throat kept swelling, and he was having a hard time swallowing; it often hurt when he ate. The doctors had started him on some new pills that they hoped would reduce the swelling and the pain. He was living in the barn at Jen Voss', helping Tom, who now had several horses of his own in training.

By 6:30 a.m. I was up on Tambourine Man — my own special horse now. I let my stirrups down low and hacked him for half an hour up and down the paths around the backside of Delaware. I had my rowel spurs on, and the stick with the knotted coat hanger in my grip. I tempted him with situations where he might want to wheel or misbehave. I was ready. He never made a wrong move. Onto the track, riding long, I jogged him once around, ready at any second for him to stop or wheel or rear. I let him ease into a canter. Around we went. Slow. Not a wrong move.

All through July, I arose at 4:15, poured a mug of coffee, drove to Mom and Pop's, and then headed up the road with Pop at the wheel. Some days Pop stayed up at Delaware at the Skyways Motel. But I was the newlywed, and I'd drive back down the road with Ricky Hruska — Pop's new foreman who was striving to become Pop's assistant trainer — who had a book of American poetry and was memorizing the poems and deciding if he really wanted to spend his life on the track, or wasn't there something more significant to which he could dedicate his talents. Like his brother Jamie, he was a gifted pianist. He was an artist and had an artist's temperament combined with a romantic and idealized vision of a racehorse trainer's life. At noon, as soon as we got outside the gates of the track, Ricky and I would stop and buy a six-pack of cold ones, and sip on them, reciting poetry and planning our futures the whole way home in the non-air-conditioned car, the windows open, the air flowing through drying our sweat-soaked clothes. And we might have argued a little about Wild Amber: Ricky was one of those who wanted to keep Amber running on the flat and not run him over hurdles.

Soon, Pop, Carol, and I were in Saratoga. Pop had just brought a small string: Wild Amber, Tambourine Man, a South American gelding, and two fillies. We'd never had it so easy. Emmett — who still hadn't regained his strength — had found us a sharp young groom, Michael Warner, who was working his way through college by "rubbing horses" and who couldn't stand the cockiness of all the jumping riders, many of whom he'd grown up with in Virginia. Michael was the son of "Dude" Warner, known as one of the best horseman/grooms in Virginia.

Pop had rented a small house not far from the track. Every morning Carol and I awakened to Pop coughing in the bathroom. Carol would tense and hold me as he coughed. It was a painful, body-wrenching cough. It pulled up stuff from inside Pop's chest, and Pop had to clear his throat and force himself to cough even more so he could spit it out.

One morning I'd gotten up not feeling too great from the night before. I was rushing around and had not taken Aaron, our spunky, broad-shouldered silky terrier whom I loved, out for his morning walk. You had to go with him or he would run off. "Paddy, when are you going to let Aaron out?" Pop asked, watching Aaron dance around by the kitchen door.

"He'll be all right," I'd replied, putting the kettle of water on the stove for coffee. I wanted that first mug of coffee in my hand, and then I'd take Aaron out.

"How would you like it if you got up and couldn't take a leak first thing in the morning?" Pop asked.

I went back into the bedroom, pulled on a bathrobe, and took Aaron out onto the back lawn.

The three of us would sit at the kitchen table, and Carol would try to talk Pop into having a glass of milk and a piece of toast for breakfast. He'd been getting weaker all summer and had lost much of his appetite. He'd also had a seizure in the early summer, and the doctors were at a loss for a diagnosis. Pop disregarded his weakness and just kept pushing hard. Before we'd come to Saratoga, he'd been arising at 4:30 every morning, setting the kettle on the stove and waiting as a whole string of would-be jumping riders and young trainers and men who just loved Pop all showed up at our house to make an Irish coffee for the road and catch a ride up to Delaware Park. He was getting to the track by six, sitting outside the tack room, having a cigarette, writing in his yellow legal pad what each horse would do that day, tacking up horses, brushing off horses, walking hots, joking with the men, going out to the track to watch his horses gallop and school, enjoying his work as never before, training his own stable of horses, and winning. He was staying on the move. He was winning flat races at tracks up and down the East Coast, at Gulfstream and Hialeah in Florida; Laurel, Bowie, Timonium, and Pimlico in Maryland; Aqueduct, Belmont Park, and Saratoga in New York; Delaware Park; Monmouth Park; and even the new track not far from home, Penn National in Pennsylvania. Winners on the flat included Voltage Clamp, Dreamily, Osage River, Ash Blue, Dubious Debutante, Vastno, Indian Ben, Individual, Ramsey's Brutus, Dashing Prince. Winners over jumps included North Country, who won at Monmouth Park; Victory Step, who won at Belmont equaling the track record; Curator, who had won the International Steeplechase Handicap at Belmont Park, setting a track record with jockey Dave Mitchell in the irons, and with whom, one year, Pop accomplished the impossible. Toward the end of the fall season, Curator won the prestigious Rolling Rock Hunt Cup over the big brush fences one afternoon and three days later won the International Gold Cup at Rolling Rock over the big brush fences again. Everyone had said he couldn't do it. The veterinarian was against running Curator — or, the Big Horse, as Tanza called him — in two races so close together because it could cause the horse's old tendon problem to flare up; Pop's assistant trainer, Sal Tumenelli, was against it because "the horse is not fucking Superman"; even the owner balked at the idea of running Curator in these two tough races with just a three-day hiatus. One man, Tanza, was all for it: "If the boss thinks the Big Horse can do it, then the Big Horse can do it."

His chair pulled up to the little kitchen table, Pop would joke with me and side with Carol on silly subjects, procrastinating drinking the milk. "Come on, Paddy. Now drink your milk like a good boy," Carol would say, tilting her head to the side and eyeing him as if she were talking to a little boy. Pop would make a horrible face, as if he were drinking a glass of cod liver oil, and would guzzle down the milk. Then, grinning, proud of his accomplishment, he would jokingly ask her for a beer.

We had the stakes-placed filly Bel Sheba at the barn. The sexy Robin Smith — this is when women jockeys first hit the big time — had been picked by our owner, who was just as interested in her good looks as her excellent riding skills, to be Bel Sheba's jockey. Robin, who later quit riding and married Fred Astaire, would stop by the barn to "breeze" Bel Sheba — let her go almost full speed for three-eighths of a mile — in the mornings.

Now that I was older and wiser, I was no longer trying to make the really light weights, 130, 135. Just doing 142, 143, and reading the *New York Times* and Hemingway's *Death in the Afternoon* in the late morning, after work, preparing for my senior year at Hopkins in the fall, preparing to head out of the horse business.

I'd get on the black, flashy speed horse, Wild Amber, first every morning. I'd ride him with my stirrups pulled up fairly short — not impossibly short, as the "flat" jockeys rode — but the length a steeplechase jockey usually rides in a race, with my calf and thigh forming a forty-five-degree angle. Pop and Carol, followed by Aaron prancing along on a leash, would walk out to Oklahoma and watch me gallop Wild Amber a mile or two.

Wild Amber pulled if you pulled against him. He was a fluid mover. He was like riding a black scarf of flying silk. He wanted to go faster and faster. It was my hands on which I concentrated. I didn't take his bait. I didn't take a hold. I stayed relaxed. Kept the hands low. Kept a long hold on the reins.

My job was to steady Wild Amber, get him going as quietly as possible and make it look easy. I'd pass Pop and Carol standing by the rail and as I took my eyes off the path before me for a split second, Pop, looking up at me with a feigned serious expression, would reach down and give Carol a pinch in the butt and she'd laugh, looking me in the eye, push his hand away. I'd laugh to myself and gallop on.

I wanted to school Wild Amber over hurdles one more time before he ran. When he galloped all out, full tilt, you could've ridden him with a glass of water balanced on your helmet. He floated. But he had been floating along too damn fast with the flat riders, burning himself out and not saving anything for the last sixteenth of a mile. I wanted to be sure I could control his speed going down over the hurdles and simultaneously have him jump well.

On National Steeplechase and Hunt Day, I rode Wild Amber out to the centerfield of Oklahoma. It was 10 a.m. The training track had just closed, and the centerfield for schooling had just opened. Dozens of horses circled around, their trainers on foot giving orders to the riders. Tourists and spectators lined the rail. Mike White, my old bicycling buddy, was up on a chestnut gelding circling around his father, Ridgely White, and I was circling around my father, and then we were schooling head and head.

We went a "turn of the field," that is, once around the schooling course. Our orders were strict. We were to go easy. Both these horses were due to run in a week. Pop didn't even want to school Wild Amber. He was a firm believer in the maxim that you do not want to waste your best performance "in the morning." You want your horse to peak "in the afternoon" — meaning at the races. But I hadn't schooled a horse for a couple of weeks, and Wild Amber hadn't jumped a fence for a few weeks. I had talked Pop into it.

I was on the outside, Mike on the inside. Over the first hurdle — nice and slow, the brush making the satisfying sound, louder than you'd think, *swish swish*, as first the front legs, then the hind legs swept through. Going into the second, we were galloping at a good pace, but we didn't want to go any faster. Inside the wings we both pushed our horses forward and asked them to stand off instead of allowing them to put in another stride. Both horses stood off. We flew side by side through the top of the hurdle. In the air we could hear the spectators "ooh" and "ah." When we landed, neither of us could hold one side of our horses. We both had our feet "on the dashboard" — we were pulling so hard on the reins that our feet were far forward of the usual position with the full weight of our bodies leaning back against the horses' mouths — and we flew over the last three.

When we returned, Pop and Mr. White attempted to scold us for hot-dogging it, but as we circled around the two of them, they were grinning at each other, and you could tell their hearts were not in it. That morning might have been the happiest I'd ever seen Mike as an adult.

Later, after the school, a cocky jumping rider whom I didn't know well, and didn't want to know well, approached me outside Wild Amber's stall, and said he'd like to talk to me about something.

"About what?" I asked, Pop and Carol just down the shed row.

"Why don't we meet for a drink and I'll tell you about it."

"Why don't you just tell me about it right now?"

"No, that won't work."

"Well, okay."

"See you at Scotty's in an hour."

An hour later Pop and Carol had gone back to our house, and here I was with this rider whose career was flattening out. He bought me a vodka and grapefruit juice and himself a Bloody Mary.

"I saw you school this morning."

"That's good. What'd you think?"

"They went well. Very well. So well that you and I have a chance here to really make some money."

"How's that?" I asked.

"You know, I have a ride in the same race you're in."

"No, I didn't know that."

"Well, I do, and my horse is a longshot."

"Yes."

"Yours looks like a shoe-in to me, and I think the gamblers might pick him."

## Chapter 19

"So?"

"So, why don't you let me talk to one of the other riders. You ease your horse up. You and the other jock let me through. I win. The long-shot wins. And we collect a bet big enough to carry us through the rest of the meet."

I stared at him.

"I'll bet one thousand dollars for you," he stated.

I was so shocked I couldn't think straight. I couldn't believe that he was approaching me with this idea in such a cavalier fashion. Was he really asking me to pull a horse? Was he really asking me "to pull" my father's horse, and not just a horse, but Wild Amber, a horse who had become my friend and teammate, a horse Pop and I had worked on all spring and summer? Yes, he really was asking me to do this. I got up and walked out.

\* \* \*

A few days later I was in the jocks' room. An older rider from out of town, from Chicago, was there that day to ride a stakes race. Most of the flat riders were from South America, and many could speak only a little English. This guy was a Caucasian and spoke English, and Dick Dwyer, my steady valet, was going to be his valet for the day. He imme-diately found out from Dick who I was, walked up with not a stitch of clothes on — he was the most bow-legged human being I'd ever seen — and started telling me of trips up the Jersey Turnpike he'd taken with Pop in a hot car, and then of races he'd seen Pop win. He was one of the old-timers — had ridden with Arcaro, had ridden with Hartack, and was getting ready to hang it up.

Chicago went into the shower and seconds later came flying out, chasing two or three young, wet, and naked riders. He had his towel wrapped up into a rat's tail just as we used to do after wrestling practice at Gilman School and was snapping and cracking it against their butts as they ran through the room, knocking over neatly set saddles and pairs of boots and causing Dick and the other valets to cuss them out.

Chicago then settled down and told stories and sang songs and made fun of the riding styles of some of the others, in particular the way Braulio Baeza would ride to the post sitting bolt upright, with his back as straight as a board. Everyone laughed and was in a great mood.

Meanwhile, throughout all the excitement, Joe Aitcheson had been sitting on the bench in front of his locker sewing up a hole in his britches. I sat down beside him, and he asked how I was doing and how my horse had been going. He was not trying to squeeze information out of me that would help him in riding the upcoming race, as some riders would do. He wanted to help. I explained Wild Amber's history of going to the front and the flat riders not being able to "rate" him. I explained that I'd thought I had him all figured out, but a few days earlier I'd schooled him head and head with another horse, and he'd taken off with me. "I couldn't hold one side of him," I said.

"Well, sometimes," Joe said, still looking down at his sewing, "on a horse like that, if you don't rush off at the start, if you just ease away from the start, you can jump the first two in the middle of the pack, and then 'park' your horse right behind another. Don't let him see daylight. And he'll relax, settle down."

This was a new concept for me. Pop gave me pointers now and then, but he often let me learn through my mistakes, successes, and observation of others. He was a complete natural, and sometimes he acted as if I'd been born knowing most of what a rider needs to know.

I used what Joe taught me to set Wild Amber up in a good position early in the race. Then, using what Pop had taught me about relaxing my hands and riding with a long hold, I rated Wild Amber. We won the race. Pop, Carol, my sister Sallie who was up for the week, Dick Dwyer, and Michael, Wild Amber's groom, were waiting for us when we jogged back to the winner's circle. Pop had proven the naysayers wrong. Wild Amber could be rated. We had controlled Amber's five-eighths of a mile sprint speed and used it to win going a mile and three-quarters over jumps.

# 20

## You Can't Win 'em All

We won that day at Saratoga, but there were many we didn't win. I didn't win on Limbo, and I had two chances. Limbo was the biggest Thoroughbred I'd ever seen. He was more than eighteen hands, had a huge head, and was tough as hell to gallop. Once I was up on most horses, I felt a part of them. On Limbo, I felt like a little flat rider; I felt like a kid trying to steer an oversized speedboat. I rode him with my stirrups as short as I could jack them up to get as much leverage as possible.

Galloping around the track, whether at Delaware Park or Saratoga, he pulled like a train. He lunged and leaped one direction, then the other. He took gigantic strides and wrung his head. Railbirds stopped whatever they were doing — stopped reading their papers, stopped sipping their coffee, stopped looking at their stopwatches — and stared at us.

On the morning of July 24, 1970, we had finished up work at Delaware Park. I was to ride Road Trap that afternoon at Monmouth Park, and Dougie Small — who had ridden with my father and whose younger sister and brother were Sue Sue's and my childhood friends — was to ride Limbo. We were "on the card" in a betting entry — meaning that because Pop trained both horses, they would be entered in the program as 1 and 1A, and a bet on one of us was actually a bet on either of us.

Dougie picked me up early at the barn in his high-powered El Camino — a car with the back cut out like a pick-up truck. I got in. Tall and thin, Dougie was an incredible big shot to me.

"We're good and early — okay if we stop by the Brass Rail before we head up?"

"Sure," I said, "That's fine."

A few minutes later I was sitting beside one of the country's leading riders on a barstool at the Brass Rail. Bernie — on the other side of the bar — fixed Dougie a big Bloody Mary and me a virgin Bloody Mary. Dougie had a *Racing Form*. He relaxed and spent some time flipping through it. I talked to Bernie. It was still early and the regulars weren't in yet. Bernie asked about my father and Tom. Tom Voss had looked so dirty and worn out that summer when he came in after galloping each morning that finally Bernie had volunteered to wash, dry, and fold his clothes for him. They took care of you at the Brass Rail. Dougie put the paper away and nonchalantly ordered another Bloody Mary. He sat there, perfectly relaxed, as if we were going to have this drink, then lunch, and go back to the Skyways Motel and take a nap. A few of the starting gate crew came in. These were tall, strong men who'd been pulling and pushing horses in and out of the starting gate all morning and now had a few hours off before they went back to the gate for the first race. Dougie's brother Dickie had worked on the gate, so Dougie and the crew struck up a conversation.

I was getting a little nervous. I didn't want to do anything against the grain — to appear like an old nanny to Dougie — but finally I said, "Maybe we ought to hit the road."

Dougie said, "All right," as if I were certainly being overzealous, ordered a jug of Bloody Marys to go, and then we were out in the glaring parking lot. He turned the key, revved the engine of the El Camino, the whole car shook, and we were instantly flying down the road. He drove with the accelerator on the floor, passing every car we came up behind, in and out, and yet spoke calmly in his mellifluous Ricky Nelson voice as I fixed him one Bloody Mary after another.

We sped onto the grounds of Monmouth Park, walked fast through the parking lot. This was my first ride at Monmouth Park. In fact, I hadn't been there — especially to the jocks' room — since Pop's fall.

Into the jocks' room. We were late. The man running the jocks' room had a little talk with Dougie, but Dougie just shrugged him off, told him we'd gotten caught in a traffic jam.

Then, I heard this grumbling and cussing and something being thrown down on the floor. I heard someone say, "Come on, Lacey. Cool it, Lacey."

Then, an older gravelly voice, "That brick-headed, stubborn, crazy sonofabitch. Who the hell does he think he is? I know the doctors told him never to ride again. Jesus fucking Christ, can you believe those stewards are allowing this ..."

Dougie and I were standing there with our tack bags. I remembered him now from the last time I'd been in this jocks' room, but I wasn't positive. He looked so old.

With one eye on this cyclone of fury, I asked the head of the jocks' room who my valet was and he said, "You're looking at him, son. A recent graduate from the Emily Post School of Manners. He made a special request to work with you."

I approached Lacey. He continued to cuss and grumble as he set up some tack for one of his flat riders. "That Paddy Smithwick — when he walks in this door I'm going to ..." I set my tack bag down on the bench outside his lockers. He stopped grumbling and moving things and stared at me with his eyes popping out of his fleshy, pock-marked face.

"Who the hell are you?" he said, first looking me in the eye, then moving his eyes down my body to my feet and back up again as if I were ten feet tall. "We don't have any fucking elephant races here."

"I'm A.P. Smithwick," I said, knowing that's how he would've seen my name in the program, "and I'm riding in the jumping race."

"You're who?"

"I'm A.P. Smithwick Junior," I said. "Paddy Smithwick's son …"

He cut me off. "You are. You are! And I'm … Jesus fucking Christ Junior!"

I didn't say anything more.

Lacey stared at me for another few seconds. "I've seen you before. I know I've seen you before. Okay, why don't you get out of those clothes and check your weight. We have a swimming pool here now, you know. Jump in the pool or take a shower. I'll get your tack straight."

I picked up his program. There Dougie and I were listed on Limbo and Road Trap. Limbo got in with 145. I wondered how Dougie could do that weight so easily, steadily sipping Bloody Marys and not having to drive in a hot car or hit the hot box. My horse also got in with 145. I had weighed myself countless times, including that morning before work, and I knew I was in good shape. Just then I saw Dougie walk by with just a towel around his waist. He took the towel off, laid it on a table, and stepped up on the scales. He was six feet of bones. You could see his ribs, his collarbone, his shoulder bones, and his hip bones all poking sharply from his skin. He stepped off the scales, wrapped the towel around his waist, and walked up to me, this big shot steeplechase jockey, this older brother of two of my best friends.

"They had the weight wrong in the paper," he told me. "I'm six pounds overweight, and I only have time to lose a pound or two at the most." I wondered what this had to do with me.

Suddenly, I was meeting with Pop at the door of the jocks' room. "Dougie's overweight," Pop said, looking me in the eye. "You two are riding an entry. You can make the weight for either horse, so you now have a choice: You can switch and ride Limbo or you can ride Road

Trap. The stewards told me you can switch horses. Limbo has a shot of winning, especially if he carries the correct weight."

I pictured myself on Limbo, galloping around the track at Delaware in the mornings, just barely keeping his gigantic body and wrecking ball of a head in control. In my imagination I ran the film of the last time I'd seen Dougie school Limbo over hurdles. There wasn't much he could do in the way of control. Dougie rode short, really short. Limbo was rank, thrashing his legs, throwing his head as they headed into the first hurdle. Dougie dropped his hands and let Limbo go. Limbo had taken huge, long unhorse-like strides, not paying the slightest bit of attention to the hurdles, just galloping headlong into them and then shooting over them. And Dougie, showing incredible calm, nerve, and skill, somehow had him jump each hurdle just right.

I knew Road Trap well. I'd already ridden him in one race, and I'd schooled him over and over. He was well mannered, calm in the paddock, easy to ride to the start, a good jumper, but he didn't seem to have the zip, the flash, the brilliance to get to the wire first. Limbo had that brilliance. The owner had sent him to Pop because she knew he could take this previously unmanageable horse — who actually did not fit in the starting gate — and mold him into a winner. This was Limbo's first race over hurdles.

"I'll stick with Road Trap," I said. I knew that I was not following Pop's code of always going with the flashier, riskier, faster horse; I was going for the old and steady campaigner, but in this case I felt I was making a good decision, and, after all, I was following Abraham Lincoln's dictum, "It is unwise to switch horses in midstream."

It was a wild race from the start. We were heading into the second hurdle. I was in the back of the pack, and suddenly, looming on my outside was Limbo. Oddly, my horse was taking two strides to Limbo's one, and Limbo was eating up the ground, passing me, pulling Dougie's arms out. I watched as he sailed over the hurdle. Then, we were picking up the pace. I passed a horse. We were heading into a hurdle on the backside. The horse to Dougie's inside dived over the hurdle, swerving right into Limbo's path, and shooting up a barrage of brush. I focused straight ahead on the hurdle, riding Road Trap steadily into it. Out of the corner of my eye, I saw Limbo jump low and to the right, with Dougie sitting back in the saddle, just before we took off. Road Trap jumped it fine, and I started pushing him. I looked twice at Limbo, in front of me and to my outside, sensing something was wrong and saw that Dougie was calmly galloping along in his usual Irish-jockey's style, but he did not have his left foot in the stirrup. Dougie had come up from almost falling with both feet on the right side of the saddle. In an acrobatic move he somehow got his left foot back on the left side of the saddle and took the lead. Limbo held the lead until the last couple of fences, jumping well, and finished second. With three hurdles left, I made a move, passed half the field, and finished sixth.

I galloped Limbo the rest of the summer, but it was always Dougie who schooled him. The naysayers condemned Limbo to complete failure, saying he was too big and too rank to win as a steeplechase horse, but Pop paid them no attention. A race came up early in the meet at Saratoga, and at the last minute we found out that Dougie couldn't ride him that day. Pop got Joe Aitcheson to ride Limbo. The pair went to the front immediately, led all the way, jumped well, and won by two lengths. Joe always made it look so easy. I rode Road Trap in that race, as an entry with Limbo, pushed him to keep him up closer to the pace, but again finished sixth.

A week later another race came up for Limbo. Joe had to ride a horse for Mrs. Phipps. That night at dinner Pop said, "You know him. I'd like you to ride him."

"Okay," I said, "I'll do it."

The day of the race came up. I usually rode in Pop's favorite light saddle. It only weighed about a pound, and it was strong and had a long seat. When a horse got in heavy, I used Pop's old "timber saddle" — called that because he used it in timber races where the weights are heavier — which I loved. It weighed five pounds, had a comfortable and long seat, and had nice leather flaps for your knees to grip. Limbo came up with an in-between weight of 142, so I chose an in-between saddle I'd never used. It was a good-looking lightweight saddle, but it also had a long seat and a substantial flap of leather on the sides. It had a slight crack in the tree — the wooden framework — but that was far back from the pommel, and I didn't think it would make any difference.

The starter dropped the flag. I only weighed 136 and was not as strong as I liked to be. I went ahead and let Limbo run away from the start. I didn't really want to be behind all these miniature-looking horses and then have to mow them down, but that probably would've been a better riding tactic. We picked up speed heading into the first hurdle alongside a few others. Approaching the hurdle, I pushed, asking Limbo to extend his stride — which he did in a powerful way I'd never experienced — and we took off, soaring over the hurdle, gaining two lengths on the other horses, and when we landed, he took a hold of the bit and jetted away from the field. I had a good hold of the rubber-sheathed reins, my feet were practically up on his shoulders, and I was pulling against him as hard as I could, feeling each stride yank and reverberate through my arms and body. Approaching the second hurdle, right in front of the clubhouse, I couldn't slow him. I didn't want to take any chances of falling, so I did it again: asked him, one two three, for a big one, and we soared over the hurdle, but something was wrong.

We had now opened up about eight lengths on the field, and he was still pulling as hard as ever. The saddle was slipping. With each stride, as I pulled against him, the saddle slipped farther and farther up onto his withers.

We jumped another hurdle. Landed. Now, I couldn't really pull against him. The saddle had slipped up over his withers. I was leaning against the reins, but there was nothing for my feet and legs to grip. Instead of my calves gripping Limbo's sides or his shoulders, they were swinging out in thin air on either side of his neck.

This was scary. It would be like sitting on a runaway Harley-Davidson motorcycle and every time you tried to ease up on the gas, you flew faster and faster down the highway and the seat slipped forward another inch until you were riding with your rear end over the gas tank and your feet sticking out on either side of the front wheel. I had to just keep going. I couldn't pull him up. I couldn't steer him off the course — he'd just keep running right through the outside rail. We were locked in. By the time we'd reached the fourth hurdle at this unreal pace, we had opened up ten lengths on the field. Then, nearing the last hurdle down the backside, I could feel him fall apart beneath me. Suddenly, he was exhausted; he felt wobbly, leg weary, wrung out. We clobbered that last hurdle, and the entire field passed us.

We didn't win that one; we finished last — and it was a tough defeat. Limbo had such a long neck that no one could tell from just watching the race what had happened. Everyone just thought I'd screwed it up. Owners, trainers, valets, gamblers, other riders don't want to hear any excuses. You go on and win the race or you don't and you shut up about it. I lost and I learned. I learned to be more careful with my tack, never to ride in a saddle that is not in perfect shape, and, who knows, maybe it was all for the best — for that lesson could've been learned from a ride with a far worse outcome.

I still hadn't learned to rate a horse by sticking him behind a few others early in the race. Joe Aitcheson would teach me that. But first he would teach me another lesson.

It was early March of 1973, about a month after Pop had pulled me away from my desk and asked me to come down and gallop Tambourine Man. It'd been drizzling and sleeting on and off all morning, and I was soon to experience another defeat. We were stabled at Pimlico, and it was a miserable day for galloping. No matter what you wore, your hands got wet and froze, and you were sweating one minute in your rain suit and freezing the next. It was after the break —

the track had just been harrowed. Pop threw me up on a quiet, well-mannered gray horse called Mr. Brookside, who was to run in a flat race in a week. It had stopped raining and sleeting, so I took off the bulky, uncomfortable rain suit and felt clean, streamlined and light, walking in just jeans and my favorite, recently cleaned, light-weight blue jacket as I walked out to the track on Mr. Brookside.

I was to wait at the gap, go on the track the second the gate was opened, jog back the wrong way to the three-eighths pole, turn, gallop easy to the wire, get him on the bit, break him off at the five-eighths pole on the backside, and breeze him a steady first half-mile, making him really run the last furlong.

I went onto the track, my irons jacked up short like Braulio Baeza's. I could do this on Mr. Brookside because he was so quiet. I followed all directions. I galloped under the wire, around the turn, past the starting gate chute. I was wearing my hunting cap. I reached up and pulled the visor down and made the cap snug against my forehead so it wouldn't blow off. My race-riding helmet, with two pairs of goggles on it, was at home in the tack bag.

We'd beaten the rush, and only a few horses were on the track. I kept my eye on them, making sure no one was in our way. One horse was ten lengths ahead of us; he was out in the middle of the track, so I didn't think he was going to breeze. I gave Mr. Brookside a squeeze, making him pick up speed while simultaneously I took a hold of the bit to get him pulling against me, and we started drifting in toward the rail, preparing to break off at the five-eighths pole and to pass the horse up ahead on his inside. But the horse up ahead was also picking up speed and was drifting in to the rail.

We broke off at the five-eighths pole and closed in on the horse ahead, and then, as we approached the half-mile pole, the horse up ahead — and I could tell by the riding style that it was Joe Aitcheson in the tack — dropped down onto the rail and broke off to breeze. Mr. Brookside and I were four lengths behind him, and the wet dirt, feeling as if it'd been laced with pellets, was flying back, a never-ending stream of it, making a ripping sound as it lashed into my jeans and jacket, and hitting, smacking, slapping me in the face so that I couldn't see a damn thing. No goggles on the hunting cap. I had to get down lower and lower, put my face in Mr. Brookside's mane. I pushed Mr. Brookside, but the faster we went, the faster Joe went and the more mud and sand lashed at us. Making it worse, I'd been too cocky and had jacked my irons up so high, that now, having to push Mr. Brookside — who wanted to back away from this stream of mud — my thighs were on fire and I was starting to blow like a fat man.

Going around the turn, I could see we weren't going to pass Joe. I was losing ground being out a few lanes. I had no choice but to pull in behind him and to take the gushing dirt. Once around the turn I pulled Mr. Brookside out into the middle of the track. Looking like a fool breezing a horse way out there, and unable to keep my tuck, I rose higher and higher in the saddle as I struggled to push Mr. Brookside down the stretch while Joe calmly, cleanly, low in the saddle, not even knowing I was there, finished his breeze right on the rail.

Pop, Uncle Charlie, Emmett, and Sal greeted me back at the barn. Sal was shaking his head and grumbling to Emmett. He had his stop-watch in his hand, and I was sure it didn't catch us in any world-beater time. He raised his head, looked at me and then at the watch, and shook his head some more.

Pop was grinning, looking as if he were about to break out laughing at any second. Uncle Charlie had a smirk on his face, and Emmett, who was calling out, "Come on, Al, bring him over here, Al — he'll be all right. You can't pick 'em up and carry 'em ..." was the only one showing any sympathy. I knew what I looked like. The entire front of me — face, chest, thighs, calves — was encrusted with a half-inch thick layer of Pimlico's finest dirt, sand, and ground-up horse droppings.

"What happened out there, Bud?" Pop asked.

I hopped off the horse. On landing, my legs gave way so I had to take an embarrassing step or two to regain my balance. I was still huffing and puffing and spitting the dirt out of my mouth, and I was squinting and blinking my eyes because of all the scratchy stuff in them.

"I broke off at the five-eighths pole. Everything was going fine. And then that Joe Aitcheson broke off at the half-mile pole right in front of me, shooting back all this damn mud and I couldn't see a thing."

Sal was busy pulling poor Mr. Brookside's eyelids back and blowing into his eyes, trying to get the dirt out. Pop and Uncle Charlie were now chuckling. Pop grabbed the tack from me. I wasn't seeing anything funny about this; in fact, I could barely see at all. "That's all right, Bud," he said. "Don't worry about it. That won't be the last time you'll have to worry about Joe kicking dirt in your face. Now go on over to the men's room and clean up."

"Yeah — dunk your head in the toilet," snapped Sal, "and while you're at it, take this horse with you and put him in the shower."

"Got any change?" Pop asked.

I slapped my blue jeans pockets. "No."

He reached into his front pocket, pulled out his silver money clip, and handed me a twenty. "While you're over there, stop by the cafeteria and get yourself and the rest of us a cup of coffee."

I didn't win that one, but I learned a little more. One, watch out for Joe. Two, gallop with goggles at the ready on your helmet. Three, be prepared for all contingencies, and don't go out there all cocky with your irons jacked up unless you know you can ride that way when the unforeseen occurs.

* * *

That fall I was riding a little bay South American horse for Pop in a hurdle race at the Fairfax hunt meet in Virginia. I had won a timber race at Fairfax on Count Walt two years before, and I'd finished second in a flat race, riding the great Tuscalee for Mr. Aitcheson, Joe's father, the year before. I felt comfortable as soon as I set foot on the Fairfax course. I was also good and fit from riding races at Saratoga.

Galloping into the last fence, we were on the inside, and Joe Aitcheson was on our outside, practically bumping us, just a head behind us. This was something very hard to do — get the inside from Joe — and I was feeling confident galloping into the hurdle. The last fence was on a turn. You jumped it, then turned to the left and headed around a slight bend and straight down a short stretch. Galloping into the hurdle, I didn't turn my horse's head to the left to angle the hurdle as you normally would. I just kept going straight and since the hurdle was on a turn, this had the same effect as drifting out would on a straightaway. As we neared the hurdle, I did let my horse drift out just a little. Joe and I jumped the hurdle together, and the second we landed, I pulled on the left rein and cut back in to the inside rail, leaving Joe hanging on my outside. We gained a length on him and galloped down the stretch the winner.

I was weighing in by the stewards' stand after the race, preparing to accept the trophy and glad to win this hurdle race because I needed my 10 percent of the purse to help pay the Hopkins tuition that fall, when Pop came up. "Hold on, Bud; Joe's claimed a foul." I laughed inside and re-ran the film of that last hurdle in my mind. I didn't think the stewards would uphold the foul, and I was flattered to have a foul claimed against me by the most experienced and accomplished of jockeys riding in the country at the time.

Joe and I milled around the stewards' stand, waiting for the decision. Finally, it was announced. The stewards disallowed the foul. Pop, the little South American gelding, and I were the winners. Joe walked up to me, shook my hand. He'd just been conducting his business in the most professional of manner, as he always did. We turned to walk away and he patted me on the back before he headed back to the jocks' tent and I headed to the trophy presentation. That pat meant he understood that my little bit of drifting out had been fair and square and, in fact, good race riding; he didn't hold it against me.

# Chapter 20

I didn't win on Wadsworth at Belmont Park. Wadsworth's riders had not been able to hold him in a race. Rank and powerful, he'd leave the tape, churn his legs, go straight to the front and fly over those first three hurdles like a racing motorcycle, but then he'd run out of gas at the end of the race. I'd heard gamblers yell out "Chicken!" at him when the jock had jogged him back to the stewards' stand. Pop's stable rider, Dave Mitchell, had done an excellent and nervy job controlling him and had won a race, but then Wads had "broken down" in another race — had badly bowed the tendon in a front leg — and the owner had given him to us. Mom and I had worked on him all winter, schooling him cross-country, even bringing him foxhunting, trying to calm him down, and it'd paid off, though our first few hunts were not too successful. One time he took off with me going through a narrow, twisting path in the woods, passing hoity-toity members of the hunt standing there quietly on their well-behaved horses. Heading into a sharp turn, his nose on the ground, he turned so sharply, and jammed on the brakes so suddenly, that I was thrown off and landed in the branches of a sapling. Someone ahead grabbed the reins of Wads' bridle, returned him to me, and I hopped out of the tree onto his back.

We knew Wadsworth was no chicken. I'd ridden him in two races, and we'd been pleased with his performance. He'd been relaxed, jumping better and higher over the hurdles, and finishing strongly from off the pace. Mom had fallen for him, and so had I. We trained him together, right on the farm, where he was relaxed. I'd exercised Wads in the cold on many winter evenings after classes at Hopkins, and Mom had jogged him up hills all spring to strengthen his legs. Over the summer Mom had stood him in a pool in the stream to cool off his legs. The vet said that it was almost as if the tendon had never bowed.

Mom, Pop, and I drove up the night before the race, went out to a nice dinner, and spent the night in a hotel near the track.

The next afternoon Wadsworth and I left the tape at Belmont in front of the stands. I pulled Wads in behind a few horses, and he galloped along, jumping great. I'd never had so much confidence in a hurdle horse's jumping. The second time around, approaching the clubhouse turn, I asked him to pick it up. We were passing a couple of horses and I felt as if I was on the winner when suddenly his right shoulder crashed downward, his head went down, and he took a horrible lurching stride, then another and another and I was standing up high, pulling him to the outside. I hopped off before he came to a stop and looked at the tendon. It had given out. Wads was lunging and leaping. I held the reins steadily, depressingly. The leg was beyond repair. Mom and Pop had gotten Wads for me. They'd let me bring him back to the races. He didn't have to come back and be a hurdle horse; he could have just been a hunter. I blamed myself. I felt sick. Mom was sitting up there in a box in the clubhouse with Pop watching all this. I imagined her putting her program in front of her face and asking Pop what was happening. The race went on. I tried to calm Wads. The crowd cheered as the horses ran down over the last hurdle and up the stretch. A car sped up to us, a vet jumped out, and the track's horse ambulance was coming around the turn toward us. I knew what was going to happen. We didn't win that one. We lost a great friend. A great friend with a big heart. He would have "galloped" that day.

* * *

I didn't win the second time I rode Tote'm Home at Saratoga, after just winning on him two weeks earlier. As the race neared, Pop and I had a disagreement, and perhaps even a misunderstanding. He told me to ride him just as I had the week before, stay way "out of it," wait and wait, and then, at the last possible moment, make my move. I was uneasy with this. I wanted to be up closer and make my move earlier. It was one of the only times Pop had given me explicit directions. Usually, when he gave me a leg up on the horse, he would say, "You know what to do," and I'd feel relaxed going to the post, knowing I had a loose plan for riding the race, but if something unusual occurred

— if the speed horse fell or if the pace was slow — I could react and do what was best. But this time the starter dropped his flag, and we were off, and I felt stuck. There was little pace, but still I stayed back and waited and waited. The instant I made my move going down the backside, I could tell I had waited too long. The whole pack in front of me, having kept a slow pace, had plenty left in reserve and they picked it up, and I couldn't catch them.

Back untacking, Pop asked, "What were you doing, Bud? Why were you so far out of it?"

I wanted to give a detailed explanation. But Jack, the groom, was there, and Dick Dwyer was there, and I felt like a fool, and I couldn't explain it in just a nutshell, and I didn't want to look even more like a fool by trying to blame Pop for the tactical error. Feeling shame and defeat sweep over me, I couldn't think of what to say, and so I didn't say anything.

* * *

I also didn't say much when I lost on a horse at Aqueduct trained by my childhood idol Tommy Walsh. And this time it was because I did not obey the trainer's directions. Standing in the paddock, Tommy had said to me, "I like the way you ride into a hurdle and make the sonofabitches jump. That's why I'm putting you on this horse today. Now listen, Little Paddy," and then he looked me in the eye quizzically, his mind having switched to a different thought, "You're not riding dry are you?"

"What?" I asked, perplexed.

"Your father didn't let you come out here without first giving you a taste, did he?"

"Ah, no. No, he didn't."

"Okay. Now, don't let this horse get a fast start. Drop in close behind some horses going into the first hurdle. Don't let him see daylight. Then let the bastard skip through the first. Let him hit it. That'll settle him down and then you can gallop around in the pack and do your job. Got it?"

"Yeah, I got it." But I hadn't. I had never heard such directions. I had never heard of such a tactic. The Smithwick tradition — Pop's, Mom's, Mikey's — had always been to get the horse to jump every fence as well as possible.

The horse behaved all right going to the post. At the start he was no more nervous than any other horse. I lined him up. The starter dropped his flag. There were two horses in front of us. I gave him a squeeze, and instead of tucking in behind the horse on the inside, I let him "see daylight" — the space between the two horses in front of us. He charged up between the two horses, spotted the upcoming hurdle, and took a hold of the bit. As we neared the hurdle, instead of letting him chip in and hit it, I asked for a big one, we flew over it, landed and took off, immediately opening up five lengths on the field. We flew around the first mile and a quarter of the race in front, too fast, running and jumping. With three-eighths of a mile to go, four or five horses passed us, and we finished back in the pack.

After I untacked and weighed in, I headed toward the jocks' room. Tommy walked alongside me as two Pinkertons helped us make our way through the crowd. No kids were asking for my autograph. "Little Paddy," Tommy mumbled, looking down at the ticket and cigarette-and-cigar littered cement.

"Yes," I replied, feeling terrible.

"I told you not to let him see daylight."

"Yes, you did."

"And to let him hit that first hurdle."

"Yes."

"Guess your father never gave you those orders."

"No, he hasn't."

"That sonofabitch can run and jump, now can't he?" he said. "Shit," he continued, grinning, "he stood off from here," he pointed down at our feet, "to there," and then at the wall of betting windows ten yards away, "at the hurdle going into the clubhouse turn."

"He sure did," I said. I'd actually heard the spectators take a huge gasp, and then go "Wow," when we'd rocketed over it.

We walked along. "He can get rank." He looked over at me, knowing we'd been rolling right along down over the first four or five hurdles and it had taken a little nerve to hang on.

"Yes — he was tough to hold."

"That's why I wanted you to let him hit that first one."

"Right," I said.

"The bastard'll win next time out, Little Paddy."

"I'm sure he will," I said.

The bastard did win next time out, but not with me in the tack.

# 21

## In Honor of a Horseman

In the fall of 1972, after the win on Wild Amber at Saratoga, I returned to Hopkins. I hung up my race-riding tack but continued to gallop for Pop through a beautiful autumn and into the winter. In February, one night, I got a call from Tom Voss. It was bad news. There was no one around who would understand. Who could you explain it to? My classmates — would they understand? One minute Emmett Grayson was our uncle, our godfather, our mentor, our comrade, and my father's most loyal supporter. Next, he was gone. It was the end of an era. There were no more horsemen coming along like Emmett.

The Virginia countryside flashed by our windows. Tom was driving. MiMi, with whom Tom had fallen wildly in love, was sitting beside him. I was seated in the back with Carol. We were rushing. Carol and MiMi weren't pleased with Tom's driving. Tom was totally focused on getting us there on time. He smoked his Pall Mall, leaned forward into the steering wheel, worked the clutch, brakes, accelerator, and stick shift. We shot down the narrow country roads. The same roads that Pop had sped down, Mom by his side, and Sue Sue and me in the back, on the way to the Middleburg races the day he won the timber race on Valley Hart. The same roads Carol and I had sped down the day I won the timber race on Sand River. The scenery was the same, but it was not spring and we were not on the way to win a race; it was February and we were on our way to a funeral.

We were on narrow asphalt strips that cut right through huge coarse fields. Grit and gravel clattered up against the sides of the car. Barbed-wire fences with Civil War-era cracked locust posts shot by just a few feet from our windows. Cows stood bleakly between moss-covered rocks lumped here and there in the cold, brown fields. The cows didn't move. They didn't graze. Some lifted their heads and watched as we rocketed by. Going around sharp turns, Tom pushed in the clutch, went through the gears, gravel shot up hitting the underside of the car, and I either leaned into Carol when we turned one direction or I was thrown into the side of my door when we turned the other. I could remember the feel of these curves throwing Sue Sue and me into the sides of Pop's car when we were kids. The feel of it, the centrifugal force pushing me one way, then another, was pleasing, like returning to see an old friend, like bicycling down a steep, winding hill you've gone down a hundred times before and letting your body fall into the rhythm of turns it knows so well.

I could see MiMi's hand tightly gripping the handle of her door. "Thomas," she said. "Thomas, Emmett would not want you to have an accident on the way to his funeral ..." Tom kept looking straight ahead. We had had a quick bourbon before we left Maryland. "Come on and have one," Tom had said. "Yeah, I guess Emmett would approve," I'd said. I felt a little fuzzy-headed. Huge gray-bottomed battleship-like clouds floated above us. One minute everything was dark beneath the hull of the cloud. The next, the sun shot brilliantly through the gaps between the battleships. A little clapboard gas station/country store came into view. The white paint had almost entirely chipped off the clapboard. Tom downshifted through two gears and pulled under the extended roof of the building, beside a row of rounded, 1950s-looking gas pumps. Rusty metal signs hawking chewing tobacco, cigarettes, Coca-Cola, Amoco and Esso gasoline, cow feed, horse feed, and tractor parts were nailed all around the building, partially covering up holes and gaps. Tom jumped out to pump the gas; I went inside to get directions.

We were close. After a few miles we skidded to a stop on the gravel on the side of the road. I stepped outside, and the sunlight and the cold both struck me. It was February in Virginia — one of those still days when the cold makes your feet feel like they're being squeezed tight against a slab of ice as you walk on the lumpy, frozen ground. Tom and I vaulted the rickety post-and-rail fence and ran to the graveyard where we had seen a fresh mound of dirt encircled by flowers when we overshot the church entrance. Carol and MiMi stayed in the car.

We stood reverently over the grave for a moment. Everything appeared bright and shiny. Tom and I couldn't figure out if it was Emmett under all that dirt or someone else. But we set the flowers our mothers had given us on the mound anyway.

Carol joined us, and I talked her into going into the church. We stayed for five minutes until we realized it was the wrong church. There was not a black person in it or anyone we knew. The preacher was telling us all we were on our way to eternal hell. By the time Carol and I slinked out of the church, Tom had found out where Emmett's funeral was.

Again we parked on the shoulder of the road. I ran up a dirt road overflowing with empty parked cars. I sidestepped and shouldered my way through the wave of people walking down the hill and rushed to a canopy. A group of soldiers in their dress uniforms, one carrying a bugle and the others, rifles, was leaving. A coffin lay alone under the canopy. People were milling around outside the canopy, about to leave. There must have been three hundred people there — all black except for us and a few others.

I saw Emmett's wife, Catherine, standing by the canopy. I approached her, and as soon as she saw me, she opened her arms and gave me a long hug. Some men I had known from around the race-tracks when I was very young came over closer to the coffin to say hello.

Everything was going wrong. We were just arriving and everybody else was leaving. I had wanted to stand near the coffin and look at it and think about Emmett. I had wanted to stand straight and endure the cold and think about Emmett while the preacher rattled on and the twenty-one gun salute cracked the sky and the bugler played taps. It would have been nice because I would have been a part of all those hundreds of people who were doing the same.

Instead, all I did was stand next to the coffin and make small talk with old acquaintances. Everybody was scurrying around, women crying and men looking sorrowful but as if they understood and would endure what had happened.

The next thing I knew we were caught up in a vortex of people leaving, and my aunt, Dot Smithwick, for whom Catherine had worked for years, invited us back to her father's farm. We were in the car and being drawn down the dirt road along with hundreds of others and then breaking away from the long line of cars and following Dot to the farm where we had drinks and lunch before driving home.

* * *

I had seen Emmett a week before he died. He was in the Veteran's Hospital in Baltimore, not far from Johns Hopkins.

I walked down a wide corridor to the information booth, the hard leather heels of my riding boots making each step ring out on the tile floor and echo off the bare walls. I asked the clerk for Emmett Grayson's room number. I knew only relatives were allowed in and it would be a bit tough getting by the clerk. The clerk asked if I were from out of town, as Emmett told me he would, and I said yes, I was from New York. Then he asked if I were a relation and I hesitated, thinking that I might not get away with lying. He stated that maybe I should try later because only relatives were allowed to visit Mr.

Grayson at this time.

I finagled the room number from the clerk and ducked into a poorly lighted stairwell. Once on the correct floor I began to walk down the corridor. I saw a dark, unlit phone booth. Someone was seated in it. I saw a dark face and bent down to see the person more clearly.

The man was wrapped in a white robe. The body looked too shrunken to be Emmett. I moved closer. The profile turned toward me. The face was square and symmetrical, the lips thin, the cheeks sunken, and the skin stretched tight in a shocking manner across the cheek bones, jaw, and chin. He looked up at me. "Hold on, Catherine; it's Al."

He spoke a few more words and hung up. He held on to the inside handle of the door, slowly pulled himself up.

"How ya doin, Al?"

"I feel like I'm about to be carted away," I said.

"What're you talking about?"

"The man at the desk wouldn't allow me to see you."

He moved to face me by turning his shrunken shoulders. "Oh, that's a lot of shit." He turned back, facing down the hall and grinned. "You come up any time you want, Al."

He started taking short steps down the hall. I walked beside him, feeling tall and awkward. He had shrunk in size as well as weight. The muscle on his powerful shoulders and arms had deteriorated. His columnar neck was now stalk-like. In one way he looked younger, his thinness making him appear boy-like, but in another way he looked like an ancient man. His formerly black hair was longer than usual and sprinkled with white.

He held his head high and grinned as if he were going to give a tour of his new house. "Well, Al, what have you been up to?"

"Going to college, mainly."

"How's married life treating ya?"

I reached into my back pocket, pulled out my wallet, opened it, and blew into it — blowing out the dust — something Emmett did when he needed a few bucks. "Pretty good. Rough on the pocketbook though."

He kept moving. He stopped at an open door, put his arm out against it and waited for me to enter in front of him. It was a high-ceilinged room with yellow paint flaking off the walls and two tall windows that were admitting almost no light; they looked out on the solid brick wall of another building.

I walked past an occupied bed to the foot of an empty one parallel to it and rested my hands on the gray steel footboard. Emmett walked slowly up to the bed and turned around. He put his hands behind his back, on the mattress, and strained to lift himself up onto the bed.

I sat in the chair alongside the bed and looked over at the man in the other bed. He had a long tube running out of his pajamas into a quart-sized jar hanging below his bed. The jar had an inch of yellowish foam in its bottom. The man was lying there on his side as if a heavy weight were pushing down against his body. His huge stomach lay like a sack alongside him. His bristled face stared blankly at me.

"How you doing?" I asked the man.

He kept staring at me. Finally, he said, "I'm all right as long as that jar's not empty."

I nodded and looked back at Emmett. The back of his bed was up. He was seated on the bed and was stiffly lowering his torso. The muscle strands of his neck jutted out until his head rested on the mattress. He pushed off his slippers with the heels of his feet. Elastic bandages were wrapped around his insteps, ankles, and on up. His feet were swollen and the skin of his heels was dry and scaly.

"Hell, I didn't know you were in here till I found out last night," I said.

"Oh, been in an' out for three months now."

"Your boss Tom told me."

"Tom …," he said slowly, accenting the "ah" sound, and then fondly letting the name roll off into a humming sound. "He's a hard-working boy." Emmett had gotten so weak that he'd been forced to quit working for Pop. He remained living in his room in the Vosses' barn and helped Tom out as much as he could.

I was about to reply, but he was straining to push himself up with his arms. I got up and gripped my hand around his bicep. It was like holding a bone wrapped in skin. I gently eased him forward.

"I got to show you something," he said.

He lowered himself to the floor, put his feet down softly, walked to the window sill, and unwrapped some papers.

"Look at this, Al." He held up a three-foot rubber tube, thick as a hose. "I got to put this down my neck three times every day. Here, hold it." He handed it to me. I took it with my thumb and forefinger and almost dropped it. The end had a blunt steel tip and the tube must have been filled with mercury.

"Damn, that is heavy."

"Couldn't get anybody to do it at home. Had to do it myself first thing every morning. It's to keep my throat from clogging up."

"How about my partner, Tom? He'd do it."

"Naw, he's a'scared of the sight of blood."

I helped him back onto the bed.

A middle-aged nurse who'd catch your eye jauntily walked in. She started folding the newspapers lying at the foot of Emmett's bed. Only the sports section was opened, and that to the racing results. "Emmie, looks like you have company. All right if I borrow these for my lunch break?"

"Sure."

"You getting along all right?"

"Oh yeah."

"Okay — see you a little later." She pranced out.

"Em-mie …," I sang out. "I'm going to have to tell Catherine on you. Can't have this going on in here."

"Ah," he beamed. "She's an old girlfriend, a Virginia girl, you know

— from before I got married … She stops by around lunch time and we go over the racing news together. How 'bout a little something to drink, Al?" He nodded and directed his eyes toward his closet.

"No thanks."

A big white nurse marched in, put a tray down on the old man's bedside table. He started eating immediately. She returned with a tray for Emmett.

"Now what are you going to eat?" I asked.

"Ah no. I don't want none of that stuff. Wouldn't give my dog that stuff."

On the tray were a pot of coffee, a bowl of clear soup, a scoop of mashed potatoes, some mashed meat, and a cup of grape juice.

"Come on, you've got to have something."

"Okay, put a little pepper and salt in the soup."

I fixed it and gave it to him.

He had a couple of spoonfuls. Then, as if he had a neck brace on, twisting his shoulders, he swiveled his eyes as far right as possible. "Hey, old man," he said, grinning. "Want some more?"

The man had finished all his food. He stared at Emmett.

"Al, hand him the tray."

I handed the man the tray, and he eagerly began on it.

"God-damn, Emmett, what do you eat?"

"Have Cream of Wheat for breakfast."

"You've got to start eating more."

He put his hands on his stomach and didn't reply.

A tall black nurse strode in, clipboard in one hand, pen in the other.

Emmett was grinning like a kid caught doing something wrong. She looked from Emmett to the old man. "All right now, Mr. Sedgewick, let me have that." She reached for the tray. "Come on now, Mr. Sedgewick." He stared at her and gripped the tray with both hands. She stepped forward and took hold of it. He looked up menacingly at her.

"Now, Mr. Sedgewick, it's for your own sake." She took the tray, turned her attention to Emmett. "Now as for you, Mr. Grayson."

"I'm sorry. I won't do it any more."

"How do you feel?" she asked.

"My stomach's starting to swell up and it's burning a little. I guess I don't look so good, do I?"

"Oh, I don't know," she said. She smiled, then turned and left.

"You're going to be in trouble now, Emmett."

"Yeah, I'll be on the list now. They'll be watching out for me." Emmett thought he was on several lists: First, there was the IRS list, for not paying taxes. The IRS man did visit our barns occasionally wherever we were stabled. Somehow, Emmett always received advance notice when "the federal man" was coming and would vanish for an hour or two. Second, Emmett had gotten a speeding ticket or two over the summers in Delaware. He was sure the state cops had him on their list, and one more conviction could lead to being "put on the bean farm," where he said the white prison guards forced the black prisoners to work like slaves. Third, he was positive the boxing officials in Delaware had put him on a "hit-list" years ago for winning too many matches, and that this was why he'd been matched one night not against one of the usual racetrack grooms but against "one of the deaf-and-dumb boxers" from a local club whose incredibly fast left jab combined with an iron jaw caused Emmett to hang up his gloves.

He started coughing. He spit into a cup on the bedside table.

"They've got to have it to examine," he said. He leaned back and shut his eyes and remained still for a moment. He opened them. Seemingly relieved, he looked at me. "What do you got to ride this spring, Al?"

"I'm quitting riding," I said, the words sounding strange, not going together right. I wanted to rephrase the remark.

"What!"

"Yeah, had to."

"N-o-o-o-o-o-o-h," he frowned, looking me in the eyes, slowly shaking his head.

"Well — between galloping every morning and going to the hunt meets every weekend and all the drinking after them — I couldn't keep up with my classes at college."

"You'll start up again." He smiled.

"I don't know. I'm just helping Pop out now, getting on a few in the mornings. When the second semester starts in a few weeks, I plan to stop altogether. I'm doubling my course load so I can graduate this spring."

We sat there awkwardly. Emmett stared at the foot of the bed and shook his head, frowning. I stood up. He looked up into my eyes.

"Well, maybe I ought to let you have some rest," I said.

He seemed to sink farther into the mattress.

"How long you supposed to be in here?" I asked.

"Supposed to get out tomorrow, but they say that 'bout every day."

"You going to go back to your room in Tom's barn?"

"No-sir-ee. I want to go down to Middleburg."

"You still own that house on the corner, right before you go into town?" I asked, lowering myself back onto the chair.

"You bet I do. After I get better, I want to go down there and live." His eyes fell from me to the foot of the bed.

"You can't do that and leave Catherine up here," I kidded.

"What you mean? She's going to quit her job and come with me. In a while those kids will be grown up, and Miss Dot won't need her anyway."

"How's Tom going to survive without you?"

"Yep, they're going to build a racetrack down there, and I'm going to get a job as a Pinkerton — easy work and good pay. Tom ... he'll be all right. Don't you worry ... Damn, as soon as I get a little better I got to go up to Pimlico and make sure we have some stalls for the meet — that boy — he'll never do it."

A priest hurriedly walked in and came to Mr. Sedgewick's bedside. He crossed himself and mumbled a few words. He asked Mr.

Sedgewick something. Mr. Sedgewick slowly looked up at the bottle and in a whisper, said, "I'm all right as long as I can keep filling that bottle."

I looked back at Emmett.

"Some pitiful people in here, Al," he said, "A man across the hall just had his leg cut off." He turned to his side and made a slicing motion from beneath his crotch to his right hip bone. "Right here. Took one whole side of his ass off. Just barely left his asshole."

"What do they want you in here for?"

"They stick needles in me all day long."

"Have they operated on your neck?"

"All they did was cut it open and let the pus out."

"You were going to do that yourself once."

"I did, last winter. I got a razor blade and burnt it so's it'd be sterile and made a cut in that big lump and the pus and shit just flew out. Yeah, they said if I had've come in earlier it wouldn've been so bad." He looked down and we were quiet. He raised his head back up. "Al, when you going to have some kids?"

I wondered, for the first time, why he and Catherine had never had any. "Not for a while," I answered.

"You gotta have someone to give your money to."

"Well," I laughed. "We got a puppy the other day."

I looked down at my watch. It was five minutes to one. I had a philosophy class that started at 12:30. It was a great class, a seminar, with an inspiring professor who treated us like adults, like young philosophers.

"Emmett, I'd better get going. I've got to try to make my class."

"What time's it start?"

I hesitated. "One-thirty," I said.

"Oh, you'll be on time. What're you learning?"

"I've been studying how to pay attention to all the little things in life, to every little moment." He looked at my quizzically. "I've been learning that it's best to make up your mind and go full tilt, like in riding a race, for whatever it is you want in life."

"That's a mouthful, Al. Hasn't the Boss already taught you that?" He gave me a frown like I had gone a little crazy, and then started to ease himself off the bed.

"Where you going now?" I asked.

He smiled, got his feet on the floor and into his slippers and headed, crouched over, away from the bed. "I am going to see you to the door, Al," he said very clearly, enunciating each word. He reached the door and leaned on the door jamb. I put my hand out to shake his. He hesitated. This was odd. I didn't know if we had ever shaken hands. He put his hand out. He did not tightly grip my hand and vigorously pump it up and down, as I'd been taught at Gilman. He gently gripped my hand. His palm and fingers felt warm and alive and fine-boned. He didn't pay much attention to the shaking. His eyebrows were furrowed, his lips closed, and he had a dimple in one cheek as he forced a barely discernible grin and gently squeezed my hand.

"I'll see you soon, Emmett. Start eating more, will you? You look like you're light enough to start riding over jumps again."

"Over jumps? Hell, I could ride on the flat. I only weigh ninety-five pounds."

I waved to him and headed out.

I started down the corridor. The leather heels on my riding boots again made my steps ring out and echo off the bare, sterile walls. I felt alone. Emmett seemed sharp, alert, I told myself. He'll be all right, I told myself.

I'd call Tom and inform him that he was crazy telling me Emmett wouldn't last another week. I would go to my class now, and I would live in the present, I thought, as I strode out of the Veteran's Hospital into the cold air and down the hard, marble steps. I would finish up this semester strong, very strong, and Emmett would be back working in the barn in a month.

I reached the sidewalk and turned to walk the three blocks to my car.

An elderly woman was helping a frail old man out of her car. He was probably another veteran, preparing to get a bed in the hospital. I slowed, thought of saying something to cheer them up, even thought of assisting. They stopped their struggles against age and gravity and stared at me and I picked up speed, realizing that tears were running down my cheeks.

# PART V

# DOING LIGHT WITHOUT POP

# 22

## Blind Switch

*A jockey is coming around the last turn, getting ready to make his move, sitting on "all kinds of horse." He hasn't yet tapped down fully on the gas. He's on the inside of a few horses. He's "saving ground." He's "going good." Around the turn, he's ready to stomp down on the accelerator, but suddenly he realizes he's trapped. The horses in front of him are tightly bunched. The horses to his outside "aren't going anywhere." The rider is sitting on a winner but has no place to go. This rider is in a "blind switch."*

The fall of my senior year at Hopkins, I was still galloping horses for Pop at Pimlico but had left riding races to concentrate on my studies. Late one rainy fall night, just a couple of weeks after I'd decided to stop race-riding, the phone rang. It was Mr. Aitcheson, Joe's father. He offered me two rides at the race meet that weekend, one of them on Tuscalee, a legendary steeplechase horse who was a sure winner. I had ridden Tuscalee once before in a flat race, and it felt like being on a high-powered motorcycle that had been programmed to do everything, including surging to the front and winning. I told Mr. Aitcheson I couldn't do it, I had stopped race-riding. I got back into bed and told Carol about the conversation. She was quiet. We lay there, apart. I listened to the cars forlornly whoosh by on the road outside our little one-story house.

And then in early spring, 1973, I left riding altogether. I stopped galloping for Pop in the morning before classes — the job that had paid my way through Hopkins — and doubled my course load so I could graduate that spring. This was tough on Carol. We'd just been married one year, and suddenly I was entirely changing our lifestyle. Carol and I had gone from being immersed in the excitement and adrenaline rush of Thoroughbred racing to me studying, reading, and writing all the time, in addition to locking myself in my writing room and applying to newspapers all over the country. Anywhere, I was thinking, as long as I got my first job. My letters took flight to as far north as Alaska and as far south as Louisiana.

All that spring, while I was finishing up at Hopkins, Carol was getting up at four every morning to drive the twenty minutes over to Mom and Pop's and then to drive Pop the hour up to Delaware Park. She talked and joked with him and worked around the barn, gradually gaining the respect of the grooms and riders. I was holed up, sending out short stories, studying newspapers, calling editors for interviews, typing out rhetorical letters-to-the-editor, thinking they might help me get noticed. I went to the extreme of going to services at the Christian Science Church with my grandmother a few times so that in my application to the Christian Science Monitor, a great paper in those days, I could say I was a member.

Carol would arrive home at noon, dirty and sweaty, smelling of the sharpness of manure and liveliness of horse sweat and the scent of shed rows and hay and straw and a horse's coat. Exhausted, she'd shower, and before she'd take a nap, we'd lie on the bed for an hour and watch the Watergate hearings in disbelief.

In early May, Mom and Pop attended my Hopkins graduation — we had a bright, sunny, cheerful, champagne-sipping lunch afterward. Later in the month Pop's health deteriorated. He was coughing more, feeling weaker. He began to go to doctors. He missed days of work. I went back and galloped horses at Delaware Park when Pop needed me, but most of the time I was pounding the sidewalks, interviewing for newspaper jobs. Mom supported me. Pop supported me. Yet, neither of them could refrain from expressing the desire to have me back on the farm and at the track.

One morning I galloped eight horses at Delaware, took a shower at Pop's room in the Skyways Motel, rushed down to Cambridge, Maryland, in Dorchester County as if I were going to ride in a hunt meet, and had a Bloody Mary or two at lunch with a group of editors and publishers. Soon I had my first non-horsey job as a writer and photographer on the *Dorchester News*, a weekly paper, edited by Howard Gillelan, a big, burly, bearded, hard-drinking, bow-hunting, and deep-sea-fishing author and photographer who looked like Ernest Hemingway, had Hemingway's dedication to precise and clear prose combined with a far better sense of humor, and taught me most of what I know about journalism and photography. In June, I moved across the Chesapeake Bay to Dorchester County, a two-hour drive, rented a bedroom from the nicest little grandmother, and worked day and night. Carol continued to work for Pop. Colleagues at the track criticized me for not returning to help with Pop's horses, as well as for moving to Dorchester County and leaving Carol in Baltimore County. They gossiped. They stabbed. They had no idea. I had returned to the track so many times. This time I had made my break on graduating from Hopkins, and I was determined to make the best of it. I wanted a fresh start. We knew so many people at home that it was hard to find time to write; we were invited here, invited there; friends stopped by; the phone rang; everyone wanted to have a few drinks, then a few more. I wanted to move to a place where we didn't know anybody and I'd have time and peace and energy to write.

The doctors couldn't diagnose Pop's illness. They thought he'd been working too hard. They said it was the drinking. At one point, after he'd had a seizure, they'd considered he might have epilepsy. Finally, a friend of the family told Pop to go see her doctor, a general practitioner who had a little office in her house. Pop and I got in my car. I drove the short distance down Manor Road, pulled into her long, pine-tree lined driveway, and coasted to her house at the bottom of the hill. The doctor was a sweet woman. Pop took off his shirt. She did the usual with the coughing and a stethoscope. I sat to the side, watching hopefully, and drifted back to an image of Pop and me in a doctor's office at Saratoga. Pop had had a fall and a concussion, and he needed a doctor's clearance before the stewards would allow him to ride again. The doctor had held a sharpened pencil up beside and slightly behind his right eye, and then his left, and asked both times if Pop could see the tip. Pop had answered no, and the doctor refused to allow him to ride the next day — said his peripheral vision had not yet returned from the fall. Pop was furious. We went back to our rented house, and he told Mom all about it. "Paddy," said Pop, "didn't he hold that pencil practically behind my head?" The next morning the owner of the horse Pop was to ride that afternoon made some calls while we were at work. We went to see another doctor. He shined a little flashlight into Pop's eyes and said he was fine. Pop rode that afternoon, and he won. That's what was going to happen here. This sweet, even pretty, doctor whom Pop seemed to feel at ease with, was going to tell us that we had gotten through the tough part, Pop was now healing, and yes — he could ride tomorrow, he could live.

That's not what happened. She looked over the reports we'd brought, asked about his health problems, gave him a detailed physical, and told us that he had cancer, most likely lung cancer. She explained how she'd come to this conclusion. She gave us the evidence, even the proof. It seemed so simple. She was shocked that none of the previous doctors had diagnosed this earlier. In just a few days Pop was put in the Greater Baltimore Medical Center, where he started chemotherapy. He stayed in for a week, came home to recuperate, and then went back. Back and forth he went. It was tough, but he held on, and we thought the chemo would knock the cancer out of him.

I was "under the influence" of H.L. Mencken at the time. The "Sage of Baltimore" was my exemplar as a journalist and Hemingway as a short-story writer; you couldn't find two more opposing styles of writing. I set fantastic goals of prolificacy for myself. I wrote letters home every night, late, my fingers rattling the keys of the old manual Royal typewriter in the empty newspaper office, telling Pop and Mom about my adventures working on the paper, using long, energetic sentences filled with the fun-sounding polysyllabic words that Mencken used in his diatribes. I arose at 5:15 and worked on short stories constructed of short words and simple sentences in the style of Hemingway. At work, I strived to write narrative pieces reflecting the novelistic techniques Tom Wolfe espoused in his book *The New Journalism*.

Pop trained from his hospital bed by communicating to Mom what the horses should be doing. Mom had half a dozen racehorses to deal with on our farm, plus fifteen or so at Delaware Park, an hour's drive north, in addition to attending to the bookkeeping end of the business. She was more and more upset. Pop's medical bills were piling up. She worried we would lose the farm. Finally, the Horsemen's Benevolent and Protective Association of Maryland stepped up and paid the bills. Mom was forever grateful. Carol started to drive up to Delaware Park by herself at 4:30 a.m., and then back to the hospital, where she reported to Pop how the horses had gone.

I was reading Gay Talese and Hunter S. Thompson, and Ken Kesey's *One Flew Over the Cuckoo's Nest* and studying the headlines, stories, and layouts of the *Washington Star*, *Washington Post*, *New York Times*, *National Observer*, and *Christian Science Monitor*. I totally immersed myself in writing features, hard news, and editorials for the paper — relishing it, loving it, thinking Pop would overcome his illness as he always had with the bruises, the broken bones, the concussions, the paralysis.

## Chapter 22

But the doctors told Pop the chemo wasn't enough. They told him: We can operate. If it's successful, you'll get six to twelve more years; if it's unsuccessful, the cancer will spread, and your life will be shortened. If we don't operate at all, you'll live one to two more years.

Pop and I discussed this nightmarish scenario. Pop stuck with his code: Always go for the brilliant horse, even if he is riskier, go for this ride over the drone that is sure to make it around, sure to be in the money. Ride the riskier one that has a chance of falling at the third or fourth but — if you ride him well, if you control his speed — should win by twelve lengths. Like Babe Ruth, Pop didn't bunt. He went for the home run.

They operated. Pop and I were told it was successful.

We'd been through all this before. He'd start improving soon.

Carol and I were having difficulties. She didn't want to move to Cambridge. I had a hard time fully communicating with her over the telephone. I was focused on trying to launch my new career. I was not paying attention to what was happening to our marriage. One week in July I thought Carol was being particularly quarrelsome. To have some privacy, I left the office and called her from a hot, stifling, sticky-floored phone booth on the corner. She immediately started crying. I begged her to tell me what was wrong. People merrily walked up and down the sidewalk of Gay Street. One or two waved to me. I had to shut the glass door. A policeman I knew well waved as he walked by. (A week earlier he had protected me from two accused murderers who had forcefully entered my office and sat on my desk after their photo appeared on the front page.) The policeman turned around, stopped, and squinted at me, checking to see if I was all right before he continued his patrol. I gave him the thumbs-up sign. I had been writing some not-so-subtle front-page stories showing that the Cambridge police needed a pay raise, and the chief of police, as well as his subordinates, looked out for me. Cars stopped and started at the traffic light, the blistering Eastern Shore sunlight reflecting off their heavy strips of chrome and stabbing me in the eyes.

No, she couldn't tell me. No, she'd promised not to tell me. Okay — but I had to swear that I would not tell anyone …

There, sweating in the phone booth, I learned what she had known for weeks, for months. The operation had been unsuccessful; the cancer would spread fast, and my father only had several months to live. My sister Sallie, who had just turned fourteen, had been too young to tell. My sister Sue Sue was away in Spain, on a college program, and hadn't been told. And the doctors hadn't told my father or me. They thought they were protecting us. They thought I wouldn't be able to take it.

I now understood what Carol had been living through. I went back to the office, tried to work on a front-page editorial about the mayor and city council attempting to screw the police force out of a raise. The work seemed meaningless. I got in my car and drove madly to the hospital. I pushed the car to the limit. Tears blurred my vision. I met Carol in the room with my father. He was in bed; she was sitting in a chair in the corner of the room. He was kidding her, urging her to lie down on the bed with him. She must be so tired …

"Ah no, Paddy!" she said, laughing. I got the bottle of Early Times out of the closet, poured a shot into a plastic cup for me, a shot into another cup for Pop. I looked over at Carol. "No thank you," she said.

"How about some ice, Bud?"

"Hold on a minute," Carol said. "I'd better get going."

"Ah come on," I said.

"No, I've got to get back to the house and let the dogs out."

"All right," I said.

Carol gave Pop a peck on the cheek. We walked out into the hallway. She looked me in the eye. "Don't wear him out, Patrick. A doctor came by earlier and said that he definitely needs his rest."

"All right, don't worry."

"And you behave," she said.

"I will. I'll see you back at the house. I'll spend the night and drive back to work early in the morning."

I gave her a hug then walked down the hallway, looking for the ice machine. When I returned, Jack Graybeal, Uncle Charlie, Tiger Bennett, George Clement, and Betty Bird had taken over the room. Betty Byrd, about whom Pop had written so beautifully in his child-hood diary, was sitting at the foot of Pop's bed, looking him in the eye and talking quietly to him. Jack Graybeal, Pop's close friend, who worked as the whip of the Elkridge-Harford Hunt, and Uncle Charlie were finding a place to sit. George Clement, immaculately dressed and looking like an English gentleman about to spend a day at the races, was standing off to the side, by the window, with his hands behind his back, looking out at the sunset. I hadn't seen George in months; when he spotted me, he walked across the room. Tiger was watching as George, his face drained of color, shook my hand. George hadn't seen Pop for a while, and it looked like he was in shock. He was one of Pop's most jovial friends, stopping by our house on winter afternoons and drawing in other visitors who, to Mom's chagrin, lingered with him in front of our fireplace through the evening. Tiger suddenly proclaimed, "The crown prince has arrived with the ice. Sir George, would you please do the honors." George turned, and Tiger handed him the bot-tle. Tiger set up a row of paper cups, I dropped in the ice cubes, George poured a shot of bourbon in each, and some of us had one drink and then another and forgot for a moment where we were as George, com-posed now, his face flushed from the bourbon, gradually took the floor: "... It was at a mint-julep party at the club. Don't you remember, Paddy? Some sort of Sunday afternoon affair in the spring. Suzie had just won the championship of a show the week before on Clown. Someone was saying he was the best jumper they'd ever seen."

"He was," Betty languidly interrupted, in her husky Lauren Bacall voice. "He was the best jumper I ever sat on." We all knew that Betty bought Clown later on.

George took a sip of his drink. "Someone else said he didn't believe Clown would jump worth a damn once outside of the show ring. Jack Graybeal and I snuck down to the barn, tacked Clown up, walked him up on the club lawn. Everyone came outside and looked him over. Paddy walked out in a pair of loafers, jacket, cap. Jack gave him a leg up. Paddy lit a cigarette, pulled the visor of the cap down, and headed for the nearest fence. We stood up on the hill and watched as Paddy schooled Clown all around the barns, going in and out of the paddocks, over the four-foot fences. It was a stunning performance. While Paddy was walking Clown up the hill to us, Jack went in a closet and pulled out a broom. I took one end; he took the other. When Paddy reached the lawn we held it up. Jack hollered, 'Hey, how about this Paddy?' And then, it looked as if we'd rehearsed it. Jack and I stood as far apart as we could, with the broom held over our heads and Paddy gave Clown a squeeze, cantered toward us, and sailed over the broom."

* * *

Soon, Carol moved down to Cambridge, found an interesting job, and came to enjoy Dorchester County. We rented a cottage on Higgins Mill Pond out in the country.

That August of 1973, Pop was inducted into the Racing Hall of Fame at Saratoga Springs. I had become the editor of the *Dorchester News* — as well as the sole reporter, photographer, and layout specialist. Pop was too weak to go up to Saratoga for the induction. The Hall of Fame people asked that I come up to accept the honor. The induction fell right in the middle of the week, my busiest time, and I told the director of the Hall of Fame that making the trip would simply be impossible. Paddy Neilson called me at my office. By this time, Paddy — a successful investment banker — was a top amateur timber jockey. He was as graceful and stylish a rider — whose career I had followed — as he was articulate and persuasive a conversationalist. He sent a plane to get me.

I flew up and went to a brunch, where I met Winston Guest, whom I knew to have been an old hunting and fishing buddy of Hemingway's. I also knew that he and his flamboyant wife, CZ, employed Pop's great friend Bobby Burke, who had recently retired from show-ring riding, as their racing stable manger. Mr. Guest shocked me when, surrounded on all sides by horse-racing people, he struck up a conversation with me about writing and asked how my job was going. He then mentioned he had read a short story of mine that had appeared in the August issue of a racing publication and said he had thought Ernest would have liked it. This was a fictionalized account of going to work with my father at Belmont Park my first summer of galloping horses, of his being paralyzed from the fall at Monmouth Park, and of my visiting him at the New York hospital. It was my first published short story. I was very flattered by Mr. Guest's comment about Hemingway, especially considering the backlash the story had caused among some young steeplechase people.

The editor had tossed my title for the story and had renamed it, "Remembering Pop," making it seem to a small group of my racetrack contemporaries that I had written the story as if my father had died or that I was foretelling the upcoming death of my father. This was the same clique that had gossiped I was being disloyal and an ingrate by not returning to exercise and perhaps even train Pop's horses. They had spoken behind my back to Carol, on both topics, when she was working at Delaware Park and I was working on the *Dorchester News*, and this had not helped our relationship. A few of the pushier ones had grumbled something to me early that morning when I had arrived at Saratoga and had been walking around the barn area. At first I was so shocked I could not comprehend what they were talking about. They had completely misunderstood my motivation for writing the story: I wrote it by hand, typed it up, revised it over and over, and gave it to my father as a Christmas present to show him my love and admiration. And he had loved it.

At the Hall of Fame lectern, I looked up at an audience of forty, fifty, one hundred? It was a blur. I told them Pop would've liked to have accepted the honor himself. I told them he rode because he loved to ride. It was his life; he never did it to break any records. He wanted me to say that he was very honored. I thanked the Hall of Fame for inducting my father.

After the induction I spoke to one after another of Pop's riding and training friends. Dick Dwyer, Pop's New York valet, shook and shook my hand, told me he wanted to send me a photograph he'd had made of Bill Boland, the talented New York flat rider; Jimmy Murphy; Pop; and himself — "the four brothers." Dick had been the valet of all three riders. Just then, Bill Boland approached, patted Dick on the shoulder, and shook my hand. Looking directly into my eyes, he asked how Pop was doing. I told him, and he said he would fly down soon to see him. A tall man in a suit then interrupted our conversation and shook my hand. "Son," he said, "your father was a great steeplechase rider and a wonderful man." Others were approaching me. Bill gripped my hand again, looked me in the eye again, and said, "Remember this, Little Paddy: Your father wasn't a great steeplechase jockey. He was the greatest." And then his eyes left mine and he walked out of the room.

Feeling alone, I went with a dozen others to the house of Mr. and Mrs. Ogden Phipps. We had an elegant lunch. Mrs. Phipps was kind to me, and I was reminded of when she had taken me to Brooks Brothers and then to the hospital to see Pop after his fall at Monmouth Park. She had owned many of the great horses Pop had ridden, including the greatest, Neji — also in the Hall of Fame. Mrs. Phipps invited me to the races, where she had reserved a table for Fred Astaire, his child-bride Robin Smith (our former jockey), and the rest of us.

When I returned home, I immersed myself in making deadlines and writing feature stories and taking photographs and organizing an AFL-CIO-sponsored strike of the police force so that it coincided with my weekly go-to-press deadline and I could scoop the competition, the *Daily Banner*. Few of my newspaper associates, none of the members of the Cambridge City Council, and none of the members of the Cambridge police force knew anything of my father and my life in the horse world. That ended when the Baltimore Sunpapers published an article on the front of the sports page a few days later:

**Smithwick's Incredible 'chase Feats Recalled following Installation into Racing Hall of Fame**

**by Dale Austin**

*Paddy Smithwick was inducted into the Racing Hall of Fame last week at Saratoga with the same low-key kind of ceremony that reflected his life style.*

*After 20 years in the game, in which he overshadowed most of his rivals for years, Paddy should have been a national hero, like Ruth, Gehrig or Thorpe.*

*But Paddy is in racing, specifically, a special segment called steeplechasing, and there are not many opportunities to gain adulation.*

*At his home in Monkton last week, Paddy, now training a few horses on the flat, tried to explain his success.*

*"I didn't fall off much," he said. "That's what you're not supposed to do. I guess that was it."*

Later in the article, Bryce Wing, whom Dale dubs, "the patron saint of steeplechasing," says, "Paddy was an artist. He could get horses around a course that would have fallen flat with anybody else."

He adds, "But you know, it was more than just his talent. Of course, he had plenty. Paddy, if he lost, did it in such a sportsmanlike way. He was a thorough gentleman."

One magazine quoted the 1958 issue of *American Steeplechasing*:

*In all his years of riding, Paddy has incurred official wrath only once, and that resulted in a fine by starter George Palmer. In a way this is a key to Smithwick's character. In a profession where the competition gets pretty keen and the going rough at times, his good sense and spirit of fair play keep him out of the trouble spots. In fact, it would be hard to say that he ever won a race by taking unfair advantage.*

*If a popularity poll were taken among steeplechase riders, the name Alfred Patrick Smithwick would lead the list. Quiet, unassuming, but a man with very articulate ideas about horses and riding, he is the personification of a gentleman, a race rider and a great credit to the Sport.*

Articles kept coming out in newspapers and racing publications about Pop's career and his induction into the Hall of Fame:

**Paddy Smithwick: Courage and Class**

*Dick Dwyer … visited him last week and knew the end was near.*

*"He asked for some pain killers," Dwyer said. "That was the first hint. It was the first time I knew him to admit that anything ever hurt."*

*"He hurt plenty, too. He took all the spills and falls and never complained. They talk about football players playing hurt … he lived with that for years and still was the greatest….*

*"One day, shortly after his release from the hospital, he told me he just had to get back on a horse to see if he could still do it. I learned later that he had popped a few over low hurdles, just to prove to himself that he wasn't afraid. I know all of us who knew him never questioned his courage …*

*"When people thought Paddy might be too big to ride, trainer Burly Cocks was the first to note, 'They never measured his heart. That was the biggest part of him.' "*

That Thanksgiving Pop died. The cancer had been close to his heart, and when the doctors operated, they found it had spread. I was twenty-one; he was forty-six. He was gone, and with his departure the horse world also was gone for me, or so I thought.

My marriage to Carol was unraveling. By spring we were separated and heading for a divorce. My father, my wife, and my way of life were all gone in under a year. I didn't know what to do.

# 23

## Flying Change

*The canter has two stride patterns, one on the right
lead and one on the left, each a mirror image of the
other. The leading foreleg is the last to touch the
ground before the moment of suspension in the air.
On cantered curves, the horse tends to lead with the
inside leg. Turning at liberty, he can change leads
without effort during the moment of suspension, but
a rider's weight makes this more difficult. The aim of
teaching a horse to move beneath you is to remind
him how he moved when he was free.*

— the first stanza of Henry Taylor's
two-stanza poem, *The Flying Change*

In the late spring I quit my job at the *Dorchester News* and set out to
make a living as a writer of short stories and novels. I went down to
visit my old girl friend, Phini, at Hollins College in Roanoke, Virginia. I
took her out to a boozy (on my side of the table) dinner and told her I
didn't know what to do with myself. I had looked into the creative
writing program at Johns Hopkins but had been too late to apply for

the fall. She recommended I apply to the creative writing department at Hollins College. I had been unaware, first of all, that Hollins even had such a department and, secondly, that any males were enrolled at Hollins. I discovered that the college was all girls, but the graduate departments were coed. I would never have known any of this, nor would I have applied to Hollins, had it not been for this late-night dinner with Phini.

Returning to Dorchester County, I nervously called the creative writing department at Hollins, prepared to ask the secretary if there was still time to apply for the upcoming academic year. The secretary politely asked me a few questions and then said, "You need to talk to Richard."

"Richard?" I said.

"Richard Dillard," she laughed. "You know, the head of the program. Wait a minute. I'll transfer you."

The phone rang and rang. I felt I was not doing something right. The head of the program!

The secretary was back on the line. "He must not be in his office. Hold on."

I heard her set the phone down. I heard a step or two taken toward her doorway.

"Richard!" she called out. Then I heard, "Oh, there you are. A young man's on the phone ..."

I could hear the two of them laughing as they walked into her office, and I thought, here I am interrupting this important man's activities with a ridiculous, even ludicrous question. And then Richard Dillard picked up the telephone and all my worries vanished. He asked me about my background, sounded positive about my prospects, joked with me a little, and seemed to have an incredible joie de vivre. I immediately liked him. He had an unusual, very quick, off-the-wall sense of humor. I had to stay on my toes to keep up with him. The next day I mailed Richard a letter, transcripts, copies of my published newspaper articles, and a clip of my published short story on Pop as well as a manuscript of a short story I'd written about Emmett Grayson, which had been accepted but not yet published by a literary journal. My background was different from that of others applying; I was accepted and given a full scholarship and a generous grant. To come up with some cash, I sold my car and bought a sexy ten-speed bicycle, which I soon named Esmerelda.

I had serious misgivings about going to Hollins. I associated it with "going down the road" from Washington and Lee, taking dates to the Hollins Inn, and Hank Slauson and I being shot at by the cops and then outrunning the police as we merrily blazed through the windy Hollins roads in my Ford Falcon, only to be met by two state trooper cruisers at the entrance to the college, put in handcuffs, and tossed in the clink for the night, waiting to be bailed out in the morning by Joe Bosley, my "big brother" at the Beta House. That part of my life was over. How could I go back to Virginia, back to Hollins, as a writer?

I left Dorchester County and lived with Mom over the summer. I cleaned out the smoke house, set up a desk, shelves, and a typing table, wrote stories, started a novel, and read Faulkner's *As I Lay Dying*, James Agee's *A Death in the Family*, and Malcolm Lowry's *Under the Volcano*. I galloped some freelance horses, worked in Mom's garden (we lived on beets: beet leaf salad, beet soup, beet slices. My urine was beet-red most of the summer), and in a desperate search for love and female companionship, I had two intense relationships with young women. I kept track of what Carol was doing, sometimes called her late at night, and a few times visited her, unannounced and uninvited, late at night.

I also saw a great deal of my grandmother Um. I'd bicycle the twelve miles over to Hydes, and we'd go out in the back field, have a picnic, and talk about writers and literature. She loved reading biographies, especially on Churchill and Lincoln, and was always full of surprises. One afternoon, sitting on a log jump in the hundred-acre field, I was discussing my interest in Fitzgerald and Hemingway. Um patiently listened to my monologue and then remarked that she had had lunch with Hemingway in Paris in the 1920s. (She had worked in Paris as a Red Cross nurse during the war.) She knew he was a good writer, but she thought he drank too much, talked too much, and in general "thought too highly and too much about himself." No, "Winnie," as she referred to Churchill, was the ideal — she'd read most of his works and had met him several times — though he also sometimes drank too much. Um had subscribed to the *Dorchester News*, and we had corresponded the entire time I worked on it. When I waffled on my decision to go to Hollins, Um pushed and spurred me, and informed me she would send an occasional check to help with expenses.

Granny Whitman also subscribed to the *Dorchester News* and acted much like my literary agent. She cut out articles and sent them across the country to friends who were journalists and writers. She even sent a magazine story I wrote on foxhunting to the queen of England and received a nice note back from the queen's personal secretary. Granny cut out every lengthy newspaper piece that I wrote, taped it to a white sheet of paper, and mailed it to her friend and former colleague Nancy Offutt, past English teacher and retired headmistress of Garrison Forest School. Ms. Offutt would then mark up the article with a pencil, comment on the grammar and style, and mail it back to me. Granny urged me to go to Hollins.

Soon it was two o'clock on a Monday morning in September. I had to be at Hollins at nine to start classes. I bicycled home to Mom's from a party held by one of the young women I was romancing. I had a half-loaded U-Haul parked in Mom's driveway. I finished packing, gently rolled my new, bright yellow, sleek touring bike between the couch and the mattress, and started off on a new life, heading to Harper's Ferry, then to Charles Town, West Virginia, and down Route 81 through the Shenandoah Valley, past Lexington and Washington and Lee, to Roanoke. I had never had such a drive.

I'd been reading a book belonging to Sue Sue — an art major — on the revolutionary art of the American painter Edward Hopper, a member of the wonderfully named movement, the Ashcan School. I'd been studying Hopper's paintings and at the same time poring through a coffee-table-sized edition of Walt Whitman's *Leaves of Grass*, each page thick and textured, and each poem accompanied with stunning, sensual illustrations of Americans at work and at play out-of-doors, by majestic rivers and mountains, with vistas stretching out into infinity behind them. The sun came up as I entered the Shenandoah Valley. My eyes were eerily sensitized to the infinity of colors from studying the Hopper book, and I could see everything much better high up in the cab of the truck than in a car. It felt like the U-Haul was an airplane and I was floating on wings through a valley of greens and blues and reds. I had the Whitman book beside me and I was memorizing and reciting aloud sections of "Song of the Open Road" — as Ricky Hruska and I used to do driving home from Delaware Park with a six-pack of beer resting on the emergency brake between us.

I had a fresh cup of black steaming coffee beside me and I was starting anew:

*Afoot and light-hearted I take to the open road,*
*Healthy, free, the world before me,*
*The long brown path before me leading wherever I choose.*

*Henceforth I ask not good-fortune, I myself am good-fortune,*
*Henceforth I whimper no more, postpone no more, need nothing,*
*Done with indoor complaints, libraries, querulous criticisms,*
*Strong and content I travel the open road.*

I didn't have a cent to my name. But I didn't owe a cent either. I had a bike. A grant. A few boxes of favorite books. Three chairs, a writing table, a typing table, a mattress, and a sofa. A briefcase filled with dozens of partially completed short stories, and the rough draft of a novel — which I wanted to hone, polish, revise, receive criticism on, and finish at Hollins. Hundreds of books I wanted to read. Hundreds of young women I looked forward to meeting. New fresh minds. When people had asked about me going there, I told them, oh yes — it is all girls, but they decided to make an exception in my case. (This reminded me of Mark Twain's comment, when, lying on his death bed, he was asked by a reporter, "What do you have to say now?" And Twain replied, "I was hoping, in just this one case, that God might make an exception.") Later I would explain that the undergraduate school was all-women, but the graduate programs were coed.

I was leaving behind a marriage, a way of life, and a place that reminded me at every step of an experience, an adventure, or a conversation with my father. I planned to ease up and even, perhaps, completely stop the drinking. I planned to take undergraduate courses in modern American literature, modern Irish literature, the English novel, and to write and write. I had driven down over the summer with Sallie, and we had picked out an apartment. It was a one-story, two-car garage; the owners had pulled the cars out, nailed sheets of wallboard to the inside frame, put in a sink, refrigerator, and toilet, and declared it an apartment. It was perfect. The price was right, it was secluded — high up on a hill and out in a grove of trees — and it was just a mile's bike ride from the campus.

At Hollins I immediately met Kathy Raley, an inspiring, energetic junior. We became good friends. All fall she kept telling me how she could not wait until a classmate from Florida returned from her year in Paris. Ansley Dickinson was her name. Kathy went on and on about her: Ansley Dickinson was beautiful; Ansley Dickinson was tan and had stunningly straight, long brown hair; Ansley Dickinson had the most incredible figure, and she was smart, really smart; Ansley Dickinson was majoring in Russian studies and was studying the Russian language with French students through a French-speaking professor. We would be perfect for each other, Kathy said. And Ansley could dance; I wouldn't believe the way she could dance. At bars or nightclubs, whether in Paris or Roanoke, the managers often came out and asked if she'd like to dance professionally. Kathy was insistent, and I got so I paid no attention to her.

I worked hard all fall. I fell in love with Hollins. I had amazing professors. I did not regress to the life of a Washington and Lee fraternity boy. I arose early, at my old racetrack hours, and wrote every morning, went to classes in the afternoons, went for long runs and bike rides through the mountains at dusk, and spent the evenings either reading or getting together with fellow graduate students. I had no car, no money, and no financial worries. I befriended a wonderful man called Poopsie who worked in the Hollins cafeteria. He called out "Hey!" and waved to me every time he saw me entering the cafeteria; if I saw him first, I called out "Hey!" to him. Poopsie helped me get free breakfasts, and at the conclusion of my morning feast, he'd slip me a paper bag of food to make it through the rest of the day. My grandmother Um lived up to her promise and sent me a small check, with an accompanying letter, each month.

I was reading *Adventures of Huckleberry Finn* again, studying it in a class on American literature taught by Richard Dillard. As Hemingway said, "All American literature comes from *Huckleberry Finn*." Richard made the relationship between Huck and Jim, and the many decisions Huck had to make about what was right, come alive. Twain was writing about how to come to the right decision, and how to live, way before the existentialists I'd been studying at Hopkins. I was reminded of what Emmett had taught me about loyalty, about working hard, about not worrying about getting the credit but just focusing on getting the job done right, about learning a craft, an art, about discipline — being at work at 4:30 every morning no matter what. Flat tires, flooded roads, blizzards, speed traps, you just have to prepare ahead. And about racism. It was behind the scenes on the racetrack. But my father set an example by treating every man as an equal. And Emmett showed me that there was no difference between the soul of a black man and the soul of a white man.

Early that fall at Hollins my short story on Emmett came out on in a literary magazine. A group of us took the check for twenty-five dollars I'd made on the story and went down to the Hollins Inn to cash it. At first the owner/bartender refused. He wanted to frame it and hang it on the wall and give me the twenty-five bucks. We laughed and insisted he cash it, and in no time we blew it all on beer. Between ringing up the cash register and pouring draft beers, he began reading the story from behind the bar. When he came across a paragraph he liked, he'd hold up his hand, stop pouring the beer, wait for the noise to settle, and read it aloud. We laughed and drank, and he kept the beer flowing way past what the twenty-five dollars would buy, predicting more glorious times to come. I'd been editor of a newspaper; I'd won awards on the paper for the writing of short stories, features, and hard news; my short story on Pop had been published in a glossy paper over a year earlier; and now my story on Emmett had come out in a new literary magazine. I was on a roll.

Nevertheless, by this time — despite Kathy Raley's optimism about my upcoming relationship with Ansley Dickinson — my love life was a mess. One of the Maryland girls from over the summer was attending another all-girls college in Virginia, and I was occasionally seeing her. Then, in one of my creative writing classes, there was this southern, sophisticated Hollins senior, who had a fondness for black leather pants and heavy eye shadow; we were having a fling — which she was writing about and then reading to our creative writing class. And there was Carol, back in Maryland, whom I was still thinking about, dreaming about, writing a novel about, and to whom I was still married.

One night in January, Kathy Raley ran half a mile across the fields and up to my refurbished garage. "She's here!" Kathy announced. We decided to have a couple of beers to celebrate. I poured them into shapely pint glasses given to Carol and me by Tom and MiMi as a wedding present. The conversation shifted. Kathy started telling me about the difficulties she was experiencing with her boyfriend Patrick — she called him "Patrick One" and me "Patrick Two," not my favorite nickname — and we never got to see Ansley Dickinson.

The next night I was in an apartment-dormitory complex with my slow-talking, heavy-smoking Southern femme fatale. I was trying to get her up to my refurbished garage, and she'd informed me she was not going to ride up on the cross-bar of "Es-mer-el-da," nor was she going to hike across the dark and murky cow pastures through which I so loved to run. A bunch of us were sitting in a cramped washing-room/kitchenette, drinking scotch. The Rolling Stones were on and this girl walked in and someone introduced me to her. Ansley Dickinson. She had just returned from Paris. Then, the Rolling Stones record was spinning, and the washing machine was chugging along, and this Ansley Dickinson was facing away from me. She was wearing snug blue jeans and a turtleneck, and she was fixing me a scotch and water on the chugging washing machine, and she had the most beautiful figure. Her hips were catching the rhythm of the Stones, and the scotch was on its way, and her hips were swinging, the back pockets winking, and Mick singing, and it drove me wild. In a terrible move on my part, I asked her to drive my femme fatale and me up to my garage. I ducked my head and squeezed into the back of her VW bug — reminding me of the old car pool days with Ronnie Maher. My girl in black sat in the passenger seat, and Ansley Dickinson got in behind the wheel. They started to chat, and I began to regret asking this Ansley Dickinson to give us a ride, but what the hell. They talked stiffly about Paris and the Hollins Abroad program, and then this Ansley Dickinson asked my girl in black something about where we had met, and my girl in black laughed, took a drag of her cigarette, and came out with a snappy sounding French expression. Ansley Dickinson laughed, and came out with another French expression, and with that, they chatted away in high-speed French, which I couldn't keep up with, all the way to my garage.

A week later, on January 17, 1975, I was seated at a large round table in the Hollins cafeteria. As a favor to Kathy Raley, I had escorted a friend of hers to a ball the night before. I had gone with a group, fallen off the wagon, which I'd been on since January 1 — with the exception of a few late nights with my creative writing classmate who, with her love of Southern Comfort, was not the best influence. I had drunk too much Usher's Green Stripe (the scotch I drank when the horses weren't winning). The whole group of us who had attended the ball was having breakfast together the next morning. We were laughing and they were kidding me about my love of dancing — apparently I hadn't left the dance floor once the entire night, except to get a drink. I stood up and walked over to the gigantic, sparkling coffee urn. Poopsie spotted me, and sang out, "Hey!" before I could react. We both laughed. I poured the rich, black Hollins cafeteria coffee out of the gigantic, sparkling urn into a thick, white porcelain cup, and turned to walk back to our table. I looked down at my hand, holding the saucer, and saw that it was so unsteady the coffee was spilling out of the cup and into the saucer. I looked up, and there was Ansley Dickinson. I had never met anyone who seemed so mysterious.

She was sitting at a long dark oak table, all by herself. She had light brown hair, parted in the middle and swept up into a ponytail that fell between her shoulder blades. She had a long, slender neck. She had high cheekbones and sat up very straight. She wore a square-fitting, washed-out, checkered men's workshirt. She didn't say a word. She just sat there with a cup of coffee before her and looked me straight in the eye.

The toxic by-products of the Usher's clamoring through my veins, the cup clattering against the saucer, I began to walk past her. She watched me, quietly, Sphinx-like, as I headed back toward my table of bantering couples, and then I changed my course.

Mystified by her calmness, her serenity, her smile, I sat down directly across from her, set my cup and saucer down, curious about what physique lay beneath that baggy boyish shirt, and what thoughts were going on behind those quiet dark-blue eyes.

The coffee drinking and conversing, the immediate trusting, led to us leaving the cafeteria together for my garage apartment. On the way out one of the girls I had just been dancing with the night before ran up to me, and in a blitz of frantic words, notified me that her younger sister was having a nervous breakdown, was leaving Hollins on this very day, and was telling everyone it was all because of me. She explained that her sister thought she and I were somehow destined to be lovers. Ansley Dickinson heard the whole thing. I was in a jam. I brought Ansley Dickinson and the sister with me to the girls' room. I'd only met her a few times. She was on the bed crying. She told me that she had been standing at the third fence of the Hunt Cup the year I rode in it, had thought I'd been killed, had run out and put my head in her lap. On her first day at Hollins, she'd seen me walk into the cafeteria, immediately recognized me, and had thought this was all some sort of preordained plan. As gently as possible, I cleared myself of all wrong-doing. Ansley Dickinson and I headed up to my apartment — she, in her yellow VW bug, following behind me, on Esmerelda — and the non-stop talking developed into wine and dinner and more wine and more talking.

I sat on a small vacant patch of the couch, which was overflowing with stacks of Sunday *New York Times* to scan and novels to read. She sat a car-length across the garage room in my favorite reading chair, an old La-Z-Boy patched with yards of duct tape. Between us was my father's battered army trunk, on which I had thrown our coats and hats. A rain and sleet storm was whipping up outside. The aluminum sliding door — trapped above our heads in the drop-ceiling — rattled with each gust. It rattled so hard that it shook the wall against which Esmerelda leaned and caused her to come to life and start rolling away from the wall before I jumped up and saved her from crashing. Ansley Dickinson and I had a good laugh.

We conversed into the early hours. I told her about my marriage to Carol and the separation we were going through. She told me about her boyfriend in Paris. I talked about the death of my father. She talked about her father — a tough, hard-working, high-powered cardiologist; her mother — a sensitive, artistic, and beautiful woman; and their marital difficulties. I explained to her how Pop had inspired me, detailed my many wild, almost impossible to fulfill ambitions, and described the fires inside me that were fed most of all by the example set by my father but that were also fueled by the lives of the heavy-drinking, incredibly gifted Ernest Hemingway, F. Scott Fitzgerald, William Faulkner, and Thomas Wolfe. She explained that she'd originally thought she would major in biology and then go into medicine, but her love of language had taken over and she was now majoring in Russian studies and minoring in French language and history.

I walked outside to water the oak tree, to cool off, to look up into the clouds and try to comprehend all that was happening, returned, and saw the newspapers neatly stacked behind the couch, the books and manuscripts up on a shelf, our coats hung from a door knob, the wine bottle and glasses up off the floor and on my father's old army trunk, and this mysterious woman, Ansley Dickinson, seated on the couch. I sat down beside her, and the next morning there we were, Ansley and I, in our garage.

By late morning we were in her dorm. She was assertively telling her roommate and friends that yes, she was leaving the dorm, she was moving in with this "Patrick." They eyed me suspiciously, and my name suddenly felt sharp and angular compared to hers: "Ansley" — it sounded smooth, strong, the syllable "Ans" like the curve from her rib cage to her hips, and when you added the "-ley," and got Ans-ley, it had a kick, a swing, a swivel of the hips, a nod to get out on the dance floor. She was a real person now, no longer the "Ansley Dickinson" I had pictured for months whenever Kathy Raley had told me about her. This Ansley was decisive. One or two friends took her aside, gave her a talk, but she didn't waver in her decision. Soon, we were entering the cafeteria together, and Poopsie, happier than ever with my choice of a girlfriend, was calling out "Hey!" to the both of us. Then, I started calling out "Hey!" to Ansley when I spotted her walking out of a class on the campus or when she returned to the garage apartment, and she began to use the same salutation. We picked up this habit at Hollins, and another one: Each of us began to address the other by the endearment "sweetheart" as if that were actually our names.

I received my master of arts "with all the rights, privileges, and honors appertaining thereunto" from Hollins College that spring, and a year and a half later, Ansley and I were getting married in Ansley's hometown of Winter Park, Florida, near Orlando.

The night before the wedding — Labor Day weekend of 1976 — Tom Voss, my best man; Hank Slauson and Tom Whedbee, best friends and ushers; and I had the hell beaten out of us in a huge old-time Wild West brawl that took place on the streets of Orlando, in front of Rosie O'Grady's, right across from the police station. I'd stirred up a little trouble in this replica of a Mississippi steamboat, and it just so happened that a few undercover cops were there that night of my rehearsal dinner to make a big drug bust. The bust never happened. Instead, they busted us. The fight spilled out of Rosie's, onto the street. Policemen poured out of the police station. It was the ushers and I against the cops. Cops smashed Hank's head against a hubcap. Tom Whedbee, at six-foot-six, was a sure target. The cops kept knocking him down, punching him, and then strangling him until he broke away. Two bouncers yanked me away from the melee, threw me up against a cop car, and a third used me for a punching bag. The one huge undercover cop had it out for me. Over and over, he wrestled me down, put me in a stranglehold, and choked me until I was just on the verge of passing out, at which time I would somehow escape and deliriously dive back into the brawl. Tom Voss leaned back on his heels, pointed his finger at this behemoth, stated, "Don't you touch my friend again or I'll beat the living shit out of you" and seconds later was down on the asphalt with two or three officers on him. They almost met their match when they encountered my sister Sue Sue. She jumped on an undercover cop who was pummeling me, grabbed him by the little hair he had with one hand, and by an eyeball with the other, yanked that poor bastard off me and told him he'd better leave her brother alone. (In the end the policemen told me that Sue Sue had been the toughest brawler in our whole group.) We put up a good fight, but they prevailed. Hank, Tom Voss, Clay — Ansley's middle brother, Pam — Ansley's maid of honor, and I were all thrown in the city jail. Even Sue Sue was forced to put on a striped prison outfit. Tom, Hank, and I were the last to be released, on a steep bond of thousands of dollars, having had no sleep, only several hours before the pre-wedding brunch at the Country Club of Orlando.

Ansley had cried her way through most of the night, and her parents — who were going through a divorce — had some second thoughts about their daughter marrying this jailbird.

After our honeymoon, I returned to my steady — and rewarding — job as a feature writer and photographer on the *Star-Democrat* in Easton, Maryland. The paper was the flagship of a large chain of Eastern Shore papers, of which the *Dorchester News* was one. I'd picked up the job in the spring, and I was working for the same editor-in-chief, Greg Romain, as I had been at the *Dorchester News*. He was pleased with my work at the *Star-Democrat*, as he had also been with my work at the *Dorchester News*, and treated me as the high-energy, nervy, boy-wonder feature writer on his way to the big time.

Our house on the Miles River was a cross between a local tavern, a bed and breakfast, and a sailing/canoeing country club. We had friends and relatives spending the night, staying for a week, even moving in for full months, from all over the country. We partied and philosophized and dreamed of our grand futures and flirted around and skinny-dipped and sailed naked on through the night until the dawn's early rays reflected off the water, then drank black coffee and went to work.

Meanwhile, I was writing more and more stories about the Chesapeake Bay crabbers and oystermen. Three weeks after returning from our honeymoon I quit the nice, civilized job on the paper that had retirement benefits, a medical plan, and paid vacations, and went to work on the Chesapeake Bay as a waterman. I wanted to live, to fully experience the life of a waterman. And that's what I did, with the added privilege of a few times coming close to experiencing the death of a waterman.

That winter of 1976–77 was the worst of the entire century to work on the water. Boats sunk. Watermen drowned. Ansley was nervous about my surviving. My skipjack, *The Virginia W.*, sunk, the bay froze, and suddenly I had no job. I turned to bartending and carpentry until March when the ice melted and I was finally back out on a skipjack, *The Stanley Norman*, dredging for oysters with the excellent captain Ed Farley. James Michener came out on our boat one morning; he was researching his novel *Chesapeake*. I chatted with Jim — as he told all us dredgehands to call him — taught him how to cull oysters and answered questions about working on the bay and on the way watermen pronounce certain words. I asked him how he'd managed to write so many books. As he and I stepped forward on the deck to tend to the backbreaking, mind-numbing job of culling yet another pile of oysters — throwing behind us the good ones, shoveling overboard the shells and mud and rocks and broken glass and toadfish that'd like to bite your fingers off — he said, "It's like what you've taught me about culling oysters. You just bear down and do it, and you don't stop until you're finished."

The following fall Ansley and I moved to Petersburg, Virginia, south of Richmond, where we were going to start life fresh. We both had our first teaching jobs. I had decided that teaching English would be the way for me to earn money and have time to write. I thought of it as my "panacea." Little did I know that the school, Bollingbrook, would have me teaching English, philosophy, photography, journalism, coaching tennis and soccer, editing and sponsoring the newspaper and the year-book, and advising the senior class, plus teaching an SAT course in the summers, and that our house would soon become a favorite socializing spot for many of the seniors. We were leaving the carefree and wild, hard-drinking watermen and journalism days of Talbot County, Maryland. We were organized, focused, and had our plans drawn up. This was Ansley's first real full-time job — she'd be teaching French, history, and geography. Most importantly, I had plotted for us to move down two weeks before school started and had extremely high expec-tations, which I kept to myself, about the romantic time we'd have out on a sprawling dairy farm, west of Petersburg, in Ford, Virginia, with no friends or relatives visiting. Our only responsibilities would be to study our glossy new textbooks, prepare our lesson plans, and take soothing naps.

Within three days of moving to Petersburg, we inherited Ansley's eleven-year-old brother, Graham, who would live with us for the next two years. Ansley's mother was over-drinking and her health was dete-riorating. Ansley's father thought it would be best for Graham to live with us and attend the school where we taught. About this time Ansley constantly felt sick to her stomach. There was no positive response to my invitations for naps to relieve the fatigue from studying. Romantic overtures in the evening were ill fated. My wife didn't feel well. Day after day.

Finally, we dropped off a urine sample at the Petersburg health clinic early one morning before school. That afternoon Ansley, Graham, and I drove to the clinic. I walked in and the receptionist handed me a sheet of paper, with a box checked and the word "positive" beside the box. Driving back to the dairy farm, I quietly drank a six-pack of Pabst Blue Ribbon. Now I had one instant-kid, Graham, who had taken to chew-ing tobacco, keeping snakes in his bed, and knocking on our bedroom door at all hours. He had recently informed the headmaster of our school that we had no problem with our long commute. First, he explained, we drove so fast on the country roads that when we hit a bump we were often "airborne," with all four of the car's wheels off the road; secondly, he pointed out, when we got on the highway our red VW Rabbit would do eighty-five with no problem. And we had another child on the way.

Soon we befriended too many fun-loving faculty members and were dancing the night away at faculty parties, where cute, bespectacled teachers in their twenties showed a different side of their personalities from that which I saw in the classroom. I'd left the hard-drinking race-track lifestyle for journalism, only to discover that newspapermen liked to sit at a bar just as much as horsemen. Then, I'd left the drinking and brawling waterman lifestyle for the effete lifestyle of a teacher, only to discover that these educators enjoyed cutting themselves loose from society's restraints, whether they were mixing up a batch of strawberry daiquiris or opening up a few bottles of homebrewed ale, just as much as anybody else.

With the exception of a few parties, Ansley and I worked day and night and through the weekends to keep up with all the material to learn and the papers and tests to grade. And we instantly acclimated to being parents: We attended Graham's soccer games, met with his teachers, went to his plays, served as his chauffeur, checked out his new friends.

Then, in January of 1979, Ansley's mother, Ann, went into kidney failure. She was hospitalized in Florida, but her health continued to decline. She died on January 21, just four years after Ansley and I had met. She was forty-six — the same age of my father at his death. Ansley was twenty-five years old, six months pregnant, holding a new full-time job, and now, for better or worse, the matriarch of her family — her father, younger sister, and three younger brothers. She threw herself into caring for her father and siblings and into the organizing the funeral and its aftermath.

I thought Ansley was handling the pressure just fine. I didn't make any adjustments or changes in our day-to-day living. It was Graham about whom I was worried. I had promised Ansley's mother that I would look out for him, and when we returned from the funeral in Florida to Petersburg, I dedicated myself to getting Graham through this rough period.

Graham and I joined the Boy Scouts. Every other Saturday I was up at six making the two of us a full breakfast of eggs, bacon, toast, and grits. Then, we were eating and rushing around to find the equipment — bicycling, hiking, camping, canoeing, spelunking — whatever was needed for that day or weekend's excursion.

\* \* \*

On April 22, 1979, the faculty of Bollingbrook School took on the student body and parents in a tennis tournament — all doubles. The moment the last car load of parents and students drove off the campus, we rolled kegs of beer onto the courts and continued to play.

Ansley hadn't been a seeded player in the tournament. She was a few days overdue and we all kidded her about the size of her protruding stomach. Finally, she had a cup of beer, stepped out on the court, and rallied with our close friend, James Minter, head of the Classics department. We finished off the kegs and played until dark, and then we all went to the headmaster's — where he allowed me to have too many of his potent homebrews, and Ansley and I had a dance or two.

Back at our place I was sound asleep when Ansley awoke in the middle of the night, exclaimed that her water had broken, started pacing all around, getting ready to go to the hospital. I told her everything was fine and to go back to sleep.

Finally, she got me up. No doubt her playing tennis and dancing had shaken things up, as she'd hoped they would, and made the baby realize it was time to leave his sanctuary. I felt terrible. We called James Minter. He saved me. He immediately drove over and helped us get to the hospital.

## Chapter 23

A.P. "Paddy" Smithwick III made his way into the world April 23, Shakespeare's birthday.

Having Paddy gave me drive, purpose, and focus. Yet, it did not change my lifestyle. The headmaster of Bollingbrook gave me a "promotion." On top of my load of teaching and coaching, he added the new title, director of communications, which came with a 10 percent pay raise and plenty more work. Graham, jealous of all the attention the cute little baby was receiving, needed more love now than ever. He and I raced back and forth to school and sports practices and Boy Scout meetings, often with him on my lap steering the red VW Rabbit. Ansley took care of Paddy, taught part-time, and tutored Harrison Woody, one of our favorite students. I pulled out my old carpenter tools Granny had given me and turned a shed in the back yard into a writing room. I went out and wrote whenever I could find the time. Students and teachers stopped by — we caroused and partied and danced, and somehow Ansley kept the whole show afloat.

# 24

# A Deep Seat and a Long Hold

*When riding a race, as in living one's life, sometimes you get into an unpredictable situation, a contingency for which it is impossible to plan. A spectator suddenly runs out onto the course in front of a fence. A horse crosses in front of you, blocking your horse's line of vision, as you approach, at a fast pace, the largest fence on the course. In these cases, and in many others, the expression on the track that Pop rode and lived by was "take a deep seat" — get your rear end back and deep in the saddle, "and a long hold" — let the reins slide through your fingers so that if your horse starts to fall, and his head goes down and his nose skims on the ground, you don't go flying over his head. You lean back, balancing against his mouth with your long hold on the reins, keep him from falling, gather him back up, and go on and win the race, as my father did for twenty years.*

By the time I was in my late twenties, I had built up a portfolio of newspaper and magazine pieces, and I decided to leave teaching and go full-tilt back into journalism. I interviewed for jobs all over Virginia. One night I was talking to Tom Voss on the phone, telling him of my switch in careers. He urged me to come to Maryland. Baltimore was going through an exciting renaissance, and he was sure I could find a position on a Maryland publication. Ansley, Paddy, and I could move into the old tenant house on his grandmother's place, Atlanta Hall Farm, and pay a minimum rent while we got settled.

We moved from Petersburg back to Maryland in August of 1980. Graham went back to Florida to live with his father. Ansley got an excellent job teaching French at Oldfields School in Glencoe, near both Atlanta Hall Farm and Mom's farm. I could not, at least not right away, find a full-time job in journalism. Funds dwindled. Next thing I knew, I was galloping a few horses for Tom. By September, I was working for him full-time in the mornings and writing in the afternoons. Ansley was settling into her job at Oldfields. And we had finally found good daycare for Paddy.

On September 26, 1980, Ansley's charismatic brother Tom died in a small-plane crash, with his fiancé, his fiancé's sister, her boyfriend, and the pilot with his young son, whom he had taken up for the first time. Tom was twenty-five. This death, added to the unhealed scars from the death of her mother, riddled my free-flying Ansley with anguish and depression, and combined with my non-angelic behavior, sent our marriage into a tailspin. Those early years were tough. Elmer Delmer would have had the odds against us. What made me hang on at this time with more guts and more strength than I had ever shown in my life was the gift of our son Paddy.

I enjoyed galloping for Tom for a year and then spent two wonderful years teaching at Oldfields School before going back to horses, combined with part-time teaching and freelance writing.

In the spring of 1984, I went on a camping trip with my son Paddy, a good friend, Rob Deford, and his son Phineas. During a run through the wooded mountains I was planning the beer I would soon be rewarding myself with when I suddenly saw with pinpoint clarity that I'd been planning all our activities around my vacation-drinking schedule: beers driving to the mountains; beers after running; smooth, smoky scotches by the fire before dinner; a nightcap before bed ... and that I'd often been coaxing Rob into having "just one more" with me. Running along the narrow rocky path, carefully picking my steps, I thought, "I'm addicted to three things: running, coffee, and alcohol." Turning, pumping my legs, and heading straight up a steep slope, I thought, "I'm definitely not going to stop running. And I'm not going to give up the ritual of making my early morning coffee before anyone in the house is up, and sipping and savoring it alone. That leaves alcohol."

As I ran, I realized that the damn stuff was ruling my daily schedule. Whenever I was free from mental work, whether driving a car, playing tennis, splitting wood, planting the garden, playing ball with Paddy, or talking to Ansley, I had to decide whether to have a drink. Splitting wood on a ruddy autumn day, I would rationalize that I should have another mug of hard cider to drink in the essence of the outdoors and to remind myself of old times with Tiger. Pulling on tennis shorts, I'd think back on that one time I'd had two beers and then served three aces in a row. Going out to dinner with Ansley, I wouldn't be looking forward to the food or the conversation. I didn't even really want to converse until I'd had those first two margaritas. Only then could I let my guard down, discuss subjects that mattered. Furthermore, I was visiting more and more of my old friends from the horse world — not at the neighborhood pub but at drying-out centers with four-week programs that cost ten thousand to twenty thousand bucks. Not one of them had gone willingly. The term "intervention" had come to have a new meaning. Also, another good friend, a heavy drinker, had recently died. He'd been drinking at his father's funeral and reception all day and had gone to sleep late that night. There was a fire, but he never woke up. I wanted to be alert for the safety of my son, my wife, and the child to come — Ansley was pregnant and due in June. This pregnancy was affecting me in a different way from the first. I felt pressure from it — but good pressure.

I made a loose plan. I would ease up on drinking but not think about attempting to quit entirely. I'd already done that unsuccessfully dozens of times. And I wouldn't try to quit on New Year's Day, as part of a New Year's resolution. That tactic had always been a disaster.

I would wait, and then on my thirty-third birthday — the year of change, growth, rebirth, the year Christ was crucified — I would have my last drink, and I'd make it a good, strong scotch late at night by the fireplace. First, I would shoot for a day, then a week, then perhaps a month. In the back of my mind was the farfetched dream of a year without drinking. I would tell no one, not even Ansley. I'd made that mistake before. When someone offered me a drink, I wouldn't say, "I've stopped drinking," or the equivalent, which would necessitate an explanation. I'd just say, "No thanks, don't feel like one right now."

I planned the drying-out period to occur at a time when I could isolate myself. Ansley, on spring vacation from teaching, took Paddy to visit her father in Florida. I remained in Maryland and let friends think I'd gone to Florida. The night of my birthday, March 13, I had a few very nice scotches by the fire. For the next ten days I wrote, went for long runs, split wood, and read. I didn't see a soul. I didn't have a drink.

When I rejoined my family, I was over the hump. I could handle going out to parties. I learned to dance without drinking. I learned to make love without drinking. I began to discover the dozens of reasons I had for drinking: insecurity, boredom at parties, something for my hands and mouth to do at a deadly social gathering — sip, jiggle ice, small talk, escape ... "Excuse me. I need another drink ..." And there was the physiological craving: the feeling of every muscle in your body tightening, your cheeks sucking in, your eyes burning inward, your whole being anticipating that first, second, ah-lean-back let-it-hit third scotch that would ease the pressure and put you off to yourself in another plane of existence. One more and click. Or as Brick says to Big Daddy in *Cat on a Hot Tin Roof*, "This click that I get in my head that makes me peaceful. I got to drink till I get it. It's just a mechanical thing, something like a switch clicking off in my head, turning the light off and the cool night on and — all of a sudden there's — peace!" For the first time in my life, I realized that when I'd been reducing to ride races and hadn't eaten anything all day, I had gotten in the habit of relying on a few strong drinks in the evening to cure this craving. But now that I wasn't having that drink, I learned that much of what I had thought was a need for alcohol was actually a need for food, nutrition.

I stopped living in a delirious alcohol-and-adrenaline-fueled dream world of the present wherein I never faced my problems with the past, never looked into the future because I never counted on living long enough to get there. No longer did I worry about the example I was setting for Paddy. I began chipping away at the protective layers I'd grown to mask my insecurities and weaknesses; I began digging into my core. For the next seven years I learned and gave and listened while experiencing a productive and intriguing leave of absence from the world of drinking.

Andrew Coston Smithwick was born in June of 1984. I felt clear-headed, sharp, and helpful throughout the entire birth. Andrew's presence changed my outlook on my life and my lifestyle in a way I never would have predicted. Now, with Andrew in diapers, and Paddy age five, we had to be more organized and plan ahead. And then there were the bills. Paddy hadn't seemed during his early years to change our finances a bit. But now, with two children, the number of incoming bills rose, the need to spend more time and energy making more money increased, and the time available for Ansley and me to spend together decreased.

Ansley worked steadily at Oldfields, teaching French, becoming head of the French department, then head of the language department, and then director of alumni affairs and director of publications. I hopped among my jobs teaching English full-time, teaching writing to adults at Goucher College and Johns Hopkins University, and riding horses, but all along I was writing. I had a long, narrow garret with a high ceiling on the top floor of the old brick Monkton Hotel, in

Monkton, a little town just up the Gunpowder Falls from us, and whenever I could — nights, early mornings, weekends — I was there writing. No telephone. No one else on the whole floor. No interruptions. No bills in a pile, needing to be paid. There was a huge oak tree right outside my window, and on hot days in the summer I'd put a fan in the window, which would blow the oak-cooled country air into my garret. If I were there in the afternoon, I'd hike barefoot down to a hidden spot on the river, take off my clothes, and jump in the cold water flowing out of the bottom of Prettyboy Dam ten miles upriver. I'd hike back to my garret, hang my clothes from a nail, and write in my boxers. In the winters, the garret was cold — I wore long underwear, boots, wool sweaters, drank steaming black coffee out of a thermos, and intermittently did push-ups, sit-ups, and jumping jacks.

Around this time I was in close touch with my old friend Willie Dixon, a successful businessman now, who was married, had two sons, and was living in Pennsylvania. Willie took an interest in my writing career — I called him "Will-get-a-deal" — and I often brainstormed with him about upcoming writing projects. Neither of us had seen much of our mutual friend Mike White in recent years, but we'd heard how he had become one of the top "pony boys" at the New York tracks of Aqueduct, Belmont Park, and Saratoga. Highly respected for his ability to handle and to calm the roughest of horses, Mike would "pony" horses in the mornings — leading them with a shank while seated deep in his western saddle — and he would take horses to the post in the afternoons, leading the horse and jockey right up until they went into the starting gate. He also worked full-time galloping horses for trainers such as Sidney Watters and was known for having "good hands" on a horse. I'd heard stories about Mike being the cleanest and most fastidious human being on the racetrack. Sometimes, in the late morning, after the grooms and hot-walkers and exercise riders, and even Sidney, had left the barn, Mike would return, and clean, polish, and rehang all the halters and shanks, which had already been cleaned and hung up just hours earlier. Every night Mike shined his riding boots to perfection, and every morning he buffed them to a high gloss.

Off and on, Willie and I had heard rumors that Mike had trouble with drugs, but he was tough as they come and we were sure he'd whip the problem. I'd always thought that what Mike really wanted to do with his life was be a jumping rider for five or six years until he couldn't stand the reducing any longer and then make the transition to becoming a trainer. I theorized that he got into the drugs to dull the pain of not fulfilling this ambition.

One afternoon Willie called to give me some bad news. He'd just heard that Mike had gone clean, fought off the drugs, but had recently had a major setback after taking some bad drugs. Willie explained that the day before, our Saratoga buddy had had a fight with his wife. She went out to go shopping, and when she returned, he had killed himself.

After hearing the news, I took a long, quiet walk on the path beside Gunpowder Falls. I stopped and sat by a set of rapids Tiger and I had often canoed through. I listened to the water pour and rush and splash over the rocks. I thought of Mike as freed now, off on his own, headed to sea, headed out into infinity. I sat still, very still, feeling as if I were becoming a part of the bank of the river, a part of the water and air and sunshine, and I appreciated all that I had — my wife Ansley, my son Paddy, my son Andrew, my mother, my sisters, my friends. I returned and wrote Mike's parents a letter about our friendship.

* * *

On a winter afternoon in 1987, I danced out of a magazine office in Baltimore with four of the latest issues under my arm. It was twenty degrees out and the wind was blowing and I was ecstatic. I hadn't had a drink in three years. I was three years younger than my father when he was forced to retire from riding. I felt tall. I walked straight, no jacket, the cold having no effect on my fit-feeling thirty-six-year-old body, toughened from galloping twenty-two horses a day around racetracks and across fields and over jumps all through the cold Maryland winter.

Beneath my jeans I had on wool underwear, and beneath my red-plaid flannel shirt, I wore a turtleneck. The cold felt good. Let it come.

I was back galloping horses again, freelance riding in the mornings so I could freelance write in the afternoons. And it was working. Twenty-two Thoroughbred horses a day. Five dollars a horse. All at farms within a few miles of one another. Six nice "made" steeplechase horses at Tom Voss', on Atlanta Hall Farm; seven rambunctious two-year-olds at Corbett Farm, each ridden a monotonous seven times around a little training track; eight at a farm where the horses were wild as hell and I risked my life every day and where the hired help one day put my saddle on backward but where I got paid on Fridays with a thick stack of new greenbacks; and one, Nine Wide, for Bobby Hale at Taylor's Purchase Farm, where I was treated like royalty.

I hopped in my rusted-out piebald Ford Maverick, slammed the heavy door, revved the engine, and cranked up the radio. I took off, speeding north on the Jones Falls Expressway, flipping through the magazine pages with trepidation, waiting to see my article. I quickly read the first few lines, nervous there'd be some mortifying error or change in my wording that would render the whole paragraph meaningless. They were okay. I turned page after page, eyed my words bending artistically around the photographs. It looked good! This, my first cover story, looked good. I liked it. And I had just moments ago gotten another assignment from the editor. The writing was on a roll.

I was cruising along, steering the Maverick past the entrance to Northern Parkway that led up to Pimlico Racetrack, an entrance my father and I had taken a thousand times, all at 5:30 a.m. I was wishing he could be sitting beside me in the car. I was picturing him, sitting there in the front seat — leaning against the door — and I was wondering what he would have to say. Suddenly, it all came together: what I could do with my life even though he was no longer here. I'd return to race-riding, to being a steeplechase jockey.

I could do both now!

My mind ran off with the idea: I had devoted all these years to getting my writing on track, and now that it was on track, I'd ride, I thought. Ride and write. This time I wouldn't put my ego into the riding. This time I wouldn't be doing it professionally, as a way to make a living. I'd be doing it because it was in my blood.

I'd tell Tom tomorrow when I drove over to Atlanta Hall Farm to get on his horses. Tomorrow night I'd call all the trainers I knew. It was the perfect time of year, the races not starting for a few weeks. I could line up a good string of rides for the spring, and I didn't have to worry about getting fit: I was already fit from getting on all these damn freelance horses.

I'd ride steeplechase races. I'd missed it, craved it, more than anything else in the world, besides my father. My body wasn't battered and broken and held together by baling wire like most jumping riders my age; for the past fifteen years, while they'd been getting busted up, I'd been away from race-riding. While they had all hung up their tack, I can pick mine back up.

The next day, I talked to Tom. That night I called several trainers. I had it all lined up. The adrenaline was pumping. I felt close to Pop. Rides started in several weeks. I envisioned myself getting a leg up in the paddock of the Middleburg races. I didn't tell Ansley.

That week I played soccer each evening with my son Paddy, age seven. I taught Andrew — age three — how to kick the ball without toeing it. I made love to Ansley and listened to her stories of teaching French to her students and her plans to take a group of students to France for a full language immersion during the spring minimester. I wrote and read and lined up part-time positions teaching English and creative writing at Johns Hopkins University and Goucher College in the spring. And I told Ansley about my decision to go back to race-riding.

Ansley was dead set against it.

My sisters were against it.

My mother was against it: "Don't be ridiculous, Patrick. You have a wife and two children to support. You can't run off and start riding races. Why would you want to do that ... ? Look what happened to your father. You've worked so hard to get your writing and teaching going — now you need to stick with it. Besides, you don't have the time. You don't have the money ..."

And Granny Whitman sent me a note in her shaky handwriting that included the following:

*Patrick,*

*1. Do not try to make lamb out of mutton.*

*2. Stick to your knitting. You have spent years studying. You have had a good education.*

*3. The pen is mightier than the sword, lifting man's sights. Racing is dangerous. Vanity, vanity — it is all vanity, just a day, a moment of glorified self; it is no help to man.*

*4. You have a perfect set-up, exercising in the mornings and hours to write and to be your own man, and a future for yourself and your family.*

Those were strong, rational, practical arguments, but they weren't what turned me around. I came about-face after realizing that the euphoric feeling I had had in the car about going back to riding races was based on a false premise. Riding races would not bring my father back.

A week after I had called the trainers and talked to Tom, after I'd lined up the rides, I called the trainers back, declined the rides. I felt ashamed. This was the last chance in my life to return to riding races. In March I was turning thirty-seven, two years away from Pop's age when he had the fall. I was going to have to find some other way to come to terms with my upbringing, with my father.

# 25

## A Match Race Ending in a Dead Heat

*A match race is a two-horse race, one horse and rider running against another horse and rider. A dead heat is a finish where two horses finish together, their outstretched noses passing under the wire at the exact same fifth of a second.*

Turning thirty-nine was a major milestone for me. The age of thirty-nine was the big year, the big number. Thirty-nine, the end of Pop's life as a healthy man, as a talented athlete, as a human being with unreachable depths of endurance, the year of his fall and paralysis.

As my birthday in March approached, I took a long look at my head-and-head gallop — or was it a race? — through life alongside my father who had died seventeen years before, and I learned something. I called my mother to ask her some questions for a Father's Day piece entitled "Missing My Father" that I was doing for a magazine. During the conversation I learned that the idea I had held all my life of my father always wanting to ride "just one more year" was wrong.

I had thought Pop, like so many athletes, just couldn't stop. Yet, Mom explained over the telephone that Pop had been trying to quit riding, had been trying back before that thirty-ninth birthday to move into full-time training. He wanted to stop, but he allowed himself to be talked into riding for one more year. Do what you know in your guts is right, Pop told me again and again in his later years, about training horses — and about life. But they pushed him and he kept on riding, for the sake of his mother, brother, and family — to uphold the tradition of dominating the sport. If he had quit the sport then, and the lifestyle that went along with it, he would most likely have been there with me at my thirty-ninth birthday party.

He didn't quit earlier. The family wanted him to keep going — for where in the family business was there room for two full-time trainers? Mom told me she could remember as if it were yesterday the tears in my father's eyes as his mother sat in our living room over Christmas and told him he had to ride one more year, the year of Bon Nouvel, 1966. While listening to Mom on the telephone, I realized that Pop had needed to stand up to people, to tell them to go to hell. People used my father, they used his talents; they took advantage of his gentlemanly conduct, his trusting of others.

As I approached turning thirty-nine, it became more important to me to make it past Pop's birthday on February 11, than mine in March. I began to feel a sense of release from my father's life influencing my own destiny, and yet he was more alive in my thoughts than ever. While struggling to find a conclusion for the magazine piece, I imagined sitting beside Pop in the Manor Tavern, explaining to him this new sense of release. First, I'd turn my face toward him, and looking forward to his reaction, look him in the eye and inform him that, yes, he would be having another grandchild, a granddaughter — Eliza — and that he'd better start taking better care of himself. I'd relate to him the latest athletic exploits of his two grandsons, ask how the training was going, give him hell about his rehabilitation program, and urge him to exercise that left side. I'd scold him for having the Pall Mall, and I'd laugh inside as he allowed himself a shot of Old Grand Dad to go along with his Budweiser. Helplessly, I'd try to shrug off, elbow away, turn my back on, all the hangers-on and sycophants and friends that would circle around him, preventing me from telling him about this new feeling of release. I'd watch helplessly as he bought a round and things started spiraling out of control as they bought us a round and we were caught up in the duel, the bartender, not letting on to the others, occasionally setting up a pair of on-the-house boilermakers for the two of us. It didn't matter. I didn't have to tell him.

He didn't need to hear that I no longer felt a sense of conquest about reaching the age of thirty-nine without being battered and broken. He didn't need to know that I felt cut loose, free to make my own decisions, and yet alone.

The competition with him that had earlier driven me had faded. Instead, I was filled with unalloyed wonder and respect and tenderness for him, with a new sense of curiosity about what drove him. I compared the way I was as a father to the way he was to me. I was filled with a different feeling — no longer the image of Pop leaning on the mantle piece, grinning cockily, raising an eyebrow, and explaining to my pipe-smoking grandfather that there was this horse called Bon Nouvel and he just wanted to ride for one more year. I no longer felt I must dash off and do the most dangerous, flamboyant, and exciting thing.

Pop had been caught in a web of undiminished talent.

If only he had gotten off a horse one day, finished riding a race one day, and said, "That's it."

If only he had slid off Bon Nouvel in the shed row one morning, taken the red pack of Pall Mall's from his chest pocket, thrown it down in the manure pile, and said to the groom holding the horse, or to Mikey, or to the owner of Bon Nouvel, or to me, "That's it."

If only he had lived more moderately, not smoked so much, not drunk so much, not been banged up so much, not slept so little, not spent twenty years of doing light — then perhaps the cancer wouldn't have gotten him. And yet, then he wouldn't have been my father. That just would not have been my father.

## Chapter 25

I thought back to what Pop in his last months told me: He wanted to take a canoe trip some day, camp on an island, be with his family. He was tired. He wanted to stop pushing. But it was too late by then, he'd pushed too hard, crammed so much life into his forty-six years that it was time for him to go.

At the end of our conversation about Pop, Mom had given me Bobby Burke's phone number. She thought he'd be a good person to talk to before I finished my Father's Day piece.

I dialed the number. Bobby answered the phone. We chatted, and then I told him I was writing a piece on Pop.

"He was my best friend," Bobby said. "I loved him like a brother. He was the greatest. Scotty Schulhofer has a photo of Paddy jumping a hurdle on a gray horse in Aiken. The horse's head is on the ground! Paddy sat back, pulled that sonofabitch's head up and finished second. For a man to get a horse around a course, there never was and never will be any better."

Bobby paused, might've sipped on something. I relaxed, not minding the silence, and waited.

"You know, Little Paddy. You know, the winter after his fall — oh, Little Paddy, I could tell you stories all night about your father! — that winter, he stopped in Aiken to visit me on his way to Florida. I was shocked when I saw him. He had no strength in his left side.

"He arrived at night and we had a few drinks. The next morning we got up early. 'What do you want to do?' I asked him.

" 'Get on a horse,' " he said.

" 'Are you sure?' I asked. He said he was.

"So we tacked up two horses and went out riding through the woods. I'll catch hell from Suzie if she hears about this, I was thinking, and just then, to make matters worse, we had a clear view of a few schooling hurdles set up in a field. 'Let's jump them,' Paddy said.

" 'Come on Paddy, you're just out of the hospital ...'

" 'Bobby,' he said. 'I've got to do it.'

"We jogged out of the woods, Paddy's balance not looking great, his left side just sort of hanging. I came up alongside him, thought we might pull up, walk 'em up, and look at the hurdle, then turn and jump it. Paddy kept his eyes on the hurdle, clucked to his horse, and we galloped into it head and head. His horse stood off, and Paddy leaned way back, let the reins slide, and managed to stay on. We pulled up. He looked over at me. 'Well at least,' he said, leaning back in the saddle and letting the reins slide all the way to the knot, 'I can still do that.' "

Bobby and I spoke some more and when we were winding down, just as we were about to say goodbye, I used an old interview tactic I'd learned working on newspapers. After the interviewee and I had concluded our session, and I had folded up my notepad, and the interviewee was relieved it was over and it had all gone well and was ushering me to the door and talking about the weather or an upcoming golf game, just then I'd ask the toughest, most personal question — nonchalantly toss it out like Peter Falk used to do when he played Columbo in the television detective series. I asked Bobby, "Why was Pop so loved by so many?"

Without hesitation, Bobby answered, "I never heard him say a bad fucking word about anyone."

* * *

That night I dreamed:

I'm outside the tackroom at Delaware Park. I feel light and happy and am preparing to ride my first race in a long time. It's a skinny little filly and she's tricky to ride but I feel confident.

I need some britches. An old girl friend — Phini — brings me a pair of beautiful leather britches. They're nice and soft, good for foxhunting maybe, but they're heavier than what I need.

I'm standing there, beside the britches and some tack, outside of a barn, when I look up and there Pop is on a big, beautiful bay horse. He's riding long and looks comfortable and he's strong and healthy.

He has a long hold on the reins — a beautifully long hold, and he is walking down the path toward the race. He grins and says, "Come on, Bud; let's go." He's calm. He's professional. His broad shoulders are turned toward me. "Come on, Bud; let's go," he says, his voice deep and steady. I hear it very clearly.

And he walks on. It feels unbelievably good to see him so well. I have an inner glow of life expanding in my chest. We are going to ride a race together. He has resurfaced, walked out of the mist, and now we are going to ride together.

I prepare to pull on a pair of old nylon britches I'd dug up in the tack room. I had them just a moment ago, but now I can't find them. The leather ones would make me overweight. I couldn't ride a race in those damn things. I start to search and the dream deteriorates, the pieces fall apart, melt into one of those thousands of nightmares of little things going wrong, preventing me from even getting to the paddock, from getting to the horse, from getting close to my father.

My father, as if out of Arthurian legend, walks on, back into the mist, on the long-striding bay. The toes of his racing boots are balanced lightly in his stirrups, his long calves are relaxed against the horse's sides, and his hands are lightly gripping the reins. He exudes a wonderful, beautiful, enviable self-confidence.

I am left alone.

And then I awoke and again I was alone.

# Epilogue

Many of the people who knew and loved my father, who worked and played alongside him, are now gone. Those written about in this book who have passed away are Tiger Bennett, my godfather Garry Winants, Emmett Grayson, Salvadore Tumenelli, Uncle Charlie White, George Clement, Jack Graybeal, and Tanza. Both my grandmothers have "graduated," as they termed it. My mother is gone. She died of kidney failure in her bedroom, on her farm, perfectly lucid until the last second. She was my closest connection to my father. We shared a common knowledge and a mutual love and respect.

My sisters, Sue Sue and Sallie, are both healthy and prosperous. Sue Sue — now "Susan" — is a licensed social worker and practices psychotherapy in Saratoga Springs. She orchestrated the painting, by children, of the many murals that today brighten up the streets of Saratoga. Sallie is a licensed acupuncturist in Charlottesville, Virginia, and has spent two decades in the nursing profession, specializing in labor and delivery. Both sisters have dedicated their working lives to helping others.

Now that my mother has died, my strongest connection to my father is my Uncle Mikey. We have become closer and closer over the past decade. He stops by once a week on Thursday after his massage. I build a fire in the fireplace and he and I have a drink and hors d'oeuvres. The dogs jump all over Mikey, sit in his lap, and he laughs and pets them. Just when we've run out of cheese and crackers, Ansley arrives home from Oldfields School and whips up a huge meal. We laugh and talk nonstop, and Mikey eats and appreciates his food as if it were June and he is ending a spring of reducing to ride timber races. I listen to his stories about his and his brother's beautiful childhood, and I'm reminded by his mannerisms, movements, posture, and tenacity of Pop's same characteristics. I love the way he says the word "Paddy," with such love and longing and respect, and I drink in his gentle presence and old world charm and kindness and thoughtfulness. After dinner I drive him home, to the racing farm at Hydes. It is just the two of us, and I have discussions with him that are unlike those I have, or will ever be able to have, with anyone else in this life.

My Aunt Dot Smithwick is very busy running her 2,000-acre farm, Sunny Bank — where she was raised — in Middleburg, Virginia. She does it all, from driving the tractor to riding her own horses. Her stable is a formidable presence at the hunt meets where she is known for being able to push a horse to perform at its absolute highest potential.

My great friend Tom Voss has become one of the country's best trainers of steeplechase and flat horses, and he learned much of what he knows from working during his youth for my father. Like my father and Uncle Mikey, Tom is an old-fashioned, thorough, three-dimensional horseman whose corduroys are frayed on the inside of his calves from riding, stained with manure at the knee from feeling tendons, and ripped in his rear pocket from jamming his bandana in and out. He does not train from an office. He is on the tractor, harrowing his indoor track before the first set goes out. He is standing by the wing of a hurdle giving orders to his riders as they are about to school. He gallops and schools the bigger and stronger horses himself. Tom has been the leading steeplechase trainer of the country two times. He has won virtually every major steeplechase stakes race at least once. More importantly to me, he has won the A.P. Smithwick Memorial, now a grade II steeplechase stakes, four times — with Cookie, Mickey Free, Brigade of Guards, and Anofferyoucantrefuse, all of whom I have galloped, breezed, schooled, and known well.

From the late 1990s through 2001, Tom trained a turf horse called John's Call. At the age of eight, in 1999, John won two noted mid-Atlantic stakes. At the age of nine he stunned the racing world, winning the $500,000, mile and a half Sword Dancer Invitational Handicap at Saratoga by almost ten lengths and going on to win the Turf Classic at Belmont. That year, at an age when most racehorses are retired, he ran a magnificent race in the $2-million Breeders' Cup Turf, beaten just a half-length by the winner, and a nose by the second horse.

Speedy Kiniel, who helped me through the nightmarish week after Pop's fall, is still here, and he is still speedy! He is extremely strong and healthy. Only recently, Speedy retired from working for Uncle Mikey. The two had worked together for more than thirty-five years, and for most of those years Speedy lived on the farm at Hydes.

Pop's great friends Tommy Walsh, Evan Jackson, Jimmy Murphy, Janon Fisher, and Bobby Burke are all still at work, and Scotty Schulhofer has only recently retired.

Scotty, one of our roommates at Elmont back in the Esposito's days, trained Ta Wee, champion sprinter of 1969–70, and four other champions. Scotty won the Breeders' Cup Juvenile with Fly So Free, the Breeders' Cup Sprint with Smile, the Florida Derby with Cryptoclearance, the Washington, D.C., International with MacDiarmida, and the 1993 Belmont Stakes with Colonial Affair. In 1992 Scotty was inducted into the Racing Hall of Fame, and many thought his career had peaked. In 1998 he began training Lemon Drop Kid, who went on to win the Futurity, the Belmont, the Travers, the Whitney, the Woodward, and other graded stakes.

Tommy Walsh, an occasional Elmont roommate of ours, continued his riding career for a few more years after Pop's fall, outriding anyone who made the mistake of coming alongside him. Tommy picked up Pop's rides, including Bon Nouvel, and his career soared until he suddenly quit riding at age twenty-seven, largely because of what had happened to Pop. Tommy won the Temple Gwathmey Steeplechase three times and the Saratoga Steeplechase Handicap three times. His most amazing feat was winning the Grand National five years in a row. Tommy, who was inducted into the Hall of Fame in 2005, is a successful trainer of flat horses. Tommy is still known for his iconoclastic outlook and his non-reverential attitude toward high muckety-mucks.

Pop's great friend and riding colleague, "Brother" Jimmy Murphy, is a successful trainer on the Maryland/Delaware circuit. He usually ships his horses up for the Saratoga meet, where I enjoy seeing him. He is the consummate gentleman.

I wrote about these friends and colleagues of my father, and about my father and our family, to bring to life this time and place, in the same way Pop told me to ride the last stretch of a race. "Ride into that last fence like it's not there," Pop said, tilting his head slightly and looking me in the eye as we sat at our little table in Esposito's Bar. "Then ride from that last fence to the wire as if your life depends on it." This was a philosophy of race-riding, and it was a philosophy of life. I lifted my glass and took another sip of the last beer I would ever have with my father in the full bloom of health. Pop finished his screwdriver and added the toughest part of his code of living. "And don't look back," he said. "Don't look back. It throws a horse off balance."

This last injunction is important in riding a race. It is also important in how to live. It is how my father lived his life. It means not only not to look back at the horses behind you, but not to dwell regretfully on races lost, on mistakes made; and just as importantly, not to live in the past off races won, successes achieved. Push on. Ride hard. Pay attention to the moment. Keep your form — back low, hands maintaining good contact with the horse's mouth through the reins, calves gripping the saddle — and keep your eye on the finish line.

# Photo Credits

**Cover:** Allen Studio; Bert Morgan

**Page 1:** A.P. "Paddy" and D.M. "Mikey" Smithwick (Bert Morgan); Paddy Smithwick and Colorado Prince (Bert Morgan); Weighing in (Mid-Atlantic Thoroughbred)

**Page 2:** Paddy and Mikey Smithwick and their parents (Freudy); Suzie Smithwick and her children, Paddy and Suzie Smithwick (courtesy of the author)

**Page 3:** Paddy and Patrick Smithwick, house at My Lady's Manor (courtesy of the author)

**Page 4:** Paddy Smithwick and Neji, Paddy over a water jump (Bert and Richard Morgan); Paddy and Bon Nouvel (The Blood-Horse)

**Page 5:** Crag, Paddy, and Patrick before the Rochelle Tin Cup (Jean Firth Tyng); Paddy and Patrick before the Maryland Hunt Cup (Skip Ball); Paddy and Jackie Kennedy (courtesy of the author)

**Page 6:** Tanza, Curator, and Dave Mitchell (Freudy); Tin Cup win (Jean Firth Tyng); Moonlore winning (Peter Winants)

**Page 7:** Paddy and Patrick at Saratoga (Bert and Richard Morgan); Patrick at the typewriter (Skip Ball)

**Page 8:** Hall of Fame ceremony (The Blood-Horse); Ansley and Patrick (Skip Ball); Mikey and Patrick (Douglas Lee)

# About the Author

Patrick Smithwick has been working with horses all his life. At a very young age he began working with his father, the legendary steeplechase jockey, A.P. Smithwick, who became a trainer after retiring from riding. Smithwick then worked his way through school and college by exercising Thoroughbreds at major East Coast racetracks and riding steeplechase races at such venues as Belmont Park and Saratoga Race Course, and hunt meets such as the Maryland Hunt Club and the Grand National.

Smithwick received a bachelor of arts from Johns Hopkins University in 1973 followed by a master of arts in creative writing from Hollins College in 1975. After working in the newspaper business for several years, Smithwick began teaching English, philosophy, photography, and journalism at both the high school and collegiate levels. In 1988 he received a master of liberal arts from Johns Hopkins University and in 2000 he received his degree in education for ministry from University of the South. During this time, Smithwick taught as well as held the position of director of publications and public relations at two different schools.

He has now turned his two biggest passions into two businesses — riding and training Thoroughbred steeplechase horses and writing. He also gives talks, teaches part-time, and does freelance writing.

In addition to *Racing My Father*, Smithwick has written *The Art of Healing: Union Memorial Hospital* and *Gilman Voices, 1897–1997*. He has also written for many publications including *Mid-Atlantic Country*, *The Maryland Horse*, *Horsemen's Journal*, and *The Chronicle of the Horse*.

Smithwick resides on the horse farm where he was raised in Monkton, Maryland, with his wife Ansley. They have three children: Paddy, Andrew, and Eliza.